P9-DNB-748

TRIALS
WITHOUT
TRUTH

TRIALS

WITHOUT

TRUTH

Why Our System of Criminal Trials
Has Become an Expensive Failure
and What We Need to Do
to Rebuild It

WILLIAM T. PIZZI

 NEW YORK UNIVERSITY PRESS
New York and London

NEW YORK UNIVERSITY PRESS
New York and London

Library of Congress Cataloging-in-Publication Data
Pizzi, William T., 1943–
Trials without truth : why our system of criminal trials has
become an expensive failure and what we need to do to rebuild it /
William T. Pizzi.
      p.   cm.
Includes bibliographical references and index.
ISBN 0-8147-6649-8 (acid-free paper)
1. Criminal justice, Administration of—United States. 2. Trial
practice—United States. 3. Criminal courts—United States. I. Title.
KF9223 .P58 1998
345.73'05—ddc21   98-25530
                                     CIP

New York University Press books are printed on acid-free paper,
and their binding materials are chosen for strength and durability.

Manufactured in the United States of America

10   9   8   7   6   5   4   3   2   1

To my three great loves:

my wife, Leslie,

and my daughters,

Anne and Elise.

CONTENTS

ACKNOWLEDGMENTS

I have written a book about the American trial system. But the book comes out of a decade of studying the trial systems in other countries. For that reason, I owe an enormous debt of gratitude to many people who have helped me with comparative research over the years. There are too many at this point to mention all of them, and I am sure I would end up leaving some out. But I must thank specifically Luca Marafioti, a professor at II University of Rome at Tor Vergata, and Walter Perron, a professor at the University of Mainz. I have coauthored articles with each of them and I learned a great deal in the process of working with two such knowledgeable scholars.

I want also to thank Murray Richtel, a former faculty colleague, who went on the bench and has been one of the best trial judges in Colorado for the past twenty years. Murray read a draft of the book and gave me many helpful suggestions. I also very much appreciated his enthusiasm for what I was attempting to do in the book.

I was aided enormously at all stages of this project by Jane Thompson, the faculty services librarian at the University of Colorado Law School, who always seemed able to find exactly what I wanted and get me a copy very quickly. I thank Ingrid Decker and Katrina Jones for their excellent research help as well. Finally, I would like to thank the faculty secretaries at the Law School for their help at every stage of the editing process.

Acknowledgments

Chapter 1 is an expanded version of an essay, *Soccer, Football and Trial Systems*, which appeared in the *Columbia Journal of European Law*. I am grateful to the editors for permission to republish it.

TRIALS
WITHOUT
TRUTH

INTRODUCTION

Up until the 1990s, American lawyers and judges seemed to have many reasons to be proud of our criminal justice system. While none of them could have been naïve enough to believe that the quality of justice was uniform around the country or that the system did not have problems, the improvements in the fairness of the system over the last thirty years seemed staggering and obvious. No longer was it the case, for example, that defendants charged with relatively minor crimes spent months in jail awaiting trial, sometimes longer than they would ever spend in jail if convicted. Bail reform statutes passed in the 1960s and 1970s meant that the vast majority of those arrested were quickly released on bail. For those not able to make bail, speedy trial statutes assured those in jail that they would receive a trial within months of their arrest, not years, which would have been the expectation before and is still the expectation in many other countries.

Another source of pride to lawyers and judges were the many decisions of the United States Supreme Court protecting the rights of defendants. These decisions seemed to go a long way toward assuring all Americans that certain minimum standards of fairness applied to the way they were treated by the police and to the trial they would receive if charged with a crime. Many of the most famous of these decisions represented sharp breaks with past precedent and it appeared that our system was making progress toward a criminal justice system that was both strong and fair.

1

However, looking back from the perspective of the late 1990s, there were clear warning signs in the 1980s that there were serious problems with our trial system. One was the emergence of a powerful victims' rights movement in this country. The tremendous anger that crime victims in this country expressed toward our trial system should have alerted those in the system to the fact that all was not well. But it was hard for those in the system, after so much had been accomplished to protect the constitutional rights of defendants, to comprehend the anger of victims or to understand how a trial system that seemed a model of fairness could possibly do more for victims at trial than it was already doing. Thus, it was easy for many, including even many prosecutors, to conclude that victims were looking for some sort of solace from the system that no trial system could ever give them.

The system's self-confidence, bordering on complacency, was shaken by the acquittal of the officers who had beaten Rodney King and by the riot that followed the acquittals. While there had been riots before following the acquittals of police officers charged with assaulting citizens—the Miami riots in 1980, which had led the President to call out the National Guard, were sparked by the acquittals of four white officers charged with the beating death of Arthur Mc-Duffie—what was different about the Rodney King case was that everyone had seen the tapes of the King beating. Thus even some police officers expressed shock at the acquittal of the four officers.

It was against this background that the trial of O. J. Simpson took on tremendous importance. Defenders of our trial system were confident that this case would show the country what a trial system can accomplish when it has sufficient resources and when a trial is conducted by excellent advocates before an excellent judge. The *Simpson* case stunned the system out of its complacency. From every angle—the trial attorneys, the judge, what went on in court, what went on out of court, what went on in the jury room—the case showed very little of which we could be proud.

While there are still occasional apologists who insist that our trial system is strong and that the *Simpson* case, or whatever shocking case is presently under discussion, is "not typical" of American trials, there are now too many trials with too many problems occurring in too many states to deny that our trial system has serious structural flaws. Instead of confidence, the mood of those in the system as an important criminal trial approaches is one of anxiousness as they pray that the trial does not derail in some way and turn into yet another public relations disaster.

This book is about our trial system and, as the title suggests, is strongly critical of the way the system has evolved. Put simply, it shows a trial system in which winning and losing are badly overemphasized and in which the quality of one's lawyer or the composition of the jury can be more important to the outcome of the case than the quality of the evidence.

This book is highly critical of the roles of lawyers and judges in the system. Some famous cases, such as the trials of O. J. Simpson and Louise Woodward, will be discussed to back up the criticisms offered. But the book is not a rehash of particular trials, such as one hears nightly on lawyer talk shows, nor does it focus on individual lawyers and judges. It is rather an exposition and an attack on the structure of the American trial system that permits and encourages extreme behavior from lawyers, that makes it very difficult for trial judges to control that behavior, and that ends up undervaluing truth.

While the book is about the structure of our trial system and the roles of lawyers, judges, and others in that system, chapters 2 and 3 discuss the restrictions on the way crimes are investigated by the police in the United States. These restrictions have very important consequences for our trial system. Chapter 2 deals with the way the system enforces restrictions on search and seizures by police officers through the exclusion of evidence and chapter 3 centers on the restriction on the questioning of suspects by the police.

Discussion throughout the book is heavily comparative. Thus, for example, when I assert that the limits on advocacy in American courtrooms are few and that the system encourages extremes of advocacy, I will not only give examples of such extreme advocacy, but show why such advocacy would be unlikely or less likely to occur in other western trial systems. I rely particularly on the trial systems in four western countries in the book: the Netherlands, Germany, Norway, and England. The first three have strong trial systems and yet each is quite different from the other. As for England, the United States shares a common legal heritage with it and yet, the trial systems in the two countries differ in important respects. Besides showing how extreme our trial system has become, it is my hope that the book's comparative approach will convince readers that it is not just desirable, but possible to reform our system.

CHAPTER ONE

Soccer, Football, and Trial Systems

Understanding Ourselves

In a book that attacks our criminal trial system, readers rightly expect that the author will discuss topics such as juries, the jury selection process, the appalling behavior of trial lawyers, and a trial system that emphasizes winning much more than truth. Yet this introductory chapter is largely about sports. One reason for approaching our trial system initially through the medium of sports is that we cannot begin to understand our criminal justice system until we understand ourselves and our culture better. We—lawyers and nonlawyers alike—tend to think of ourselves as a pragmatic, "no nonsense" people who abhor bureaucracy and "red tape," and who like to keep things simple and informal, especially when it means getting the job done efficiently. Perhaps this self-image is part of the reason the public is so frustrated when it looks at the American criminal justice system and especially at our trial system. Not only is the reliability of the system questionable, but it is also incredibly expensive as lawyers and judges in important criminal cases eat up hours and sometimes even days of what should be trial time in debate over technical evidentiary and procedural issues.

But trial systems do not evolve independently of the social and political values of the countries in which they exist. One objective of this chapter is to force us to face up to the fact that our self-image is not accurate in important respects. We have many strengths of character but we also have some flaws that we need to recognize and acknowledge. One of them is that we love procedure. Or, to be more blunt, we are procedure addicts. To convince readers of this fact, I intend to spend much of this chapter in the world of sport, comparing two types of professional football, namely the American version that culminates in the Super Bowl each January and the type of football passionately followed by Europeans and much of the rest of the world, which Americans call "soccer" to distinguish it from what we consider to be "real football." (Being an American who continues to love football and only began to appreciate professional soccer during World Cup 1990, I will use the American terms "football" and "soccer" to refer to the two sports.) I will use the two sports to show that Americans have a "procedure problem," to put it euphemistically.

Another objective of this chapter is to use the two sports and the strong parallels they have to different trial traditions to provide a general overview of what I will refer to in this book as "European" or "continental" trial systems, meaning by these terms the countries on the continent, including the Scandinavian countries, but excluding England, Scotland, and Ireland. (In chapter 5 I will expand on this comparison between our trial system and those on the continent.)

A final reason for beginning this book with a somewhat humorous and tongue-in-cheek look at ourselves and our favorite sport is that Americans badly need to let down their guard and take a look at themselves with a sense of humor, a commodity that is all too often lacking in public discussion on controversial issues these days. In fact, I am tempted to say that we have no public discussion of important issues having to do with the American criminal justice system today; instead we shout at each other and too often prefer to substitute an attack on the motives of those with whom we disagree for argument about the issues. Suggest that we ought to cut back on the exclusionary rule (which requires the exclusion of evidence unconstitutionally seized by police) and one is likely to be accused of tolerating police violence such as we saw in the Rodney King case or the abuse of minorities. Suggest that the privilege against self-incrimination is too broad and the orderly questioning of suspects should be permitted and encouraged and one is likely to be dismissed as someone who is proud of the fact that we have long passed the one million mark for those in prison or that a very high percentage of young blacks are in prison or in some form of probationary status.

It is my hope that what I have to say about the criminal justice system in the remainder of this book, admittedly much of it controversial and maybe even radical to some, will be better received if we all—lawyers and nonlawyers alike—begin by looking at ourselves with a sense of humor.

Our Obsession with Rules

It may seem bizarre to suggest that the world of sport can teach us about different trial systems. But, on reflection, it should not be surprising that elements of a country's popular culture, such as the sport it loves above all others, might reflect and thus help to explain the legal culture of that country as well. Games of sport are defined by rules the infraction of which must be punished by a referee or a judge. But "rules," "referees," "violations of the rules," and so on are equally part of the vocabulary we use to discuss trials and trial procedures. To the extent that soccer differs conceptually from football in its perceived need for rules, in its view of the way those rules should be enforced, and in terms of what the game emphasizes on the playing field, it should not surprise us to find that some of these basic conceptual differences exist in the respective trial systems as well.

The differences between the two sports begin with the rules that are viewed as necessary to govern play. In soccer, there are comparatively few rules and most are rather easy to express. A player can't intentionally trip someone or push someone off the ball or engage in dangerous play. The only complicated rule is that governing offsides but even that is easily expressed, even if it is sometimes difficult to determine in a game situation.

By contrast, American football has many, often extremely complicated, rules. Consider just a few: certain players on the offensive team may move before the snap of the ball but only in certain directions, others may not even flinch; certain offensive players may be blocked or impeded a certain way, but others may be blocked only if within a specified distance from the line of scrimmage; offensive tackles usually may not receive a forward pass, but sometimes they may be eligible to do so; a quarterback may not intentionally throw the ball to a vacant part of the field to avoid being tackled for a loss, but in certain areas on the field he may do so and, at certain points in the game, he is even permitted to create an incomplete pass by "spiking" the ball at his feet, though in other situations this is strictly forbidden. Even the running of the clock is governed by its own complex set of rules that stop the clock in certain situations but permit it to run in others.

Another indication of the different emphasis that the two sports place on rules and their enforcement is the difference in the number of officials thought necessary to enforce the rules. Although a soccer field is substantially bigger than a football field and, in addition, play tends to be much more spread out around the entire field and to move quickly over great distances up and down it, there is only one referee on the field. This referee has sole responsibility for controlling play among the players on the field. The only concession to the size of field are two assistant referees who follow the play from the sidelines and help the referee with decisions at the perimeters of play for which the referee may not be well positioned. They indicate by raising a flag when the ball has gone over the sideline, when players are offside, and when fouls are committed. But only the referee has a whistle and only the referee can stop play.

A professional football game, by contrast, requires many officials and many whistles on the field. There are between six and eight officials on the field, the better to observe play at all times from different positions and different angles. Any of them can stop play at any time for perceived infractions of the game's extraordinarily complex rules. In addition, there is a whole category of lesser officials off the field who are there to assist the officials on the field. They do so by keeping track of the game clock so that it can be started and stopped according to the rules, keeping track of the line of scrimmage, keeping track of a set of chains along the sideline that enable the referees on the field to decide if a team is entitled to a first down, and so on.

Part of the tremendous difference between the numbers of rules that govern soccer and football and the numbers of officials thought necessary to enforce those rules stems from the very different pace thought desirable for the two games. In soccer, there is a strong preference for not interrupting the flow of the game if possible and for letting the players play. Consequently, minor infractions of the rules are ignored and the referee is in the background as much as possible. Those who watched World Cup 1998 may recall the familiar "play on" signal the referee gave the players in cases of minor infractions. With the palms of both hands extended together below the waist sweeping up gently he seemed to say to the complaining player, "Come on, come on! Get up and get going. That was hardly important."

The strong reluctance to interrupt the game of soccer is evident in other subtle ways. For example, when a player is fouled but his team retains a strong offensive position nonetheless the rules state that the foul should not be called so that the offensive team can maintain its advantage. Moreover, a player in an offside position does not incur a penalty for his team if the offending player did not influence the play. Thus a goal that is scored on an offensive thrust by a team one of whose players was clearly in an offside position is not nullified if the player stayed at the perimeter of the action and did not influence the play that led to the goal.

In football, the penalty takes priority and the play must be run again in many situations where there would be no similar "do-over" in soccer. For example, if an offensive player such as the left guard moves just before the snap of the ball but the play is run and the running back fumbles the ball with the defense recovering the ball, the play is "nullified" by the penalty before it began. Or, as officials like to explain it, "there was no play." Thus there could be no fumble and no fumble recovery, even though thousands of people in the stands and hundreds of thousands of television viewers saw the play, saw the fumble, and saw the fumble recovery.

The idea of not calling a penalty or not strictly enforcing the rules so as not to interrupt the flow of the game seems almost offensive in football. If a wide receiver, even if improperly held or obstructed by the defense, still manages to make a catch and a big gain for his team, the penalty must still be called and discussed with the offensive team even if it is clear to all concerned that it will certainly be declined. If one team is behind by twenty points and has just failed to make a first down so that the ball now goes over to the other team with the clock stopped and ten seconds left in the game, the offensive team must come on the field and go through the ritual of hiking the ball to the quarterback who then genuflects to one knee to signal he is down. Only then can the game be permitted to end. How many of us who are diehard football fans have not seen a referee struggling to clear the field with a few seconds left on the clock when the two teams are shaking hands in acknowledgment that the game is over and one side has clearly won? Rules exist to be enforced and it is not the job of the officials to think beyond that.

Because football is governed by a much more complicated set of rules that need to be enforced by a comparatively large "officiating crew," the pace of the game is completely different from soccer. The game is frequently interrupted by the fluttering of little yellow flags, often followed by conclaves of officials trying to reach agreement on the appropriate ruling in this particular situation. Sometimes they then decide that there was no violation of the rules after all. Color commentators often praise this as "a good 'no call'" by the officials despite the fact that a penalty was called and the game was stopped for discussion of the call.

Our Obsession with Rulings and Our Insistence on Exact Precision in Rulings That Can Never Be Precise

A more complicated set of rules and a larger number of officials naturally results in many more interruptions and rulings during a game. In addition, football places particular stress on technical precision in making those rulings and in marking off penalty assessments during the game. If a penalty is ten yards, it is very important that it be ten yards, not nine yards or even nine and a half yards. To assist in that determination, the field is marked with horizontal stripes across it starting at the goal line and then continuing every five yards to the opposite goal line. But even this is not enough to yield the desired precision in marking penalties and in locating the ball for the start of play. So, in addition to these lines, the field is marked off with one-yard chalk marks at four locations. Each of the two sidelines are marked with "hash marks," as the commentators call them. And there are two more sets of hash marks ten yards in from each of the two sidelines. There are thus four sets of "hash marks" to assist officials in deciding if a team has made a first down.

But even these hash marks are often not considered sufficient for the sort of precise ruling thought desirable in football. There are two sets of chains, one at each side of the field, each of them exactly ten yards in length. At various points in the game one of the two chains will be brought on to the field to make sure the ruling is precisely correct. Sometimes when a team is found to be a few inches short of getting a first down, the official making that determination will keep his finger on the chain while other officials carry the ends of the chain over to the nearest set of hash marks and again stretch out the chain so that the ball can thus be placed on the hash marks precisely where it needs to be for the next play to ensue.

Given that the initial spotting of the ball following a play is often somewhat arbitrary as a runner fights for extra inches, or that the ball has to be extricated from beneath a pile of players grabbing for possession of it, one might think the officials would be relaxed about the use of the chains and simply use the set of chains closer at hand if they have to be brought onto the field. But the chains must yield the one true measurement and not just one that is "very close." So one of the sets of chains is designated the "unofficial set" while the other is the "official set." Thus if the measurement must be taken five yards in from the sideline with the unofficial set of chains, the official set of chains must be carried all the way across the field to the ball and then stretched out to make sure that the decision whether or not to award a first down is precisely correct according to that set.

In soccer, by contrast, it is thought preferable to keep the game moving and to that end there is much less emphasis on technical precision in rulings. If a foul is whistled, there is often hardly a break in the action as the ball is quickly placed on the turf, only very roughly where the infraction occurred, and the game immediately resumes. If a ball goes out of play, the throw-in takes place in the general area where it went out of bounds.

One may protest that soccer doesn't need the sort of precision that would be involved in marking the exact place where the ball should be put into play because it won't make any difference, given the size of the field and the nature of the game, whether the ball is spotted at the exact spot where the foul took place or a yard or two away from that spot. But there are times in soccer when a precise distance is specified in the rules and the distance may be important. One example is a free kick very close to an opponent's goal. The rules state that at a free kick following a foul the opposing players must be at least ten yards (9.15 meters) back from the ball. The closer the players are to the ball when they form their wall to try to keep the kicker from scoring, the less angle the kicker has and the more difficult it will be to score. Yet the ten-yard setback for the defending players is determined only approximately (and very quickly) by the referee without the benefit of chains or field markings or even without the referee taking the time to pace off the required distance.

Obviously, the nature of the games is different, with football emphasizing movement in ten-yard intervals up and down the field. This gives rise to a constant need for measurement that doesn't exist in soccer. But the games remain similar in the sense that in both there are bound to be difficult decisions for the official or officials, some of which may even affect the outcome: Was the ball in the goal (or over the goal line)? Did the player fumble before or after his knee touched the ground? Did the player's hand deflect the ball into the goal or not? Did the foul take place inside or outside the penalty box? The critical difference is that football is completely unselfconscious about the amount of effort and time it is willing to devote to trying to make what it believes will be perfect decisions on issues such as these.

This emphasis on false precision in marking out penalties and the willingness to stop the flow of the game in order to discuss and rule on possible penalties in the American game results in contests that are of exact "official" length but of rather uncertain actual duration. Thirty minutes of precisely kept "playing time" in football often consumes at least an hour and a half, and maybe more, of real time. By contrast, in soccer forty-five minutes of soccer is basically forty-five minutes of soccer, with rarely more than two or three additional minutes of "injury time" (when the game is stopped to permit an injured player to be treated) added on.

Several years ago the length of the games became a concern to National Football League officials. Their "solution" to the problem is itself a fascinating commentary on the American mentality when it comes to procedure. The most logical solution would have been the simplest as well: instead of stopping the game clock at various points during the game, such as when a player runs out of bounds or when there is an incomplete pass, the clock should continue to run. In this respect football would have mirrored soccer where the game clock continues to run even when a ball is kicked out of bounds or into the stands. But instead of the obvious solution the NFL came up with a far more elaborate procedural apparatus ironically aimed at speeding up play on the field. They added a second clock—a "play clock"—which counts off the seconds between plays. The offensive team is now required to start the next play within a set number of seconds from the end of the preceding play. Of course, the solution quickly became part of the problem because whatever gains were made were largely undercut by the difficulties officials on the field had communicating with the official off the field ("Will the time-keeper please put ten more seconds on the play clock?") as well as the stoppage necessary to mark off additional penalties when the offensive team was only one second late in getting off the ensuing play. In professional football, where passing is emphasized and hence the game clock is frequently stopped between plays, the game is of uncertain duration. But it is usually close to three hours for sixty minutes of football.

The conviction that adjudicative perfection is desirable and attainable if only enough time and care are lavished on rulings remains strong in the United States. As in our legal system, so in football there is always the temptation to add just a little more procedure in the quest for such perfection. For a couple of seasons the National Football League employed an elaborate system of appellate review whereby the officials' ruling on the field could be appealed to a completely different set of officials who sat in a box perched high above the field where they reviewed videotapes of the play from two or three different angles in order to decide whether to affirm or reverse the decision on the field. Often, the head of the officiating crew on the field would be called to the sideline to talk on the telephone with the reviewing officials and he would then scurry back to the center of the field to announce the reviewing body's decision. Meanwhile, of course, the game was stopped for several minutes with the television commentators filling air time with an explanation of the standard of review and how it might be applied to this particular situation.

The Insistence on False Precision in Our Trial System

The sharp contrasts that exist between soccer and football have strong parallels when one compares European and American criminal trials. At European criminal trials, the judges—usually a mixed panel of professional judges and ordinary citizens—want to hear and evaluate all the relevant evidence; to that end, there are few rules of evidence and other rules aimed at excluding relevant information. They function more as guidelines than as strict rules.

Witnesses are granted considerable latitude to give their testimony in their own words and interruptions in the flow of testimony are discouraged. Even if a piece of evidence is what an American lawyer would seek to exclude as "hearsay," there is likely to be no objection: the judges want to hear all the evidence and they don't want to be deflected from their task by having to deal with technical violations unless the issue is truly important. A day of trial testimony at a European trial is pretty much a day of hearing the testimony of witnesses and listening to them answer questions.

By contrast, the rules that govern American criminal trials are extremely complex and they must be enforced to the hilt. Objections to what a question seeks to elicit from a witness are common and even objections to the way the question is expressed are frequent. Because of the technical nature of the subject—there are in the United States multivolume treatises devoted to the subject of evidence law—a judge may not understand the thrust of the objection or may need more time to hear the argument from the lawyers. This frequently gives rise to huddled discussions, called "sidebar conferences," between the lawyers and the judge at the front of the courtroom near the judge's bench. Sometimes these sidebar discussions can be quite animated, leaving the jury, the witness, and spectators, who cannot hear the discussions, puzzled as to what is going on and why. Some of the objections may be considered so important that the judge orders the jury out of the courtroom so that fine legal distinctions can be more fully argued and analyzed. Sometimes there will even be a hearing within the trial as the judge previews the proposed testimony from the witness to see if all or parts of the testimony are appropriate for the jury's hearing. A day of trial testimony at an important trial in an American courtroom will often entail lots of legal arguments and subtle rulings, but relatively little testimony from the witnesses when compared to a similar trial in Europe.

Of course, it is not always possible for lawyers to make objections in time to stop the witness from answering a certain question. If an objection to the question should have been sustained, our trial system has the equivalent of the "no play" ruling in a football game. The judge will announce in solemn terms that the answer will be "struck from the record" (though it remains in the trial transcript) and the jury will be ordered to disregard it.

The obsession with adjudicative perfection in our criminal justice system is worse than it is in football because there is no time clock and there is always the excuse that "this is not a game, it is a trial and someone may be convicted." This justifies any additional expense so that the system is free to spend as much time as it wishes in trying to come up with exactly the correct ruling. The flow of the trial is interrupted and even its purpose is forgotten as judges struggle to make perfect rulings, becoming little referees concerned only with rules and rulings. While other trial systems understand the important lesson that there is no ten-yard marker to enable a judge to determine precisely and correctly for all time what is "relevant," "prejudicial," or "reasonable," the American legal system completely fails to understand this. It fails to acknowledge that it is trying to do something that cannot be done with precision, that reasonable people will always differ on the application of these terms to individual situations, and that it is better in such situations to rule quickly and move on without interrupting the trial. That is not the American approach to football and it is definitely not our approach to trials.

The addition of a second clock to the game of football in an effort to "speed up the game" when there are many simpler and more obvious ways to solve the problem has numerous parallels in our system of criminal trials. Everyone I know in our criminal justice system—judges, prosecutors, and even hard-bitten defense attorneys—concedes that it is way too complicated and needs to be made simpler. Yet they are constantly tempted and usually cannot resist adding new procedures and new hearings to an already over-burdened system even in the face of a crying need for more efficiency. A nice example is jury selection. Lots of countries—England, for example—have basically no jury selection process. The jurors are put into the jury box, the judge describes the case and the witnesses, and that is pretty much it. The trial begins without the lawyers questioning the jurors and without any challenges to the jurors. But in the last ten years, despite everyone's recognition that trials are too complicated and too expensive, we have gone in the opposite direction in jury selection: adding subtle legal issues to jury selection which require delicate inquiry and rulings by the trial judge as the prosecutor and the defense attorney, occasionally advised by jury consultants in big cases, each proceed to kick people they don't like off the jury. The obvious solution would be to limit jury selection. But we have a weakness: we are procedure junkies and always prefer to add more procedure.

The Differing Relationships between Players and Coaches in the Two Sports

Another striking difference between football and soccer is the very different relationship that exists between coaches and players during the actual game. In soccer, no coaching is permitted during the game. No coach prowls the sidelines to shout signals or relay specific advice; the coach is not permitted near the playing field and instead usually sits quietly on the bench. At professional soccer games in Italy I have noticed that the coaches seem to pass the time chain smoking to relieve the tension, only occasionally glancing at the field and then rolling their eyes with a look of pain at developments they can't do anything to rectify. The only decision a professional soccer coach has to make during the game is whether to make a substitution. But since only three substitutions are permitted during the entire game even that role in the game is extremely limited compared to football.

The very secondary role that coaches play during soccer games contrasts sharply with the role of American coaches during their game. Football coaches are much more involved in the play of the game. Perhaps a more accurate way of describing the relationship of the coach to the players in professional football is to say that the line between players and coaches is blurred because the coach and his staff really dictate the play of the game. Typically, they decide what every single offensive play will be. In addition, on the other side of the field, defensive formations are also determined by the coaches, not the players. Because the pace of the game is more leisurely than soccer and there are so many interruptions, all the major strategic decisions—whether to "go for it" on fourth down, whether to punt or try a field goal, or whether "to go for two" (points) following a touchdown—are made by the coaches, not the players.

At one time, it was the custom to send plays to the quarterback by whispering the play to an offensive player and substituting that player into the game. This player would in turn whisper the play to the quarterback who would then tell the other players in the huddle what the next play would be. Although there are unlimited substitutions in a football game, relaying plays from the coach to the quarterback through another player was thought too cumbersome. So football turned to technology to take the coach directly onto the center of the field. A small receiver was placed in the helmet of the quarterback so that the coach could speak to him directly through a transmitter and give him precise directions for the next play.

In contrast to soccer which wants the players to play on their own and tries to accomplish that by forbidding sideline coaching, there is constant coaching by a plethora of coaches throughout a professional football game. This is made much easier both by the constant breaks in action between plays and by the unlimited substitutions that permit coaches to sit with their offensive or defensive teams to go over what the players should do when they are reinserted into the game. Sometimes coaches can be seen on the sidelines drawing up formations for the players or reviewing with the players Polaroid pictures taken moments earlier by team personnel high up in the stadium and sent down to the sidelines showing different opposing formations.

During the game, players are expected to carry out the plays that have been designed by the coaches and that the players have been drilled in advance to execute with precision. If the coaches have done their jobs correctly, it is hoped that the players will have the answer to any defensive alignment they will face during the game. Of course, not all plays during a football game work the way they were designed, and sometimes the players must improvise. But while such improvisation can be important, the pejorative way those plays are described—they are "broken plays" and those who execute them are "scramblers"—makes it clear that they are viewed as exceptional situations. There have been excellent NFL quarterbacks who couldn't scramble at all.

Soccer is fundamentally different in concept in that improvisation and spontaneity are considered the heart of the game. (In this regard, soccer is much more like basketball, a game that not coincidentally is extremely popular in Europe, while football has been slow to catch on.) While there are different offensive and defensive alignments that teams use and there can be set plays on corner kicks or throw-ins, the size of the field and the fluidity of the game make for a game that places great emphasis on spontaneity and improvisation. There is no such thing as a "broken play" in soccer because it is understood that that sort of improvisation will occur throughout the game. With no time outs and only a couple of substitutions, teams shift quickly from offense to defense and back again, and players are expected to exploit spontaneously the fluid possibilities of whatever situation presents itself.

The Roles of Lawyers at Trial and Their Relationship to Witnesses at European and American Trials

Just as American football coaches are much more involved in every phase of the game itself—play calling, substitution decisions, deciding whether or not to try a field goal—the same is true of lawyers at American trials. Because the American trial system is so heavily proceduralized, only someone trained in the law can make the kinds of sophisticated judgments about tactics that the system calls for and fully appreciate the legal issues that arise with considerable frequency during the pretrial and trial stages of an important criminal case. While, in theory, we may think of the witnesses as the "players" at an American trial because the outcome of the case should ultimately depend on the strength of the evidence, in fact the line between players and coaches is very difficult to draw in the American trial system. The system places such heavy emphasis on lawyering skills that it seems to be understood and accepted that an excellent lawyer can affect the outcome of a case even when the evidence supporting that lawyer's side of the case is weak. Lawyers and judges commenting on high publicity cases often tell us with perfect hindsight that this or that lawyer "blew it," the plain implication being that someone as brilliant as themselves would have prevailed on the same evidence. That there is anything amiss in making so much turn on the quality of one's lawyer rather than the evidence does not occur to them.

The line between players and coaches in American trials is further blurred by the heavy emphasis the system places on the careful pretrial preparation of witnesses by the lawyer calling that witness.

In any important criminal case, the testimony of the prosecution and defense witnesses will have been carefully rehearsed by the respective lawyers. Lawyers shape the testimony for maximum effect on the jury and try to prepare the witnesses to withstand, and perhaps even counter, the cross-examination of the other side. If the witness is a particularly important one, this preparation may entail bringing in another lawyer to put him or her through a mock cross-examination. The preparation in major civil cases is often even more extensive, such cases being "pretried" in front of a group of mock jurors. In short, we have built a system so complicated that lawyers and judges dread spontaneity from witnesses, and discourage it in all kinds of ways.

In Europe trials are conceptualized very differently. While lawyers are important in any trial system, continental lawyers have far less influence on what occurs in their trials than do American lawyers on theirs. This difference rests in part on the fact that Europeans make a different set of assumptions as to what should take place at trial. Far from wanting witnesses who are prepared and controlled by the lawyers, continental trial systems start from the premise that witnesses should always be permitted to testify in their own words and in their own way about the events in question without being influenced in their testimony by others. To that end, European trial systems place a heavy emphasis on spontaneity, and not only discourage but consider highly improper the sort of pretrial preparation and rehearsals of witness testimony by lawyers that takes place routinely in the United States. Rather than testifying according to a rehearsed set of questions and answers, in Europe witnesses have the opportunity to testify about the events in question in their own words and at their own pace before questioning from the judges and lawyers takes place. This means, of course, that a witness may allow some things to slip out that are not relevant to the issue in question, or that may even be somewhat prejudicial; but

Europeans accept those risks in order to permit witnesses to testify candidly and completely.

Given the fact that a European trial differs sharply in concept from an American one, it is hardly surprising that European lawyers are assigned a more limited role in the proceedings than their American counterparts. Because European trial systems are less proceduralized and because spontaneity is desired, lawyers do not need to spend days or weeks briefing legal issues and preparing witnesses in advance of trial. They do not have tight control over what occurs at trial and their role at trial is de-emphasized, unlike American lawyers who are permitted to dominate the courtroom.

Some of this difference between the two systems can be seen in the physical movements of lawyers around the courtroom, which again has parallels with the sports of football and soccer. While American lawyers have considerable freedom to move around the courtroom, sometimes moving over to the area in front of the jury box to question a witness or make an opening or closing statement, or sometimes approaching the bench to argue a point of law, European lawyers are expected to stay in their seats, usually located at the sides of the courtroom. They ask questions from that location and they make final arguments from there as well. Like European soccer coaches, they must remain well back, at the periphery of the proceedings.

Conclusion

Our American trial system reflects many of the cultural values encoded in the rules and traditions of professional football: the worship of proceduralism, the attempt to rationalize every aspect of decision making, the distrust of spontaneous action, the heavy preference for tight control over the participants, and, above all, the daunting complexity of the rules such a system requires. Today trials in the United States are prepared for, officiated, and even reported on much like actual football games. Television, in particular, uses the same techniques for trials as it does for slow-moving football games, including video replays, color commentators, sideline reporters who prowl the corridors of the courthouse, and plenty of Monday morning quarterbacking.

But the analogy between sports and trial systems breaks down at the objectives of the two systems. A trial system does not exist for the purpose of entertaining the public or showcasing the skills of its legal players. It must strive to achieve and keep in balance much more difficult and important objectives. No trial system is strong and deserving of public respect (1) if it cannot be trusted to acquit the innocent and convict the guilty with a high degree of reliability; (2) if it fails to treat those who come in contact with the system—including victims and witnesses as well as suspects and defendants—with dignity and respect; and (3) if it fails to make wise use of limited judicial resources.

In this book, I question how well our criminal trial system is meeting any of these three objectives, especially the first. We have developed a criminal trial system that is entertaining and that places tremendous emphasis on winning and losing. But the system badly underemphasizes truth. In the long run a trial system that cannot be relied upon to find the truth with a high degree of reliability ends up hurting the vast majority of defendants just as much as it does victims and the general public.

CHAPTER TWO

Technicalities and Truth

The Exclusionary Rule

The Vain Quest for Adjudicative Perfection

Just as all football-loving Americans believe that enough time and effort devoted to rulings on the football field will yield something close to adjudicative perfection, American judges have the same confidence that adjudicative perfection is achievable in their rulings. In this chapter, I want to discuss one manifestation of the judicial obsession with adjudicative perfection, the so-called "exclusionary rule" whereby evidence unconstitutionally seized by police officers is excluded from being used at trial. This topic is a perfect sequel to the introductory chapter on football and our trial system because the attempt by American judges in applying the exclusionary rule to determine, well after the fact, individual case by individual case, whether a particular search was "reasonable," manifests the same worship of proceduralism that one finds in football.

This topic is also a nice bridge to the broader discussions that will take place in succeeding chapters. The subtle costs of the exclusionary rule to our criminal justice system—and I say "subtle" to distinguish these costs from the obvious costs of the suppression of reliable evidence—are tremendous, and I want to explain just what they are.

The Exclusionary Rule and Close Cases

On the face of it, the idea of excluding evidence where there has been a violation by the police of our fourth amendment prohibition against unlawful searches and seizures seems to make good sense. Why should the police be permitted to violate the rights of citizens in order to gather evidence with which to prosecute those citizens? One only has to think of the facts of *Mapp v. Ohio*[1] to understand why the Supreme Court felt that an exclusionary rule, although not technically part of the fourth amendment protection against "unreasonable searches and seizures," had to be creatively read into the amendment to protect citizens from police illegalities in violation of the fourth amendment.

In *Mapp*, the police ransacked the home of Dollree Mapp from cellar to attic, lied to her about having a warrant, and although they were supposedly looking for a fugitive in the house, ended up looking through her personal possessions sufficiently to charge her with the possession of obscene pictures. On these facts, one can see why the Court decided to exclude materials unlawfully seized from the evidence.

The problem is that the rule doesn't always occur in shocking and clear cases such as *Mapp*. In fact, such cases are rare in the system. Instead the sort of case one is likely to see in most courts are like the one that arose in Denver on a hot September afternoon. On that afternoon, a woman, Darlene Bergan, saw a man, whom later events revealed to be Fidel Quintero,[2] go up onto the porch of the house across the street and stand at the front door for about twenty seconds. He then went to a front window for another twenty seconds so he could peer into the house. He then left the porch and went to the side of the house and appeared to be studying the windows. Eventually, he left the house and went down the street where Mrs. Bergan saw him stop at another house before she lost sight of him. About an hour later, Mrs. Bergan saw Quintero standing at a bus stop in front of her house. He had taken off the short sleeved shirt he had been wearing and had used it to cover a television set. He was pacing nervously and trying to hitch a ride from passing cars while waiting for a bus. Mrs. Bergan called the police, thinking he had committed a burglary.

Five minutes later, Officer Freeman of the Denver Police Department, later joined by other officers, arrived on the scene to investigate the possible burglary. He asked the suspect for identification but the suspect said he had none. When the officer lawfully patted down Quintero, he found a pair of wool gloves in Quintero's back pocket. (The opinion in the case states that the temperature that day was "in the 80 degree range or above that.") At this point, Mrs. Bergan came out and made herself known to the police as the woman who had called the police to report what she had seen. The officer decided to arrest Quintero. In his pockets the police found $140 in cash, five rings (including two class rings bearing different initials and different class years), and some ladies' jewelry. Later that day the owners of a house one block south of Mrs. Bergen's returned home and reported that their home had been burglarized and a television set, eventually identified as the one in Quintero's possession, had been stolen.

The issue in the case became the arrest of Quintero. Up until the officers arrested Quintero and seized the television, there was no problem with anything they had done. But should they have placed Quintero under arrest or should they have let him leave the scene with the television? In some other countries police officers don't have this stark choice in such a situation. They may lawfully detain a suspect for several hours while an investigation is continuing. But in the United States, as the Court has interpreted the Constitution,[3] after a brief on-the-spot detention for investigation, a police officer has the choice of either arresting the suspect or letting him or her go.

The answer on the facts in *Quintero* was easy for Justice Luis Rovira of the Colorado Supreme Court. In his view, the officers would have been "derelict in their duty" had they merely released Quintero. But the majority of the court held that the officers should have released Quintero and that because his arrest was unconstitutional the television should not have been seized and was wrongly admitted at trial. They thereby overturned Quintero's burglary conviction.

One might wonder why the arrest of Quintero was unconstitutional. After all the fourth amendment only condemns unreasonable seizures and in this case the officer felt the seizure was reasonable. Why was this an "unreasonable" seizure under the fourth amendment? As the law has developed, to arrest a suspect requires probable cause and the Colorado Supreme Court differed over whether there was probable cause. But what is "probable cause"? Well, the cases tell us that probable cause exists when the facts and circumstances "are sufficient to support a reasonable belief in the officer that a crime has been committed by the person being arrested." But can't we say the officers' belief that Quintero had committed a crime was reasonable when a justice of the Colorado Supreme Court would have done just what the officers did in this case, the officers certainly believed Quintero had committed a crime, and later events proved that belief correct? Why was this an unreasonable seizure and why should the television be suppressed?

Notice that we have reasonableness chasing reasonableness in this situation. This is typical of many fourth amendment issues. What is a reasonable seizure depends on whether the officer has a reasonable belief that a crime has been committed. But all the officer on the street has to make this decision is his or her own judgment as to what it is reasonable to believe from the facts in question and, as this case shows, even judges may differ over what may reasonably be inferred from the facts and circumstances of an individual case. There is no litmus test for probable cause. No ten-yard chains as in football that an officer can stretch over the facts to see if the ball lies on one side or the other of the end of the chain. There will be many cases like *Quintero*—cases in which reasonable people differ over whether there was probable cause.

This is, of course, exactly parallel to the soccer rules on "dangerous" play, or "holding" or "obstructing" an opponent. But American courts are completely confident that they can actually illuminate and define what is "reasonable," case by case, situation by situation, so that officers on the street will have an easy job of it. This is a vain hope. I learned this lesson some years ago when I was a young law professor fresh from a stint as a federal prosecutor. A few weeks after I had finished teaching a course that centered on the fourth amendment prohibition against unreasonable searches and seizures, I was looking through the course evaluation forms filled out by the students. On this occasion one of the students had written, "I enjoyed the course very much. But one thing I never really seemed to learn from the course was what probable cause was." My immediate reaction was defensive anger: "I have taught all the major Supreme Court cases on probable cause. I even told the students about some warrant cases I had worked on as a prosecutor. What is this student talking about? It is certainly the student's fault, not mine." But the more I have thought about the point over the years, the more I have come to see what the student was talking about. And I have come to realize that this student was right on the mark with the criticism.

To make this clear, consider *Quintero* once again. I could not have helped the officers make their decision, except to say the obvious: "It is a very close question as to whether there is probable cause on those facts." Nor has *Quintero* taught us anything useful about probable cause that will help them tomorrow. Imagine the same set of facts but now in addition to the wool gloves in Quintero's pocket the officer finds a screwdriver and sees paint chips on the gloves. Or imagine instead that when Officer Freeman arrived and started to approach Quintero, Quintero turned and started to walk away quickly, leaving behind the television.

Do these additional suspicious facts justify an officer in the reasonable belief that Quintero has committed a crime? My answer to the officers would be the same: "I'm sorry, officers, I wish I could help, but it's a close question." Most search and seizure decisions are "fact bound," meaning that they are tied to a narrow set of facts that will never occur in just that way again. And, of course, judges on courts change so who knows how an appellate court will rule?

I like to discuss *Quintero* with my students because it shows the difficulties officers on the street face when they have to anticipate how courts will rule with twenty-twenty hindsight. *Quintero* is also an interesting case to ponder because the United States Supreme Court agreed to review the decision. Unfortunately, Fidel Quintero died before the case was argued. So it was mooted and the Court never got a chance to look at the issues that call into question so much of what courts around this country have been doing over the last thirty years.

Another Close Case: United States v. Bayless

Quintero is but a single case and it is now a bit old, having been decided in 1983. But close cases like *Quintero* involving search and seizure law, often where judges can't agree among themselves whether a search was reasonable or not, come along every single day. A rather notorious case—one that gained national attention for the judge in question—that makes exactly the same point about the system's vain attempt to define precisely what can never be defined precisely, arose in 1996 in New York City. In a drug-infested area of Manhattan, at 5 A.M. on a January morning, plain clothes officers observed a car with Michigan plates pull over and double park. Four males approached the car single file and, without conversing with the driver, the first man opened the trunk, the second and third each placed large duffel bags in it, and the fourth closed the trunk. When the officer approached, the four men walked off quickly in different directions. The officers stopped the car and eventually received consent to search the trunk where they found thirty-four kilos of cocaine and two kilos of heroin, a drug cache estimated to be worth some four million dollars. The driver of the car, Carol Bayless, was arrested and charged in federal court with involvement in a cocaine and heroin distribution conspiracy.

Bayless filed a motion to suppress the drugs found in her car. The issue in the case was whether the officers possessed "reasonable suspicion" to stop the car. Like "probable cause," "reasonable suspicion" is another term of art in fourth amendment law. Under this law, the police can forcibly stop and briefly detain a suspect if they have "reasonable suspicion" that a crime is taking place or has taken place. Because a "stop" is intended to be brief and temporary, a stop is permitted in suspicious circumstances even if the officer lacks probable cause to arrest.

On these facts, one might well ask, "Why wasn't the stop legal since the circumstances seemed somewhat suspicious? A choreographed delivery of luggage in the dark of night to a car in a drug-infested neighborhood by four men who quickly scatter in different directions upon the approach of the police?" But the judge in the case, Judge Harold Baer, acting as if he had a ten-yard chain he could stretch over the facts and definitively tell whether there was reasonable suspicion or not, concluded that the police officers lacked reasonable suspicion and picked apart each of the factors mentioned by the police.[4] As for the fact that this neighborhood was known for its drug activity, Judge Baer concluded that "mere presence in a neighborhood known for its drug activity . . . fails to raise reasonable suspicion that the person is present to purchase drugs." As for the timing of the delivery, nothing was suspicious about a 5 A.M. transfer of luggage because New Yorkers are about at "all hours of the day and night." Nor was there anything suspicious about a double-parked car with out of town plates as New

York has lots of visitors from other states and cars are often double parked on Manhattan streets. As for the evasive action of participants in the transfer, the judge noted that Bayless had not done anything furtive or evasive herself and, as for the four males, people in this neighborhood "tended to regard police officers as corrupt, abusive and violent" so that "had the men not run when the cops began to stare at them, it would have been unusual."

Judge Baer's decision caused a national uproar, with politicians from both political parties blasting the decision. Even President Clinton, who had appointed Judge Baer, announced his hope that Judge Baer might reconsider his opinion and there were hints that the White House might ask Judge Baer to resign if the opinion stood.[5] Judge Baer took the unusual step of calling for a rehearing in the matter and eventually reversed his earlier decision in an opinion that expressed regret over the fact that "the hyperbole" in the original decision "may have demeaned the law-abiding men and women who make Washington Heights their home and the vast majority of the men and women in blue who patrol the streets of our great City."[6]

Decisions like those in *Quintero* and *Bayless* demonstrate a legal system that does not understand that there are different types of rules: some are clear and precise, and can be easily and quickly applied; others are necessarily vague and subject to different interpretations. This is not the fault of the drafters; often this is the best we can come up with when a rule has to cover many different possibilities. Applying rules that are necessarily somewhat vague calls for experience, fairness, and sound judgment rather than technically precise rulings. We have yet to learn this lesson in our criminal justice system. In area after area, the rules and their enforcement have become ends in themselves so that the broader goals of the system are ignored—including trying to determine with a high degree of accuracy whether the defendant committed the crime in question. Our legal system spends countless hours arguing, after the fact, about particular instances when anyone can see that no definitive answer is possible. Nor is there any way to make future decisions easier in the hundreds of close cases that take place around the country every day.

The Exclusionary Rule: The Theory

According to the Supreme Court, the justification for our tough exclusionary rule that is willing to countenance the suppression of reliable evidence even in close cases like *Quintero* or *Bayless* is that it will serve as a powerful "deterrent" remedy, forcing police to obey the Constitution by harshly punishing any violations. This deterrence rationale is badly misconceived. We talk about deterrence a great deal in the United States, usually with ardor and passion but not much intelligence. Thus, we constantly hear politicians and "law and order" advocates claiming that we need a death penalty to deter murderers, or tough mandatory sentences for drug possession to deter addicts, and so on. Everything I have read suggests that it is not the occasional harshness of the penalty that deters, but the certainty that the offender will be caught, convicted, and punished appropriately.

But even if you accept that severe punishments deter, it is one thing to deter someone from violating the criminal law and quite another to think it is appropriate to use a powerful deterrent when officers are trying to enforce the law on the streets. In the criminal area we don't want citizens flirting with crime. We would like citizens to stay far back from the line that separates the legal from the illegal.

But as *Quintero* and *Bayless* make clear, we don't want police officers to be extremely cautious in stopping or arresting someone: we want police officers to intervene on the street and investigate as soon as they have "reasonable suspicion" and we want them to make an arrest just as soon as they have probable cause. This is especially true when the crime is serious. If the officers don't make the stop or arrest quickly the perpetrator will get away with his crime because he may never be identified, or the suspect may toss away and lose important evidence. If Quintero is permitted to leave the scene after being stopped, the chances of later recovering the television and using it to show beyond any reasonable doubt that he was the burglar are nil.

When officers have the minimum of probable cause and make an arrest that solves a crime, they are often patted on the back and congratulated for their work, not condemned. It would not surprise me to learn that the officers in *Bayless* received a commendation for their work in that case because their alertness led to the discovery of such an enormous cache of drugs. Yet the lines between a hunch and a reasonable suspicion, or between reasonable suspicion and probable cause, are blurry and reasonable people, even reasonable judges, can differ over whether a particular case is over the line or not. In these situations a harsh deterrent remedy that requires the suppression of all evidence gathered as the result of what is, well after the fact, determined to be an unlawful stop or unlawful arrest, which evidence may include even a voluntary confession from the suspect or crucial physical evidence, is out of place. When the public is confronted with cases like *Quintero* and *Bayless* which hold out the possibility that the offender will not be convicted of a crime, but that the police are to be punished for what is seen to be a technical violation of a rule—one that involved no abuse or mistreatment of the suspect—the public becomes convinced that the values of the system are wrong and its priorities misplaced.

One of the most disturbing aspects of our exclusionary rule is the fact that this tough "macho" rule sometimes ends up directly punishing an innocent party. *Quintero* is a case in point: who has really been punished by the *Quintero* decision? Officer Freeman and the other police officers will go on with their jobs without any black mark on their records. There is no indication that the officers treated Quintero other than politely and who could fault an officer who did exactly what a state Supreme Court justice said he should have done? The prosecutor will pick up another file and go on to the next burglary case of which there are hundreds each year in any major American city. The real losers in the case are the victims of the particular burglary who had their privacy and their sense of security violated in a much more serious way by Fidel Quintero than anything the police did to him. Yet because Quintero was arrested a few hours *before he should have been arrested*, Quintero avoided conviction and punishment for what he did to the owners of the home he burglarized.

When the crime is a very serious one, such as murder, assault, or rape, even the occasional application of the exclusionary rule is sufficient to undermine public confidence and respect for the system. I want to stress that I don't believe that cases like this are common. (Judges will sometimes credit rather incredible testimony if necessary to avoid suppressing reliable evidence. There is a cost to this, too.) But it doesn't take many suppression cases to weaken public confidence in a system that appears to care far more about the comparatively minor wrongs done by the police than it does about the terrible things the defendant has done to the victim.

The Adversary Mentality of American Lawyers and Judges

The Supreme Court has said over and over in its decisions that the exclusionary rule is not part of a defendant's fourth amendment right but exists solely by "judicial implication" to deter future violations of the fourth amendment. Given this justification for the rule, one wonders how our criminal justice system could place such a high priority on the uncertain and speculative prospect of future deterrence when the claim of victims or their families to a fair trial of the offender is so strong in individual cases.

Our tough exclusionary rule is a manifestation of the "adversary mentality" that grips American judges and lawyers. We like to say that "we have an adversarial trial system." But lots of countries have a trial system in which there is someone in the courtroom representing the state and someone else representing the defense. What is different about American lawyers and judges is that, viewing our whole system through the prism of an "adversary mentality," they honestly believe that criminal cases are two-sided contests between the state and the individual. Just as the monks of Galileo's time were sure that the sun revolved around the earth, American lawyers and judges are no less convinced that criminal trials are two-sided. It is a matter of basic metaphysics.

Looking at the world through their eyes there is ample proof that the world is as they claim. Just as the monks could point to the sky in support of the obvious truth that the sun revolves around the earth, American lawyers and judges are surrounded by "proofs" of the two-sided nature of criminal proceedings no less obvious and compelling. "Look at the caption of every legal document filed in every criminal case in this country, does it not demonstrate that criminal proceedings are two-sided battles involving the defendant and the state?" If that seems too abstract, they have concrete evidence that criminal cases are two-sided in the very structure of American courtrooms. There are two tables in the well of the courtroom, the one nearest the jury for the prosecutor who represents "the state" and the other for the defendant and the defense attorney. What better proof could there be that criminal cases are only about "the state" and the defendant?

Of course, anyone not afflicted with the adversary mentality knows that the way cases are captioned or the way a courtroom is arranged for trial says very little about the structure of the world. It so happens that we have evolved a trial system in which a professional prosecutor presents the evidence that has been gathered by the police during the investigation. But we could have chosen to do it differently. This is even more obvious if we consider the physical arrangement of the courtroom. It so happens that we set up our courtrooms a certain way—usually with two tables, one for the prosecution and one for the defense—but this simply reflects the way we have chosen to have evidence presented and tested. We could certainly imagine a courtroom that was set up differently. In some European countries, it is set up with three or four tables around the perimeter so that there is room for others, in addition to the state's attorney and the defense attorney, to participate in the trial. In some countries, an attorney for the victim is permitted to participate with a lawyer at the criminal trial on an equal basis with the prosecutor and the defense attorney.

Our extreme version of the exclusionary rule is an example of the adversary mentality. In a two-sided world, it is easy to accept the premise that if the police violate a constitutional right of the suspect, "the state" should pay the penalty for that violation. But when the "rules" turn out to be not so clear, even to judges who have the time to study all the precedents, and when it turns out that criminal cases are not two-sided and that sometimes there are victims who have a stake in seeing that the verdict at trial is truthful, an exclusionary rule as extreme as ours becomes difficult to defend.

The Costs of the Exclusionary Rule

One might think that since we have the toughest exclusionary rule in the world aimed at deterring unlawful searches and seizures by the police, we must have the best police departments in the world, certainly better than those in Norway or Germany—countries with no exclusionary rule—or Canada and England—which have much weaker exclusionary rules. But is there anyone who thinks the police in our major cities are less likely to mistreat citizens than the police officers in Ottawa or Oslo simply because there is not a similar exclusionary deterrent in those countries? We have had thirty years of a tough exclusionary rule applied to the states and where are we? Amnesty International has accused the New York City police of widespread police brutality against blacks and Hispanics.[7] Recent evidence of the serious problems alluded to by Amnesty International was the brutal attack by officers in Brooklyn on Abner Louima, a Haitian immigrant, who was sodomized with the handle of a toilet plunger and suffered, among other injuries, a perforated colon and lacerated bladder.[8] In Philadelphia, 137 cases have been overturned following the convictions of police officers who had beaten, robbed, and framed drug suspects.[9] And, of course, we are all familiar with the beating of Rodney King by Los Angeles police officers.

If the exclusionary rule is to protect citizens against police abuse it is a failure. The mistreatment of citizens by police remains a serious problem in the United States. The plain fact is that there is no shortcut for achieving a professional police force. The only way to have a highly professional police department that treats all citizens with respect and dignity is to work hard every day of the year toward this end. A lot will depend on the quality of those who are selected to become police officers, the training and support they receive, the priorities senior officials place on this goal as well as the command structure of the department, the disciplinary mechanisms put in place for punishing offenders, the civil remedies made available when police mistreat citizens, and so on. Even with many of these programs or mechanisms in place, policing the police will be difficult if the department cannot break through the "code of silence" among officers when the subject is police wrongdoing. It is sometimes remarkable how many police officers had their backs turned or were looking down when a suspect alleges he was struck and knocked to the ground.

Rather than contributing to police professionalism, a draconian exclusionary rule feeds into this "us versus them" mentality among police officers and encourages cynicism about the system and even the practice referred to by police as "testilying," meaning that officers "embellish" the actual facts in their suppression hearing testimony to avoid the possibility of suppression.[10] When the crime is a serious one and the consequences of suppression would mean that the guilty person will go free, judges are tempted to credit testimony that they have good reason to believe has been embellished, to avoid suppression. Sometimes they give in to the temptation, or even hunt for an exception that would allow them to uphold search. If Quintero had assaulted the owner of the house he had burglarized and left him bleeding and badly injured, or if the packages being put in the trunk of Bayless's car had contained a large quantity of explosives for some terrorist group, I have no doubt that both searches would have been upheld on exactly the same facts.

In short, a system with harsh rules becomes less honest all around as we struggle to avoid the harshness of the rules. Testimony and judicial opinions are less honest. An attitude of cynicism starts to pervade courthouses as the criminal justice system comes to expect and tolerate dishonesty under oath. ("Defendants lie in court? Sure, but so do police officers. . . .") At the same time, the windfall of suppression encourages the filing of motions to suppress for actions by the police that were taken in good faith and that caused little or no damage to the citizen.

Supporters of our exclusionary rule frequently assert that the police must "play by the rules." But the *Quintero* and *Bayless* cases show one of the problems with fourth amendment law: despite hundreds of cases decided by appellate courts year after year, to a large extent there are no rules that can help officers on the spot in the street. Whether police conduct amounted to a "forcible stop" requiring "reasonable suspicion," whether the officer had reasonable suspicion, or whether that "stop" blossomed into an "arrest" which would require "probable cause," and whether the officer had probable cause turn out to be difficult questions on which the responses of reasonable people, including reasonable judges, may differ. As a case progresses through the system, the officer's decision on the street may be second-guessed by a trial judge. He in turn may be reversed by the majority of an appellate court which may or may not be of one mind as to whether the police officer really had "reasonable suspicion" or not. The purpose of chapter 1 was to suggest that Americans don't have a light touch when it comes to procedure and refereeing. The result of the exclusionary rule is a system that devotes incredible resources to deciding numerous cases that no officer on the street could ever hope to recall and keep straight. Whether this is a wise use of scarce judicial resources is extremely doubtful.

I want to make it clear that I don't believe lots of defendants are walking out of courthouses around the country as a result of the exclusionary rule. And even when evidence is suppressed, it is almost always in minor drug cases where many of those who do walk out will very likely be caught again down the road. But even if cases like *Quintero* and *Bayless* are not common, the costs of the exclusionary rule for our criminal justice system are very high.

I believe our Supreme Court has never fully appreciated the seriousness of these costs. Let me start with the unspoken assumption behind the rule: it is fair to punish the police officer and jeopardize the conviction of the offender because the police and prosecutor are part of "the state" and it is their job, working together, to convict the guilty. This premise is both a product of the adversary mentality and reinforces such a mentality. Notice the picture behind this assumption: in a major kidnaping or murder case, where there may be two or three police agencies involved, perhaps even a federal agency such as the FBI, all these police forces are aligned and working "on the same side" against the suspect, who stands alone.

We ought to resist this picture of the complete identity of police agencies with the prosecution. It ought not to be the function of the police to convict the defendant. The police should do a full and complete investigation of the crime, and gather all the relevant evidence including anything that might cast doubt on the defendant's guilt. It is then the prosecutor's job to evaluate the evidence, prosecute if appropriate, and seek a conviction if the matter goes to trial.

This difference between the role of the police and that of the prosecutor may seem rather technical. But it is very important and other criminal justice systems understand well the costs of failing to distinguish between the function of the police and that of the prosecutor. A police agency that sees itself as aligned "against" the suspected criminal may neglect to investigate evidence that helps "the other side" or may fail to note in police reports or files evidence that might be consistent with the suspect's innocence or that might suggest weaknesses in the case against the suspect.

It also may lead to sloppy or even corrupt work on the part of the police. In April 1997, the Justice Department Inspector General Michael Bromwich released a five-hundred-page report strongly critical of the FBI laboratory.[11] Some FBI lab scientists were accused of giving inaccurate testimony and of having produced flawed scientific reports which were slanted to favor the prosecution. Calls are now being issued for "an independent laboratory." But criminal investigators, be they police or agents of the FBI, need to see themselves as independent. If laboratory scientists, usually far removed from the scene of the crime, are slanting reports, what about other aspects of the police investigation outside the lab?

Obviously there will usually be a close working relationship between those police officers who investigate serious crimes and the prosecutors who handle the matter if someone is charged with the crime. Precisely because of this relationship, it is important to emphasize that it is the job of the police to do a thorough, fair, and complete investigation of the crime, not to convict the suspect. Instead of emphasizing this distinction, the exclusionary rule fails to notice any distinction between the police and the prosecution.

This distinction is just as important as that between the prosecutor and the judge, or the police and the judge. Certainly, in important cases involving horrific crimes, a judge hopes that the police will solve the crime and arrest the offender and that the jury will convict the defendant if the evidence is strong. But a judge is supposed to be neutral in applying the law, even if he or she doesn't like the result.

In a 1995 California case involving the suppression of drugs found on the defendant's person and in his duffel bag, one of the appellate judges who voted to uphold the suppression confessed that his heart was with the dissent (which would have upheld the search), but that his head and his signature were with the majority in favor of suppression.[12] Here was a judge who did not like the outcome and would have liked to have been able to uphold the conviction of the offender, doing what a judge ought to do: he applied the law to the facts before him and reached the decision he believed the law demanded.

Just as the judge's role is different from that of the prosecutor, police and prosecutors also have different roles to play in the system. What is troubling about the exclusionary rule is that it sees no formal distinction between the prosecutor and the police and treats them as one. This is another manifestation of the "adversary mentality": if one is not on the side of the defendant, one must be on that of "the state." This is a mistake that encourages investigations that are incomplete or slanted to favor the prosecution and an innocent defendant may pay the price. Our tough exclusionary rule drives the police and the prosecutor closer together than they ought to be.

A Balanced Approach to the Exclusion of Reliable Evidence

As mentioned above, many European countries do not have an exclusionary rule that would suppress evidence improperly seized by police, preferring instead to keep the disciplining of police officers separate from the criminal prosecution of the defendant. But these countries often tend to be small, with only a few highly centralized police agencies. The United States presents a very different situation. Not only is the country large, but policing is very much a local matter. There are thousands of police agencies—more than seventeen thousand, according to one estimate[13]—spread out among cities, counties, boroughs, parishes, and municipalities throughout the country. Police departments range from large urban departments with thousands of experienced officers to tiny agencies with only one or two officers. The educational requirements, training, and pay that officers receive can vary considerably from city to city and the quality of policing can vary as well. Protecting citizens from police abuse is much more difficult where there is such variation among police agencies and these police agencies are largely independent and not subject to any centralized control.

But countries do not face an all or nothing choice when it comes to the exclusion of evidence at trial as one way of protecting citizens from police abuse. Many countries take a more balanced approach to exclusion than we do, permitting exclusion where there was serious abuse by an officer and denying it where the officer's violation is minor in proportion to the crime. Canada has an exclusionary rule embodied in its Charter of Rights and Freedoms, which is a rough equivalent of the Bill of Rights in the United States Constitution. Subsection (2) of section 24 of the Charter provides that evidence "shall be excluded if it is established that, having regard to all the circumstances, the admission of it in the proceedings would bring the administration of justice into disrepute." As the Canadian courts have interpreted that provision in deciding whether or not to exclude evidence, judges should consider whether the police officer was acting in good faith, the reliability of the evidence that resulted (this provision applies to statements and not just physical evidence), the seriousness of the crime, and the importance of the evidence to the prosecution.[14]

What is fundamentally different about this standard, compared to our exclusionary rule, is that it takes into consideration what the officer was trying to do and whether he or she was acting in good faith. Obviously, the Canadian approach to exclusion would not suppress evidence in situations such as *Quintero* or *Bayless* where the officers were acting in good faith and trying to apply standards that are always going to be unclear in particular situations.

The standard for exclusion in Canada is also different in another respect: the seriousness of the crime is taken into account when deciding whether to exclude evidence. This means that the same action by a police officer may result in exclusion where the unlawful arrest or unlawful search yielded a packet of marijuana, but would probably not result in exclusion where a violent crime was involved or where the quantity of drugs involved was enormous. American judges in suppression motions do take the seriousness of the crime into account when granting or denying motions to suppress, and will find some way not to suppress evidence when the crime is a serious one and the evidence is important. But the Canadian standard permits judges to do so honestly rather than in a roundabout manner.

Canada is not alone in taking a balanced approach to exclusion. In England, exclusion is called for under the Police and Criminal Evidence Act 1984 when "having regard to all the circumstances, including the circumstances in which the evidence was obtained, the admission would have such an adverse effect on the fairness of the proceedings that the court ought not to admit it."[15] The law in Australia follows similar lines in that it permits a judge to balance a number of factors, including the seriousness of the police violation and the seriousness of the crime, in deciding whether to exclude evidence.[16]

Conclusion

In chapter 1 I suggested, using football as an example, that Americans so love rules and rulings that we are willing to devote an inordinate amount of time to obtaining what we expect to be perfect rulings to the point that we end up losing track of the flow of the game. The same overconfidence in procedure that we see on the football field is present in fourth amendment law. But here the stakes are much higher and the consequences of our obsession much more costly.

While I don't think many defendants avoid conviction for serious crimes because evidence is suppressed, we fool ourselves if we think that the price of the exclusionary rule is minor. The undervaluing of truth in our trial system starts with the exclusionary rule. A criminal justice system has a skewed sense of priorities if it believes that the suppression of reliable evidence as the result of police action undertaken in good faith and determined to be unreasonable only well after the fact should take precedence over an accurate determination of guilt no matter how minor the police violation or how serious the crime or crimes committed by the defendant. The costs of such a harsh rule in terms of the honesty and integrity of the system are tremendous.

CHAPTER THREE

Truth and the Amount of Evidence
Available at Trial

Understanding a Criminal Investigation
from the Inside

Imagine that the following crime occurs and you are a homicide detective:

Neighbors in an apartment building hear a scream around 11 P.M. Then two shots ring out in a ground floor apartment. The police are called. There is no response to a knock on the door so they obtain a passkey from the manager and enter. They find a woman, who the manager later confirms rents the apartment, lying dead on the floor. She is dressed in a nightgown and has been shot in the stomach and bled to death. There is a .38 caliber handgun on the floor across the room from her body.

The neighbors report that the victim had not lived there long but that she had a boyfriend who visited her regularly, sometimes spending the night. They are able to give a description of the boyfriend and of the truck he drove. Two of the neighbors, a young couple, think they remember seeing the truck in the parking lot that evening around 10 P.M. when they returned from seeing a movie. They also say they heard a man and a woman arguing when they walked past the apartment door. Records in the apartment show where the victim worked. The next morning the police go to the office and talk to coworkers. They learn that the victim had told one of her coworkers a few days before she was killed that "it wasn't working out" with her boyfriend and that she wanted to break up with him but was afraid of what he might do. Another of her coworkers told the police that the victim had told her several times, including once just a week before she was killed, that her boyfriend was very possessive of her and exceedingly jealous and that he had once told her he would kill her if she broke off the relationship. The police obtain the name and address of the suspect from one of the coworkers.

How Strong Is the Case against the Suspect?

Although there is a lot of evidence suggesting that the victim's boyfriend committed this crime, it is not overwhelming and the investigation into the crime will need to continue. Obviously, in an ideal world, a police laboratory would find a set of fingerprints on the handle of the gun that matched those of the suspect or some other killer. There would be two or three sober and reliable eyewitnesses outside the building when the shots were fired. They would have heard the shots and seen the suspect come running from the building. The lighting would be excellent and the witnesses would get a good look at the suspect's face. A check on the handgun would reveal that the boyfriend had just purchased the gun in question two days before the murder. And so on.

But this is not an ideal world. The gun may have no prints on it—perhaps it was wiped clean. Or perhaps a neighbor entered the apartment before the police arrived and stupidly picked up the gun. Maybe no one saw the person leave the apartment, perhaps because there was no one near the main entrance to the building or perhaps because it was summer and a sliding door to a deck off the apartment allowed the killer to exit that way and flee through a dark parking lot.

Nonetheless this would seem a decent circumstantial case against the boyfriend: there seems to be a motive; the suspect seems to have had the opportunity to kill the victim on the evening in question; and there is at least some evidence that the suspect was at the apartment on that evening. But even looking at the evidence gathered so far in the investigation, the likelihood of being able to convict the main suspect of the murder is much stronger in many other countries than in the United States because our rules of evidence are far more restrictive. In most European countries, all the above evidence would be admissible and indeed it would be considered the responsibility of the judges to examine all of it in order to determine whether or not the defendant committed this crime.

But in the United States we have very tight rules of evidence and there are likely to be serious problems with the admission of the testimony of the two coworkers relating what the victim told them about her relationship with the suspect. These statements are hearsay: out-of-court statements by someone (the victim) who is not available for questioning about information in the statement. Even though there is a good reason why the victim will not testify—she has been killed—it will be an uphill battle to get either of these statements admitted at trial. Although rules of evidence differ a little from state to state, it is unlikely that testimony from a coworker that the victim had told her that her boyfriend had threatened to kill her if she broke off the relationship would be admitted. This is a very powerful piece of evidence, since it explains the victim's fear of the suspect and suggests that he was prepared to take extreme measures to preserve the relationship, even threatening to kill her. And of course, sometimes people do carry out their threats. But this statement will likely not be admissible.

The other statement to a coworker in which the victim related that the relationship was not working out and that she wanted to break up with her boyfriend but was afraid of what her boyfriend might do, also faces major hurdles to admissibility. A judge with a firm understanding of evidence law and some sophistication in the application of the exceptions that exist to the hearsay rule might admit at least part of this evidence—most likely the victim's statement about her wanting to break up with her boyfriend—but would exclude the rest of the statement. But another judge might not be willing to divide up the statement in this way and might not let any of it into evidence. Exactly how each of these statements by the victim to her coworker was worded might make a big difference.

I raise the issues surrounding the victim's statements to her two coworkers not to explain the many nuances of evidence law, but to show that if the same crime with identical evidence were to be tried in the United States and in a European country, more incriminating evidence would almost invariably be admissible in the European case than in ours because those legal systems have a different attitude toward evidence. Europeans prefer to have the best available evidence admitted at trial, which usually means hearing the testimony of witnesses. But where a witness with important information is not available—perhaps because he or she is very sick or has left the country and can't be reached—European courts will take the best available evidence. This would be statements by the witness as reported by others. In the murder case described above, since the victim is obviously not available to repeat her statements European trial systems will take what is available, namely, the testimony of the two coworkers explaining in court what the victim had told them.

A second reason for raising the issue of the coworkers' statements is that it helps explain why trials in the United States require far more preparation and why they are much more expensive than trials in other countries. The issue of the admissibility of these two statements will have to be researched by the prosecution and the defense, the lawyers will need to prepare written legal memoranda—usually referred to as "briefs"—arguing for and against their admissibility, and there will need to be argument on the issue. It is also likely that before ruling on the issue the judge will want to hear from the witnesses exactly what the victim told each of them so they will need to be issued subpoenas for the hearing to assure their attendance. If the trial judge rules against the prosecution and the prosecution feels this evidence is crucial to its case, it is likely to make an immediate "interlocutory" appeal to a higher court. This will call for additional resources as the case is briefed, argued, and eventually decided by the appellate court.

The Importance of Questioning the Suspect

On the hypothetical facts put forward above, it would seem only logical for the police to want to talk to the victim's boyfriend after they have learned his identity to see what he has to say about the crime and about the evidence that seems to implicate him in the murder. The questioning of the suspect is likely to be of crucial importance because it doesn't appear that there is anyone else with information about what took place and it would be nice to know what the boyfriend recalls about the evening. It is also not clear how the investigation should continue at the present time until the authorities hear from the suspect.

If the police can question the suspect, all sorts of possibilities may emerge. Among them:

The suspect admits to having been in the apartment on the night of the killing; he says she had telephoned him earlier to tell him she wanted to break up with him; he went to the apartment with his gun in order to kill her; and he did so.

The suspect admits to having been present in the apartment on the evening of the shooting but insists that he left around 10:30 P.M. and went home because the victim had a headache and wanted to go to bed.

The suspect denies that he was at the apartment at all on the evening in question, and claims that he spent the whole evening with his friend, Joe, watching Clint Eastwood westerns until the early hours of the morning.

The suspect admits that he was at the victim's apartment on the evening in question; they both had a lot to drink at a bar that night as well as in the victim's apartment; toward midnight they started fooling around with the victim's gun (which she had bought for self-protection); the gun went off accidentally, hitting the victim, and he panicked and fled the apartment.

The suspect admits that he was present but insists that it was he who told the victim he wanted to break up with her; she got angry and came after him with a gun and, as they struggled the gun went off, striking the victim; and he ran away in a panic.

Each of these possible accounts of what happened or where the suspect was at the time of the victim's death may be completely true, partially true, or completely false. The impact of these accounts, assuming each were true, also varies from one that supports a possible first-degree murder charge to ones that support lesser charges, perhaps second degree (no planning or premeditation) or manslaughter (a killing in sudden anger or as the result of reckless conduct), to one account that would indicate that the boyfriend had no connection with the death of the victim at all and was elsewhere when she was shot.

Getting this information relatively early in the investigation would be a tremendous advantage to the police as they can check out the information to see if it is true or likely to be true. If the suspect gives them the name or location of the bar where he claims he and the victim had been drinking, the police can go there and try to see if anyone recalls their presence or how much they may have consumed. If one of them paid by credit card, there might even be a record of how much was spent on alcohol. The police can also ask the laboratory to check the victim's blood for the presence of alcohol.

If the suspect claims to have been with a friend watching videos on the evening in question, the police can talk to the friend and try to confirm the details of the evening with that person and with other sources. ("What were the titles of the movies you watched?" "Do you own those videos or did you rent them?") If the suspect insists the victim was shot in a scuffle over the gun, the police can ask an expert to trace the trajectory of the bullet and see if the gun could have been maneuvered into a position so as to cause such a bullet path during a struggle. Or they might even try to determine whether the entry wound was compatible with being shot at such close range.

Obviously, questioning the suspect in a murder case like this would seem to be even more important in the United States, given our restrictive approach to evidence rules. In this case, this approach would likely result in a jury never hearing some powerfully incriminating information about the suspect. One might think that logic would therefore suggest that the ability to question the suspect and find out where he was at the time of the crime and what he knew about the crime would be broader in the United States than elsewhere. But while it might seem logical to balance tighter evidence rules with greater access to the suspect for questioning, in fact it is quite the opposite: the United States is far more protective of a suspect in this situation as a formal matter. Let us assume that the suspect is wealthy and has gone to a lawyer. The chances of getting any information from him if he shot the victim are nil.

In our situation, if the police go to the suspect's apartment and try to question him about the shooting and his whereabouts the previous evening, if he has consulted a lawyer or is at all sophisticated in criminal matters, he will tell the police in no uncertain terms, "Under the advice of my lawyer, I don't wish to answer any questions." He will then start to politely shut the door on the police.

Questioning Suspects at the Police
Station: Miranda

At this point, with the door being shut on them, the police have to make a choice. They could allow the suspect to shut that door or they could arrest him, since they have probable cause to believe that he killed the victim. If the police in our hypothetical case decide to arrest the suspect in the hope of questioning him and confronting him with the incriminating evidence they have gathered to this point in their investigation, they are required by *Miranda v. Arizona*,[1] the landmark 1966 Supreme Court decision, to give him the four "*Miranda* warnings": (1) that he has the right to remain silent; (2) that anything he says can be used against him; (3) that he has the right to counsel in the interrogation room; and (4) that if he cannot afford counsel, counsel will be appointed to represent him. These warnings are designed to dispel the pressures inherent in a custodial setting and to let the suspect know that he has protections available in such situations.

But *Miranda* offers more than a system of warnings. It requires that the suspect waive his rights under *Miranda* and agree to answer questions before any interrogation can take place. Thus, after being given these warnings, the suspect will be asked if he is willing to talk with the police. If he indicates that he wishes to remain silent, any attempt to question him must immediately cease. Or if he indicates that he wishes to have a lawyer present before being questioned, *Miranda* states that no questioning can take place until a lawyer is present to assist him. In short, what the Court did in *Miranda* was to shift control over whether any questioning will take place at all from the police to the suspect. The suspect must decide knowingly, intelligently, and voluntarily whether to answer questions in the interrogation room. Sophisticated suspects always refuse to answer any questions and ask for an attorney and, in the United States, any attorney "worth his salt will tell his client to refuse to answer any questions from the police," to borrow the famous line from an opinion of Justice Robert Jackson.[2]

To be a defense lawyer when a client-suspect is faced with interrogation is easy in the United States. The advice is always simple and straightforward: "It is not in your interests to answer any questions from the police: say nothing." Some evidence of this is provided in a treatise for the defense of criminal cases published by the American Bar Association and written by Anthony Amsterdam of New York University Law School.[3] Amsterdam devotes many pages in his treatise to the methods a lawyer should use to prevent a client from even being questioned by the police. He suggests, for example, that it is wise for an attorney to make and carry a supply of cards to give to clients to tell them exactly what they should tell the police during an investigation. The card starts out: "My lawyer has instructed me not to talk to anyone about my case or anything else and not to answer questions or reply to accusations."[4] When the lawyer and client confer, whether the client has been arrested or just fears arrest, he or she should always be given the following advice: "Say nothing at all to the police, tell them nothing under any circumstances, and reply to all police questions or approaches by saying that the client's lawyer has told the client not to answer questions or talk with anyone unless the lawyer is present."[5]

It is clear that once the lawyer gets into the picture there will be no interrogation. Indeed the Amsterdam manual wants to ensure that the suspect does not do anything that would assist the investigation in a positive way, from agreeing to appear in a lineup to consenting to a search of his or her premises. The lawyer's job is to try to prevent the police from gathering any information that might help solve the crime and thereby prove the suspect guilty.

The advice in the Amsterdam manual is strategically correct in our system: there is no downside to remaining silent—a suspect's reliance on his right to remain silent cannot be brought out against him at trial. The jury will therefore never know that the suspect shut the door on the police or refused to answer even a single question at the police station. And there are serious downside risks to making any statement to the police. If the prosecutor is unsure exactly what the suspect might say at trial, even if the case against him is very strong or even overwhelming, that may be just enough to help swing a more favorable plea bargain than would be the case if the suspect answered questions in the interrogation room and counsel has nothing left with which to bargain. To make the advantage of silence clear to a suspect, suppose that our suspect is charged with the crime and the trial begins. It will likely be the case that the defendant will testify as the last witness at trial. Imagine that he suddenly raises a new issue in his testimony:

> I was really frightened for the victim and I had even insisted that she get a gun to protect herself because I had seen a guy sort of hanging out near the parking lot close to the deck of her apartment two or three times over the previous two months. In fact, I had even gone running from the apartment about two weeks before the murder in an effort to catch him and find out what he was doing but it was dark and when I got outside he had disappeared.

Convincing? Maybe not. But might it not raise a reasonable doubt in the jury's mind? And how does the prosecution disprove this mysterious stalker several months after the events and on the last day of trial? It is very much to the defendant's advantage at trial not to have committed himself to any particular account of the events in question because he can then more freely explain any apparently incriminating evidence when he gets up at the end of the trial. Suppose the police uncover sales records that prove that the defendant had bought the .38 caliber a week prior to the murder. That can easily be explained: "Of course, I bought that gun. But I bought it for her and this is why it was at her apartment. I loved the victim and was concerned for her safety, living as she was in a ground floor apartment, so I bought the gun for her and gave it to her the next day. I was worried because I had seen a guy standing in the shadows across the street a couple of times. . . ." The truck in the parking lot at 10 P.M.? "I came over to visit victim about 8 P.M. and we watched television until 10:30 P.M. and I left as the victim was tired." The argument that was overheard? Easily explained, depending what the prosecution's witnesses said when testifying as part of the state's evidence. "We were arguing about politics like we always do." Or "We were arguing about her safety. I was pressuring her to let me move in with her because I loved her and what she had told me made me very, very concerned for her safety. I thought she was taking risks she should not be taking living in that apartment. . . ."

Proving a defendant guilty beyond a reasonable doubt is a very difficult task in any legal system. There are many serious crimes in every system that remain completely unsolved and many in which the authorities have a very good idea who committed the crime but have insufficient evidence to charge and prove it beyond a reasonable doubt. And proving who committed the act does not assure conviction because it may not be easy to prove what the state of mind of the defendant was at the time he acted. But the United States makes it harder for the prosecution to establish guilt because there is simply less evidence available in many criminal cases, in part because the Supreme Court views the police questioning of suspects with suspicion and it has given suspects the power to bar any questioning.

A Comparison of the Role of Counsel
during Questioning in England and
the United States

In the United States, as the Amsterdam manual makes clear, it is the function of a lawyer to prevent one's client from being questioned. As I said, it is easy to be a defense lawyer in the police station—a few minutes of legal training would be enough—as his advice is to tell the suspect to say nothing. In other countries, the role of counsel is different during questioning. I will use England as an example. But I need to explain that England has a "divided bar" consisting of "solicitors" and "barristers." In a serious criminal case, two lawyers are involved: a solicitor who does everything until the trial and a barrister who does the trial. Barristers only handle trial matters when engaged to do so by solicitors. Thus, when a suspect is being questioned, he or she is always assisted by a solicitor.

The governing body of solicitors, the rough equivalent of the American Bar Association for American lawyers, is the Law Society. A booklet published by the Law Society offering solicitors guidelines on advising suspects in the police station starts with the assumption that the solicitor's goal is not to prevent the questioning, but to see "that the interview is being and will be conducted fairly."[6] The guidelines state that "the officer should be allowed to conduct an interview in his/her own way provided that he/she does so fairly."[7] What this means as a practical matter is that the solicitor needs to watch out for questions that are confusing or misleading, that distort what the suspect has previously said, or that assume something that the suspect has never acknowledged. And of course, the solicitor may need to advise the suspect with respect to specific questions, including advice not to answer a particular question.

One might wonder why a lawyer in England would not always advise the suspect to refuse to answer any police questions, since the answers might later help the prosecution prove the defendant guilty at trial. This is a very important question to which there are a number of answers.

The first answer is that the police questioning of a suspect in England is not freighted with the same negative connotations as it is in the United States. The terminology used by the legal systems in the two countries is indicative of this difference. *Miranda* and its progeny are cases about "interrogation." By contrast, English statutes and court decisions refer to such questioning simply as the "interviewing" of the suspect. The connotations surrounding the word "interrogation" are entirely pejorative. The word conjures up images of a darkened room in the bowels of a police station where the police officers shine a light in the suspect's face and give him "the third degree." "Interviewing," on the other hand, is neutral. Lots of people conduct interviews as part of their jobs—employers interview prospective employees, college admissions officers interview applicants, newspaper reporters interview politicians—and lots of people are glad to "get an interview" or to "be interviewed." The choice of the word "interrogation" rather than "interview" suggests a system that is very unsure about the propriety of police questioning, including whether it should be permitted at all. One sees this uncertainty running through many of the Court's most famous decisions on "interrogation."

There is a second reason why lawyers in England will allow their client to answer questions: if at trial a defendant raises some matter that was never mentioned to the police when interviewed, a new English law, put into effect in 1994, permits his or her failure to have mentioned this matter to the police during questioning to be brought out at trial in order to cast doubt on this "new" defense. Reflecting this change in the law, suspects in England are now given the following warning before they are questioned: "You do not have to say anything. But it may harm your defence if you do not mention now something which you later rely on in court. Anything you do say may be given in evidence."[8]

What the statutory change was trying to stop was a situation in which the suspect gave the police no information and politely replied, "No comment" to every question, but then at trial suddenly explained that the murder must have been committed by a stalker he had seen several times outside the victim's apartment when he left at night. In such circumstances the prosecution would be permitted to show that the defendant had remained silent when questioned and the judge would then instruct the jurors that they might draw an adverse inference from the defendant's prior silence in evaluating the defense he had now put forward.

The law is thus more favorable to the police in England. Unlike the situation under *Miranda*, where a suspect can stop any questioning, in England the suspect has no right to cut off all questions. There *will* be an interview at which the suspect will be asked a number of questions, whether or not he or she wishes to answer them. The decision whether or not to answer questions is now more complicated, as the refusal to answer can be used against the suspect later at trial if it undercuts the defense.

The United States: The Trial Begins When the Crime Is Committed

There is another reason why lawyers in the United States and those in England, as well as lawyers in most other western countries, see their roles differently when it comes to the questioning of suspects. In the United States, there is no distinction between the investigation of a crime and the trial of a defendant. To understand why this is so, recall the "adversary mentality" of American lawyers and judges described in chapter 2 that leads them to see the criminal process as a two-sided battle pitting the tremendous investigative powers of the state against the individual defendant. This vision tolerates the suppression of reliable evidence *at trial* because of acts committed by the police *during the investigation* because it is only fair to punish "the state" for errors made by the police. Besides blurring the line between the function of the police and that of the prosecutor, this adversary mentality sees the investigation and trial as one undifferentiated process.

This adversary mentality, which sees no distinction between gathering evidence of a crime and testing that evidence at trial, has a powerful hold on the way American lawyers and judges view the questioning of suspects. Just as the task of the lawyer at trial is to try to keep the state from prevailing and convicting the defendant, so the job of the attorney during the criminal investigation is to try to improve the client's chances of gaining an acquittal by limiting the amount of evidence the police can assemble against the suspect. If a suspect is permitted to answer questions, even if he denies responsibility and gives the police an explanation for the crime, he is giving the state an advantage as the state can prepare to attack such explanation at trial. It is understood that one has a better chance of gaining an acquittal at trial if a lawyer can keep a suspect from making any statements to the police. The lawyer therefore seeks to limit the amount of incriminating evidence the police can assemble by urging the client, as the Amsterdam manual makes clear, to say nothing under any circumstances and, in addition, to refuse to cooperate in any way that might further the investigation.

In the United States, because the line between investigation and trial is nonexistent and because a suspect may always say something that might be incriminating, there is constant pressure on the system to extend the right to remain silent and the right to counsel back almost to the moment the crime is committed. A fascinating case in this regard is *United States v. Mesa*.[9] Mesa had shot and wounded his wife and daughter the previous day. He then barricaded himself in a motel room. Believing him to be armed (he was) and possibly to have hostages with him (he didn't), a SWAT team surrounded the motel room and a trained FBI hostage negotiator was brought in to try to defuse the situation. After three and a half hours of negotiations, Mesa was persuaded to surrender peacefully.

The issue in the case became whether Mesa's statements to the hostage negotiator should be excluded from trial for shooting his wife and daughter because the hostage negotiator had not preceded his discussions with *Miranda* warnings. After struggling with the question, a split court decided that no warnings were needed. What is fascinating about the case for our purposes is that the criminal episode that had begun with the shooting of Mesa's wife and daughter had not yet ended. The situation could still have ended tragically for the gunman, a police officer, or a hostage and, yet, the court was struggling with the possible violation of the gunman's right to remain silent in this still dangerous situation. Although the narrow issue in *Mesa* has been avoided by a later Supreme Court decision creating a "public safety" exception to the giving of *Miranda* warnings in such a situation, the conceptual framework that sees the fifth amendment as applicable here (and that requires an "exception" for warnings) is somewhat absurd. Is the hostage negotiator supposed to break off any attempt to get the gunman to put down his gun if the latter announces that he wishes to remain silent? If the gunman states that he wants an attorney are the police violating the Constitution if they don't provide one while they continue to negotiate?

Other western systems see the investigation of a crime as a distinct phase of the criminal process, quite separate from the trial. The police are expected to make a complete and thorough investigation of the crime and pursue all avenues of inquiry in an effort to determine how the crime occurred and who may have committed it. It is entirely proper for the police to try to talk to anyone who may have information about the crime and to follow up any additional leads that develop in those interviews. Citizens are expected to cooperate with the police and there is moral pressure to do so. Likewise, the police are expected to talk to the suspect about the crime in an effort to get whatever information they can and, as long as the questioning is fair and proper, it is not considered the function of a lawyer to stop him from being questioned in order to decrease his chances of being charged or increase those of an acquittal.

The "Right to Remain Silent"

I have purposely approached the issue of the police questioning of suspects from the ground up, so to speak, posing a hypothetical case and then trying to explain why it would be logical and necessary at some point to ask the suspect some questions about his relationship to the victim and his whereabouts and activities on the evening the victim was killed. I have tried to avoid addressing the "right to remain silent" or the "privilege against self-incrimination" until this point because the fifth amendment is capable of many interpretations. Its history is closely tied to religious persecution and the Inquisition. It arose in a setting in which people were brought in, tortured by the inquisitors until they confessed to heretical beliefs, and then executed for holding those beliefs. The difficulty today is to try to make sense of the privilege in modern criminal justice systems which have changed radically from what they were even a hundred years ago.

The privilege states that no one shall be "compelled in any criminal case to be a witness against oneself." Certainly its wording suggests that it was originally intended to apply to formal procedures where one was being compelled "to be a witness"—to testify under oath. This was how it was viewed until the mid-1960s. Thus the privilege was thought applicable at trial or in a grand jury hearing or at a legislative hearing—situations where one faced "the cruel trilemma" of going to jail if one refused to testify, or was forced to incriminate oneself if one answered truthfully, or committed perjury if one lied under oath. Because questioning by the police did not involve formal testimony from a suspect and there was no possibility of a perjury prosecution no matter what the suspect said, the privilege was not thought to apply to such questioning. Certainly a suspect had a "right to remain silent" because the police had no legal power to compel him or her to answer, but the privilege was not thought applicable in that setting. If the police forced a suspect to answer through physical force or other coercive means, this was considered a violation of due process, which insists that our procedures be fair and contribute to a reliable outcome, and that suspects be treated in a way that respects their dignity. Coerced confessions violated due process, not the privilege against self-incrimination.

But in the mid-1960s, during the so-called "Warren Court era" when former California governor Earl Warren reigned as chief justice, the Court was struggling to bring station house questioning under some sort of regulation and control. Let's face it: tremendous pressure to confess can be put on suspects in the back rooms of police stations and when exhausted or abused suspects are coerced in this way false convictions and terrible injustices may result. One is reminded of just one of the dangers of incommunicado questioning, namely, that of misinterpretation, by a scene from the movie comedy *My Cousin Vinny,* in which two college-age men from New York stop at a small food store in Georgia on the way to a spring break vacation in Florida and end up being accused of the robbery-murder of the cashier (which took place after they had left the store). One of the two men had mistakenly forgotten to pay for a can of tuna which he had put in his pocket in the store because his arms were full of other items. When they were later arrested, the officer questioning the man who had taken the can of tuna asked him to own up to what he did. The following conversation is a riot of miscommunication. He admitted, "Ok, I did it," which the officer took to be an admission of the murder of the cashier. When the officer told him that the cashier was killed, the suspect asked questioningly and disbelievingly, "I shot the cashier?" This was recorded by the officer as an affirmative declarative utterance: "Suspect says 'I shot the cashier.'"

This is humorous as a piece of fiction but it points to a truth: there can be enormous differences of opinion over what the suspect's mental state was at the time, what was said or done by the police in order to pressure the suspect to confess, and exactly what was said or not said and by whom. Faced with crimes, some of them capital crimes, in which a disputed confession was the pivotal piece of evidence that led to the defendant's conviction, the Court struggled to come up with some way of regulating interrogation. It ended up extending the privilege against self-incrimination to the interrogation room and subsequently developed the system of *Miranda* warnings and a series of other rules designed to protect suspects when being questioned.

Miranda remains a highly controversial opinion after more than thirty years. Some condemn it as a blatant case of "judicial legislation" and a usurpation of the authority that should be exercised by state legislatures.[10] Others attack *Miranda* from the other side, arguing that *Miranda*'s main defect is simply that it doesn't go far enough. One sees articles in major law reviews urging that suspects be given lawyers prior to any attempt at questioning in the station house so they can better understand "their rights."[11] Obviously, given the way American lawyers see their role in the system and the way the Court has interpreted the fifth amendment and the right to silence this would mean the end to interrogation in the police station. This would spell disaster in a system where already far less evidence is likely to be admitted at trial than would be admitted in many other western trial systems.

My purpose in this chapter is not a lengthy attack on the morality that undergirds the fifth amendment privilege. Readers can find those attacks stretching back even to Jeremy Bentham in 1827.[12] Nor is it to defend the status quo that existed pre-*Miranda* and that led to terrible injustices. I see nothing wrong with giving warnings to those in custody, nor with opening up interrogation so that what the suspect or the police officer said may be determined more easily. But at the same time I see nothing wrong with permitting legitimate police inquiries and some pressure on a suspect to answer questions.

While American lawyers and judges sometimes seem to assume that we are unique in honoring the privilege against self-incrimination, in fact all western countries believe they honor this privilege and they insist that a suspect must always have the right to remain silent. It is a western cultural value at this point in time. But most countries still permit considerable pressure to be put on suspects to cooperate with legitimate police inquiries. They do not see such pressure as violating the privilege against self-incrimination because there is no compulsion to answer questions. Sometimes the pressure is more cultural than formal. But sometimes it is formal, as in England where a suspect has the right to remain silent but his silence can be brought out at trial and inferences can be drawn from it in some situations.

Protecting Suspects from Compulsion in the Interrogation Room

My objection to the Warren Court decisions on the privilege against self-incrimination, as also to the exclusionary rule and to many other rights, is not to the underlying objectives of what the Court was trying to do, but rather to the extreme to which it went in the other direction. Instead of protecting suspects against compulsion and mistreatment at the hands of the police, the Court left it entirely up to the suspect to decide whether any questioning, no matter how carefully done, will take place.

One might think, given the broad sweep of the Court's interpretation of the right to remain silent, that this is the best system for suspects because they are freer to remain silent when approached by the police and can keep all their options open at trial. But there is a problem for suspects in this country: they have to assert their right to remain silent or to have a lawyer present after being given *Miranda* warnings, and it takes a certain amount of courage to do that when one is frightened and worried about the consequences of failing to cooperate. The police have also become very sophisticated about manipulating suspects so as to make it very hard for them to cut off questions. An excellent book on the American criminal justice system as it affects police is David Simon's HOMICIDE: A YEAR ON THE KILLING STREETS.[13] Simon, a reporter who spent a year with homicide detectives in Baltimore, shows that by working hard to manipulate reluctant suspects detectives are able to extract waivers and incriminating statements from them. He shows, for example, that the police even use the warnings to their psychological advantage while completely violating the spirit and intent of *Miranda* and sometimes the letter of the law as well.[14] The result is a system in which those who waive their rights and make statements to the police tend to be the poor and unsophisticated, while those who are sophisticated or who have been around the system before know that they should say nothing—no excuses, no alibis—except to ask politely and insistently for a lawyer. The *Miranda* apparatus exacts a high price in terms of police integrity. The police are often obliged to swear, under oath in court, that a suspect's waiver of rights was "voluntary, knowing, and intelligent," when they know full well that they worked very hard to manipulate that waiver from the suspect and that it was certainly not very intelligent.

I think there is a serious danger of trickery, coercion, and misinterpretation in our system which can lead to false convictions and other problems that the *Miranda* apparatus doesn't solve. Meanwhile, it permits sophisticated and wealthy suspects to avoid having to answer any questions (the better to offer creative explanations of incriminating evidence at the end of the trial). There are alternatives that would better protect the vast majority of suspects. One would be that the police be required to audiotape or videotape all questioning of suspects. Such taping of questioning is done routinely at police stations in England and Australia. (In England, audiotaping is required for most criminal investigations. There are machines in the interview rooms that permit the interview to be recorded on two separate tapes so that one can be sealed immediately and preserved to protect against tampering.)

Other countries have other ways of permitting the questioning of suspects while also protecting them from police excesses. In Scotland, a suspect may be brought before a judge and asked questions about the crime, the judge being present to make sure the questioning is fair. Although the suspect may refuse to answer any of the questions, that fact would be admissible against him or her at trial.[15]

These systems try to control the questioning of suspects in an honest and practical way in an effort to balance the need of the police to question and the right of suspects to refuse to answer. But because of the extent to which the Court has extended suspects' protection in the *Miranda* line of cases, American judges are not in a hurry to look too closely at what actually happens in the interrogation rooms. Trial judges prefer, using an analogy from David Simon's book, to view confessions rather like breakfast sausage: they want it on their plate with eggs and toast but they don't want to know too much about how it came to be.[16]

Conclusion

Whether or not the police can gather evidence of a crime bears directly on the reliability of trials in a criminal justice system. Any investigation will be incomplete if the police cannot ask questions of a suspect and confront him or her with what appears to be incriminating evidence.

This is not a plea for the abolition of warnings or a defense of the "third degree." But unless the police have some access to the suspect, and the suspect has some reason to cooperate in the investigation, it will always be hard to prove a defendant guilty beyond a reasonable doubt. It is obviously less difficult to do this in countries where cooperation with an investigation is expected, where lawyers do not see it as their function to bar such cooperation, and where some formal pressure on suspects to cooperate in the investigation is permitted.

Besides creating a system that heavily favors sophisticated or wealthy suspects, the *Miranda* line of cases results in a system that is less honest as police officers shade or sometimes distort their testimony to avoid the suppression of incriminating statements. And trial judges are only too happy to grant waivers of *Miranda* rights on the grounds that such testimony is "knowing and intelligent," when everyone knows it is neither. This makes our trial system more cynical as a certain amount of dishonesty comes to be expected and tolerated of everyone—even police officers and judges.

CHAPTER FOUR

A Trial System in Trouble

Every Criminal Justice System Needs a Strong Trial System

To be strong, every criminal justice system has to be built upon a trial system in which it has confidence. While it is naïve to think that a criminal justice system can cure societal problems such as a national drug problem, the breakdown of the family structure, pronounced economic disparities, or racial divisions among citizens, one that lacks a strong trial system can easily aggravate and exacerbate these problems. In important cases especially, citizens need to feel confident that the trials will determine guilt or innocence with a high degree of accuracy and that the punishments meted out are fair and just.

This is not to suggest that all or even a majority of criminal cases have to go to trial. Most criminal prosecutions in the west involve relatively minor crimes—traffic offenses, petty theft, drug cases, and the like—where the evidence is overwhelming (or else the case would not have been prosecuted in the first place). Most defendants prefer not to contest the charges because there is no defense and they would just as soon get the matter behind them if possible. Every western country has evolved a way of handling such cases expeditiously so as to avoid the expense of a full-blown trial. Often the defendant will be offered a lighter sentence than he or she would be likely to receive after a full trial. Usually defendants are glad to accept such sentences in lieu of a full trial.

But some categories of crimes test the strength of a country's trial system: these are the homicides, the rape cases, the sexual abuse cases, the police beating cases, the serious robbery and assault cases, and so on. Some of these may turn out to be high profile cases in which a broad segment of the public relies on the system for a fair trial and a just result. But even if not high publicity cases, they are still important because the crime is serious and there are victims to consider as well. These cases demand prosecution if possible simply because the offender deserves to be convicted and punished proportionately to the crime committed. A strong criminal justice system needs a strong trial system for these sorts of cases.

A strong trial system encourages victims to report crimes because they know that the case will be handled expeditiously and fairly. It also encourages witnesses to come forward and cooperate with the investigation for the same reasons. It even encourages suspects to be honest and candid about what they have done because they know that the truth will eventually be revealed at trial. A weak trial system does the opposite: it discourages victims from reporting crimes because they know that the system is skewed or haphazard and that the outcome of the trial may turn not on the evidence but on any number of other factors, such as who happens to be in the jury box. It becomes harder in such a system to encourage witnesses to come forward, and citizens become unwilling to make the sacrifices needed to serve.

Instead of encouraging offenders to be honest and candid in dealing with the police, a weak trial system discourages such candor. Those who do cooperate are looked down upon and viewed as stupid by those who are more sophisticated about how the system really works and know how to play it for maximum advantage. A weak trial system emboldens those who have committed crime to hold out for an attractive plea bargain that guarantees them a sentence lighter than they deserve. It also encourages defendants to "take a chance" on an acquittal at trial since the outcome of a trial is a matter of luck. Despite overwhelming evidence of guilt, it is always possible that the defendant might "walk" if the defense gets lucky. When this happens in important cases citizens may react with anger, protests, and even civil unrest or riots.

Unfortunately, despite all the time and resources that have been lavished on our criminal justice system, the United States lacks a strong trial system. The public has come to realize this over the last several years. Despite the protests of a few obdurate trial lawyers who continue to wave the flag and insist that our trial system remains "the finest in the world," we know that our trial procedures cannot be relied upon to produce accurate and truthful verdicts. In this chapter, I intend to show that even those in the system don't have confidence in our trial procedures.

Signs of a Weak Trial System

A Low Formal Priority on Truth

We have a very powerful set of defendant's rights in the United States. In the last two chapters I have discussed just how powerful these rights are compared to those in other countries. These rights impact the trial system quite directly in some cases and set us apart from other western trial systems by limiting the evidence that the prosecution can use to establish the defendant's guilt. It also leaves a defendant freer to decide how to testify at the end of trial in an effort to explain the evidence that will have been put forward by the prosecution. In the United States crucial evidence might get suppressed, allowing the offender to avoid criminal prosecution altogether. Or the task of prosecution may simply be much harder if, for example, a bloody glove were to be suppressed because a police officer was too lazy to get a warrant.

The limits placed on the questioning of suspects are even more important in terms of the number of trials they impact. Without any way to get information from sophisticated suspects or even to pin a suspect down to one exculpatory version of events, the defendant is freer to explain evidence after it has been put forward at trial. When you add this to our already fairly restrictive rules of evidence, most American trials simply have less evidence of guilt available than other trial systems.

Obviously, the Court has had a conscious set of priorities. I think it has placed too low a formal priority on truth in the system. I am not alone in this assessment: many who are familiar with our trial system as well as other western trial systems conclude that if one is really guilty, a person would prefer to go to trial in the United States.[1] This is not said as a compliment. Instead it is a reflection on the low priority our system places on truth.

The Systematic Avoidance of Trial

One sign of the comparative weakness of our trial system is the fact that we go to tremendous lengths to avoid trial. The American criminal justice system today is a plea bargaining system in which a case occasionally goes to trial, but avoids it if possible. I do not object to plea bargaining per se: if a defendant is willing to admit that he committed the crime in question in exchange for a not-greatly-discounted sentence, that makes sense. I suspect that every western system has some rough equivalent of this sort of arrangement. Given the expense of trials and contemporary crime rates, this has become a necessity.

However, it is one thing to offer defendants a discounted sentence as an incentive for an expeditious resolution of a criminal case, but quite another to plea bargain to avoid trial at almost any cost, as is happening in the United States. A system so completely given over to plea bargaining loses everyone's respect, including that of victims and defendants.

Today a defendant's "rap sheet"—the list of the offender's prior arrests and convictions—has only a very rough and approximate relationship to the crimes actually committed on previous occasions. Cases are compromised right and left. The thought that an offender ought to be convicted for what he really did and ought to be punished accordingly is to be viewed as rather quaint and romantic, as completely inappropriate in a world where convictions and sentences are compromised in "deals" to avoid trial at almost any cost.

One of the most depressing reflections of our plea bargaining culture and what it does to the system is the way guilty pleas are taken in courtrooms around this country. When accepting a plea bargain judges spend 95 percent of their time going over with the offender the various rights he or she is waiving as part of the deal. Although the defendant's lawyer should have done all this, the deal has to be repeated in open court so that the defendant will be locked into the bargain. That is the focus of the guilty plea being taken. Only at the end of a long series of questions about this or that trial right being waived will the judge bother to ask the defendant if he really committed the crime in question. Often a vague pro forma response—"Yeah, Judge, I am really sorry for what I did"— is sufficient. Because the judge doesn't want to jeopardize the plea bargain there is no attempt to get the defendant to discuss in detail what he really did on the occasion of the crime, how he planned it, or why he committed it. What is important is that the defendant be locked into *something*. The accuracy of the bargain in terms of what the offender actually did is not a priority.

A criminal justice system that is all plea bargaining—due to a tremendously expensive and not very reliable trial apparatus—becomes corrupted and the system starts to disrespect the results of its own formal procedures. Federal judges are now required to sentence defendants not just for the crime for which they were convicted or to which they pled guilty but also for the "real offense or offenses" they committed. This is determined by an out-of-court presentence investigation done by the probation office, often using FBI and other agency files. This means that if the defendant pleads guilty to one bank robbery but the judge concludes he committed three, the judge must increase the sentence because the defendant really committed three such robberies. This is controversial and has been attacked as unfair.[2] The debate over whether a defendant should be sentenced for his "real offenses" or for his "conviction offenses" is typically American. Lacking a reliable trial system the criminal justice system has to contend with tough issues like this all the time. In this case, the system ends up opting to rely on informal proof of what the defendant really did rather than what its formal procedures tell the sentencing judge the defendant did.[3] If we had a strong trial system, the defendant would be more likely to be convicted or to accept responsibility for the crimes he actually committed.

The Language of Disrespect

Another sign of a weak trial system is the disrespectful way that lawyers and judges talk about trials and trial verdicts. The metaphor most commonly used by those in the system these days when talking about trials is that they are a "crapshoot" and going to trial is simply "rolling the dice": sometimes you win and sometimes you lose. It is all a game of chance.

So accustomed are those in the system to talking about trials this way that this metaphor is even creeping into the appellate opinions of prestigious courts. In *United States v. Ruiz*,[4] the United States Court of Appeals for the First Circuit—a court that hears appeals of federal cases from the New England states—describes a defendant's decision to go to trial on certain charges as his decision "to roll the dice in the hope that he would be acquitted on all charges." Another federal appellate court, this time the United States Court of Appeals for the Seventh Circuit, which hears cases from midwestern states, also used the same metaphor in discussing a defendant's decision whether "to plead [guilty] rather than roll the dice for trial."[5]

These are not just any courts, they are two of the thirteen intermediate appellate courts that hear federal appeals in the United States. They are right under the United States Supreme Court— courts on which any good lawyer in the United States would aspire to sit. These courts have produced Justices Scalia, Kennedy, Breyer, Stevens, and Ginsburg. It is depressing to see our best courts speaking of trials as simply "rolling the dice," not because it is not accurate but because it *is* accurate. Appellate courts in countries with strong trial systems would be embarrassed to talk about trials in this insulting way. When this sort of cynical attitude begins to emanate from the system itself, its trial system is in trouble.

Structural Disrespect for Trial Verdicts

The disrespect for our trial system goes beyond words. The system itself assumes in its decisional law that trials are games of chance in which the outcome can be altered by even the slightest error. In short, the analogy of trials to dice games is fully supported by the way our appellate courts treat errors at trial. Just as the slightest alteration in the roll of the dice can turn a winner into a loser and vice versa, so even minor errors at trial can alter its outcome. The upshot? When a slight error occurs the defendant gets an opportunity to reroll the dice, meaning, of course, a brand new trial.

A case that nicely illustrates the point that trials are games of chance is a Vermont case, *State v. Doleszny*.[6] In *Doleszny*, the defendant had been convicted at trial of sexually assaulting a victim under the age of sixteen. What troubled the Vermont Supreme Court was an error that had occurred during jury selection even before the start of trial. One of the prospective jurors had stated that he was acquainted with one of the prosecution witnesses who would be testifying, a Dr. Orr, who had examined the victim after the rape. When asked if he could still be impartial in evaluating the testimony of Dr. Orr, the prospective juror had replied, "I could certainly try to be impartial but I'm not saying that I could. It might be that because of my prior knowledge of Dr. Orr I would weigh it heavily in favor of what he says."

The defense had not been satisfied with this answer and had asked the trial judge to remove the juror through a challenge "for cause," meaning that the juror was so likely to be biased in favor of one of the parties—in this case the prosecution—that he or she should be replaced by someone else. But the trial judge had refused to do so. This was an error, said the Vermont Supreme Court, and the conviction was reversed.

This might seem a sensible result. A defendant ought to have jurors who have open minds and can evaluate the testimony as they hear it without strong preconceptions. In this case, the prospective juror admitted to being more favorably disposed to give Dr. Orr's testimony credence he might someone he did not know previously. But what is startling about *Doleszny* is that the juror in question never sat on the jury that determined the defendant's guilt. After the trial judge refused to remove the juror, the defendant used a peremptory challenge—these are challenges available to each side at an American trial with which the lawyers can remove jurors "peremptorily," that is, on demand and without requiring explanation or justification. Peremptory challenges are a matter of local law; there is nothing in the Constitution that guarantees them or that determines how many a state may grant to litigants. The number varies considerably in criminal cases from state to state with some states giving each side ten, some five, some seven, and so on. In Vermont the number of peremptory challenges is six and in *Doleszny* the defendant used one of his six challenges to remove the juror in question. Thus, the only impact the judge's error had on the trial was that the defendant ended up with one less peremptory challenge than would have been the case had the trial judge removed the juror in question for cause.

It is possible that with one additional peremptory challenge the defendant might have gotten a juror who would have been more inclined to the defense and might even have hung the jury by insisting the evidence was insufficient to convict. It is also possible that the new juror might have been less inclined toward the defense. But in a world where lots of things are possible, shouldn't the error that occurred in this case be assessed by looking at the evidence and seeing whether the court has confidence in the conviction? But the Vermont Supreme Court doesn't devote a single line in its opinion to the evidence in the case. Why? Because trials are rolls of the dice and any error can affect the way the dice come up. This is so obvious to the court that the decision reversing Doleszny's conviction is scarcely longer than a page. The court briefly explains what happened during jury selection and then summarily reverses. The result is not at all puzzling, troubling, or embarrassing to the court. It is as if a bystander or the croupier had accidentally struck one of the dice in flight—there has to be a reroll of the dice. It is that simple.

It would be extremely difficult to explain this case to someone from a country with a strong trial system that emphasizes the search for truth. I can almost hear a judge or lawyer from such a system asking me in a heavily accented voice,

> But I don't understand this decision, Professor. The "bad" juror was gone after all before the trial even started and so what was the problem with the trial? Was the evidence not good? Were there not twelve fair people on the jury? Did the jury not try very hard to reach the right result on the evidence? Why didn't the appellate court even review the evidence to see how strong it was? This young victim must now testify again and go through the stress of trial and the system must absorb all the other costs associated with your very expensive trial system. For what purpose?

Lest readers think that I have chosen an oddball case to make my point about the system as a crapshoot, let me say that I could just as easily have discussed similar cases from states in all regions of the country, including Wisconsin,[7] Florida,[8] New York,[9] Colorado,[10] and Arizona,[11] to make exactly the same point. In short, extreme as the law is in *Doleszny*, appellate courts in a significant number of important jurisdictions apply the same law and would have reached exactly the same result.

All Trial Errors in a Highly Proceduralized System Become Serious Errors

What the *Doleszny* line of cases shows us is that the legal system has little confidence in its own trial apparatus. Trials are fragile and uncertain events in which any error—even the loss of a single peremptory challenge—may alter the outcome. I have used this line of cases because it is representative of a line of cases from a sizable number of jurisdictions, north and south, east and west. I want to follow up on the *Doleszny* line of cases by giving several more examples that demonstrate just how little confidence our legal system has in our trial apparatus. The cases that follow do no more than scratch the surface of the sort of reversals that descend each year on lower courts from appellate courts around the country. All these cases are relatively recent, from either 1996 or 1997. What they have in common is that in none of them—as we saw in *Doleszny*— does the particular court care whether the evidence supports the verdict. We know from chapter 1 of this book that Americans are obsessed with rules and procedures whether it is football or our trial system. When this obsession with procedure is combined with the belief that a trial is a crapshoot, almost any error becomes a very serious error even if it has nothing to do with the evidence in the case.

The first few cases, like *Doleszny*, deal with jury selection, a procedure that our trial system heavily emphasizes because of the widespread belief that the composition of the jury may be as important as or even more important than the evidence at trial. I should note by way of introduction that although other countries besides the United States use juries at least on occasion—England, Denmark, and Norway, to name a few—they seldom have an elaborate jury selection process like ours, nor errors such as the ones I will describe in the first three cases. Thus, the problems exemplified by the *Doleszny* line of cases and the three cases about to be described below are truly American in law, in outlook, and in the stunning results they mandate.

Of the three the easiest to explain is a Florida case, *People v. Brower*,[12] in which an appellate court reversed the defendant's murder and aggravated burglary conviction, despite what the court said was "overwhelming evidence" against the defendant. The error occurred during jury selection. The defense lawyer was seated at counsel table with the defendant during jury selection but went up to the sidebar to disclose to the court the defense's peremptory challenges. (Often both the prosecutor and defense lawyer exercise peremptory challenges at sidebar so that the jurors are not aware of the challenges until they have been approved by the judge, and the jurors challenged do not know which side it came from.)

The error in *Brower* was that the defense attorney was not accompanied by the defendant when he went to sidebar to exercise the peremptory challenges. Since the defendant had a right to be present under Florida statutory law and had not waived that right in open court, the court said the trial had to be reversed. Notice that defense counsel apparently did not feel it necessary for the defendant to come up to the bench, that counsel presumably was acting in the defendant's best interest in making the challenges, and that the lawyer had plenty of time during jury selection to consult with the defendant about any challenges. The trial was reversed nonetheless.

The next two cases are federal cases from prestigious circuits that need a brief introduction on the current law surrounding the exercise of peremptory challenges. One of the problems that has troubled the legal system for quite some time is the fact that peremptory challenges can be used by the prosecution or the defense to remove all minorities from the jury. This has often been a tactic of prosecutors in the past, especially when the defendant is a member of the same minority group as the prospective juror. In 1986, in *Batson v. Kentucky*,[13] the Supreme Court tried to remedy this problem by announcing that striking jurors on the basis of race violated the equal protection rights of prospective jurors. But *Batson* does not solve the problem particularly well because trial judges now face the difficult problem of deciding whether challenges which are in theory "peremptory" are being used to remove jurors because of their race. This is a very difficult task since sophisticated lawyers can often find or cite a neutral reason that could mask the racial motive for the challenge. It is not easy for a trial judge to enforce a rule which says that lawyers can strike jurors for any reason—poor eye contact with the lawyer, political affiliation, age, education level, manner of dress, the manner of the juror's responses—as long as it is not done on the basis of race, and litigation on so-called *Batson* issues abounds in both state and federal courts.

The two federal cases I will discuss here involve errors by trial judges on *Batson* issues. The first is *United States v. Annigoni*,[14] decided by the United States Court of Appeals for the Ninth Circuit, which hears appeals from federal trial courts in the western part of the United States. This case involved a bank fraud in California by Annigoni and some associates in which, in the court's words, the bank was "duped by false documents" into granting a $2.85 million real estate loan to Annigoni and his associates. The borrowers promptly defaulted, leaving the bank to discover that the collateral for the loan did not exist.

During jury selection the defense tried to use a peremptory challenge to remove an Asian-American who had stated that he had a passive interest in a limited real estate partnership. (Defendants often don't like jurors who have knowledge and experience that might enable them to understand complicated business transactions.) The trial judge refused to permit the challenge because he felt it was being made on racial grounds. The court was wrong in this conclusion, said the Ninth Circuit, and there must be a completely new trial because even a single incorrect denial of a peremptory challenge in an attempt to enforce *Batson* constitutes automatic reversible error. The court made no attempt to determine whether the trial Annigoni received was fair or whether the evidence supported the verdict the jury had returned against Annigoni.

The other federal case is even more troubling—*United States v. Huey*,[15] decided by the United States Court of Appeals for the Fifth Circuit, which hears cases from federal courts in states in the south-central part of the United States. In this case, Huey's attorney used peremptory challenges to strike five black jurors from the jury that would hear evidence of the drug-related charges against Huey and a codefendant. Huey's attorney did so because he was worried about the undercover tape recordings of Huey and his associates that would be played at trial, which would show Huey using harsh and offensive racial epithets in referring to blacks. Both the codefendant and the government attorney objected to the use of these peremptory challenges, but the trial judge permitted them.

On appeal, the appellate court ruled that these challenges on the basis of race were improper and should not have been permitted. The court concluded that there had to be a new trial. This is understandable as to the codefendant, but the court reversed Huey's conviction and ordered a new trial for him as well. Notice that it was Mr. Huey's counsel who had violated the rights of the prospective jurors, that the government and counsel for the codefendant pointed this out to the lawyer and the court, that as a result of the improper challenges Mr. Huey had a jury more favorable to him than that to which he was entitled (and the government had a jury less favorable to its case), and that he was still convicted by that jury. Yet, he got a new trial. Is it any wonder that comparatists conclude that if one is really guilty, one will want to go to trial in the United States?

I want to shift from cases presenting jury selection errors to two cases raising issues that occurred at the other end of the trial after all the evidence had been received. Although the errors seem minor—they relate to the fairness and outcome of the trial—they resulted nonetheless in a reversal of the convictions in question. The first is a New York murder case reversed by the New York Court of Appeals, New York's highest state court.[16] The error in this case occurred during jury deliberations when the judge, in order to assist the jury, gave each juror a verdict sheet that had on it a list of the alternative types of homicide charges that he or she could consider. Following each option on the sheet, the judge had put a parenthetical label describing the particular type of homicide. These two-or-three-word parentheticals which, for example, described second degree murder as "(Depraved Mind Murder)" and manslaughter in the second degree as "(Reckless Manslaughter)," were not consented to by defense counsel (although apparently defense counsel was aware of what the court was doing and could have objected). Worried that these checklist parentheticals did not fully describe the underlying law, the court reversed. The court spends no time in its opinion reviewing the evidence in the case or the fairness of the trial in order to determine whether the public should have confidence in the verdict rendered. The issue is simply whether a jury, which had twice during deliberations received full and accurate instructions on the elements required for each possible homicide charge, might have been misled by the labels on the verdict sheet.

The second case is a fraud case tried in federal court involving the owner of a car dealership in Illinois.[17] The error occurred at the end of the trial when the judge permitted, without objection from either side, the two alternate jurors who had sat through the trial to deliberate on the charges with the twelve jurors. The result was that all fourteen jurors found the defendant guilty of some of the charges and acquitted him of others. Because the court rule states that an alternate juror should be dismissed after the jury retires to consider its verdict, this was plain error, said the United States Court of Appeals for the Seventh Circuit. Though the defense had not objected to the procedure and the defendant might even be viewed as having received a substantial benefit from the error—fourteen jurors had had to agree unanimously on the verdict—the court had no difficulty reversing the conviction in a brief opinion without bothering to see how strong the evidence was against the defendant.

An Obsession with the Need for Perfect Evidentiary and Trial Rulings

None of the above series of "errors" mandating completely new trials had anything to do with the evidence in the case or even the instruction on the law that the jury had received from the trial judge. Yet each of the errors led to brand new trials at which every aspect of the trial had to be repeated. If errors so indirectly related to the defendant's guilt or innocence mandate reversal, usually irrespective of the strength of the evidence, it is not hard to imagine the amount of energy, effort, and concern that the system puts into trying to avoid evidentiary errors at trial. Anyone who spends a day or two watching an important American trial can see how defensive the system is and how worried it gets over possible evidentiary errors at trial. Lawyers sometimes huddle with the judge at sidebar conferences to debate the merits of the issues raised. But sometimes the issue is more complicated and the trial has to be stopped for a substantial period of time and the jury returned to the jury room while evidentiary and other legal issues are argued and resolved. Many of these debates will concern issues such as whether certain evidence is "relevant" or whether, though relevant, it is too "prejudicial." As with "probable cause" and "reasonable suspicion" in chapter 2, "relevant" and "prejudicial" are decisions about which reasonable trial judges can differ. But at the back of the judge's mind will always be the concern that if he or she makes a mistake—or what may be viewed as a mistake by an appellate court—the case may have to be retried.

What You See Is What We Have

I have left until last one of the best ways of determining whether a trial system is strong: simple observation of an important trial. Take a look at trials in serious cases and see what happens in the courtroom, how people are spoken to, how witnesses are treated, how well the system uses scarce judicial resources, and the like. I don't mean to claim in this chapter that all trials in the United States misfire or that the system has degenerated to the point that all trials are simply "crapshoots." But you often see a trial system that wears its insecurity on its sleeve.

To make my point, I want to consider two trials that took place at opposite sides of the country at about the same time: the trial of Colin Ferguson, the deranged gunman who shot and killed six people and wounded seventeen others on a commuter train of the Long Island Railroad, and the trial of O. J. Simpson. Apologists for the system will tell you that these are not "typical" cases. I agree, because the typical American case is not a trial at all, it is a plea bargain, and the typical American trial involves a minor crime, not multiple homicides. But, as I stressed at the beginning of this chapter, the strength of the system is best seen in the way it handles difficult cases where a lot is at stake. With that introduction, let me turn to the *Ferguson* case.

It might seem odd that I would pick the *Ferguson* case when discussing problems with our trial system, as this was a "successful prosecution." Ferguson was convicted of the crimes with which he was charged and received a zillion years in prison in a New York court. Why did I not pick the trial of Lemrick Nelson who was acquitted of killing Yankel Rosenbaum despite the fact that the victim had identified Nelson before he died and the murder weapon was found in Nelson's possession?[18] Or what about the trial of the Menendez brothers who blew away their parents with a shotgun, firing some sixteen times, yet the jury couldn't reach a verdict on the homicide charges against either of the brothers?[19]

But what the *Ferguson* case shows us is just how extreme the system's lack of priorities at trial is. Ferguson chose to defend himself and he made a travesty of his defense. But what does it say about our trial system (and our legal profession) that Mr. Ferguson was permitted to walk around the well of the courtroom and "play lawyer" as if he had suddenly become a member of the bar? Not only that, but he was permitted to cross-examine at very close range people some of whose lives and bodies had been permanently scarred by him. What does it say about our trial system that Mr. Ferguson became the butt of jokes on *Saturday Night Live* for his sad imitation of a lawyer? What is going on here? Was Mr. Ferguson *on trial* for these terrible crimes or should he more properly be thought of as the *host* of the trial? Because a defendant has a constitutional right to a fair trial, does he or she somehow *own* the trial and have the right to determine what happens there and what its priorities should be?

I have just gone through a series of cases in which any error—even errors not objected to by the defense lawyer, or in one instance even initiated by the defense lawyer—resulted in a new trial for the defendant, because our system is so obsessed with technically perfect trials. Yet if a defendant wants to make a sick joke out of the trial, that too is permitted. We don't know what we want to see happen at trial, or even what the purpose of a trial is.

I want to emphasize that I am not blaming the trial judge in the *Ferguson* case for what happened; the Supreme Court has declared that a defendant has a right to self-representation[20] and the judge no doubt felt that he couldn't do other than what he did. I don't object to the fact that a defendant should control his own defense and should have the right to ask questions of witnesses, even when the defendants have lawyers. But a trial system also has an obligation to victims and to the general public to provide a dignified trial that places a high priority on truth. The *Ferguson* case is symptomatic of a trial system whose only priority is no priority. A trial system that does not place a high priority on truth ultimately loses confidence in itself and becomes tentative and even apologetic.

The same uncertainties that were apparent in the Colin Ferguson case were also evident in the *Simpson* case. Here was a case about a double murder that went to trial after a series of high-publicity trials had resulted in stunning acquittals or failures to convict. The case was to be tried in front of a pretty good trial judge and was to be prosecuted and defended by teams of pretty good trial lawyers. It was touted by the legal establishment as a case that would prove to the American public the excellence of our trial system. Public defenders around the country insisted that it would show how a criminal case ought to be tried if only the defense was provided the sorts of resources that Simpson had. A professor at Harvard Law School announced that he would teach a course entitled "The O. J. Simpson Case" that would use developments during the trial to train future lawyers, and lots of other law schools followed suit.

You don't need to be a legal expert to know that the trial exposed very serious structural flaws in our trial system. As someone who has watched a fair number of trials in other countries, my overall impression of the case was that this is a trial system that has no confidence in itself. As with the *Ferguson* case, it was often unclear at the *Simpson* trial who exactly was supposed to be on trial and what was supposed to happen.

Leaders at the bench and bar who had built up public expectations for the *Simpson* trial were stunned by what happened, and the American criminal justice system will be a long time recovering from that case. In hindsight, apologists for our trial system have focused the blame for what occurred on the individuals. This is always the American response: the procedures never get questioned, for they are perfect. It is just that someone "blew it." For example, one reads accounts blaming Judge Ito for "losing control over the courtroom" and for being seduced by the publicity. But no one is very clear exactly which rulings Judge Ito made were wrong and exactly how he should have altered the course of the trial. When the lawyers make literally thousands of objections on which the judge is supposed to rule, what should the judge do to stop the flow of objections? Rule quickly and dismiss them in a hurry? Easily said, but I have just shown a number of cases in which very minor errors resulted in a brand new trial for the defendant. A fascinating comment on our trial system and the eggshells on which trial judges walk was a poll of American lawyers taken one month into the trial—before serious problems had developed in the case and when Judge Ito's reputation was very high—which showed that 37 percent of those polled believed that even if Simpson were to be convicted, Judge Ito had already committed a reversible error at trial.[21] In short, while Judge Ito deserves some of the blame for the deterioration of the trial, when we are unsure what the purpose of a trial is and place tremendous emphasis on procedural perfection, trials can lose their focus.

Others blame Johnny Cochran for shamelessly "playing the race card," for arguing jury nullification to the jury, and for many other ethical lapses. I don't think you would find such behavior permitted in many trial systems. But many American lawyers and judges believe that Johnny Cochran did absolutely nothing wrong and that the defense he mounted on many fronts simultaneously was in the finest traditions of defense advocacy.

Finally, lots of Monday morning quarterbacks complain that the prosecution "blew it"—that the case should have been filed in Santa Monica, not Los Angeles; that Chris Darden should never have risen to the bait and asked Simpson to try on the glove; that

Marcia Clark blew it during jury selection by not using more challenges to knock more prospective black female jurors from the jury (though, as noted above, the Supreme Court has said challenges on the basis of race are wrong).

These criticisms are largely beside the point. What these critics seem to be implying is that unless all the moons are properly aligned and each of the participants performs at near-perfect level, the trial will surely misfire, even when the evidence is strong and the resources on both sides are great. What the *Simpson* case proved is that our trial system is a frail one that puts tremendous emphasis on winning and losing and not much emphasis on truth. Is it any wonder that the system prefers to split the baby in a plea bargain, even a very unattractive plea bargain, if this means a trial can be avoided?

Conclusion

Our trial system is the most expensive and complicated in the western world, but who really respects it? Police officers? Victims? Defendants? This chapter has shown that even those who work in the system—lawyers and judges—don't respect it. Not surprisingly, prosecutors, defense lawyers, and judges try to avoid trials if possible, preferring plea bargaining, even if the result may be verdicts that do not reflect what the defendant actually did. But if the outcome of a trial is simply, as those in the system often put it, "a crapshoot," who can blame them for not wanting to gamble when very important issues are at stake?

CHAPTER FIVE

Discovering Who We Are

A Look at Four Different Trial Systems

Our Need for Perspective on Our Trial System

In this chapter, I will describe in overview the trial systems of four different western countries: the Netherlands, Germany, Norway, and England. I chose the first three because their criminal justice systems are well respected and yet they vary considerably from one another. I chose England because it is a common law country like the United States and other parts of the English-speaking world, and yet, as I will show, there are many important differences between the trial system in England and that in the United States.

The purpose of this chapter is not to make readers experts in other legal systems, nor to suggest that those systems don't have their own problems. (England, in particular, has had serious problems in recent years stemming from a series of cases involving suspected IRA terrorists in which the convictions had to be thrown out, often due to the fabrication of incriminating evidence by the police.[1]) Rather, the purpose of these short overviews of four other trial systems is to provide a badly needed perspective on our own. Writing in JOSEPH IN EGYPT, the great German novelist Thomas Mann wrote: "For only by making comparisons can we distinguish ourselves from others and discover who we are, in order to become all that we are meant to be."[2] While Mann was writing about people, his point applies equally to trial systems. Only by comparing our trial system to other systems can we get "outside" our system and see how extreme it has become.

Americans badly need the perspective on our trial system that this chapter offers. This is especially true of lawyers and judges because an American legal education is very narrow in its focus. I say this as someone who trains future American lawyers and judges and who is thus part of the problem. In a hurry to provide law students with a basic understanding of the sorts of complicated legal subjects they are likely to encounter in practice, our legal education concentrates almost exclusively on training students within our own legal system. Students become familiar with American statutes, regulations, decisional law, and the American trial system. Other legal traditions and trial systems are generally ignored.

This means that we graduate lots of law students every year who are well prepared to take the bar exam and to begin careers as prosecutors and public defenders. They know evidence law, trial procedure, the main outlines of search and seizure law, the rules of interrogation, and so on. They have also often taken courses aimed at honing their advocacy skills, or their negotiating or interviewing skills. But they end up knowing almost nothing about other trial systems or even about the evolution over time of their own legal system. Even with respect to the trial systems of other English-speaking countries such as England, Scotland, Australia, or New Zealand—other so-called "common law countries"—that share our legal heritage, students usually know very little. The sum total of what American lawyers (and law professors) know about such systems is likely to be the little they may have garnered from watching popular entertainments such as *Rumpole of the Bailey* on Public Broadcasting, or movies such as the comedy *A Fish Called Wanda*, in which one of the principals was a barrister.

When it comes to what I have been referring to in this book as "continental" or "European" countries, such as Germany, France, or the Netherlands, American lawyers know next to nothing. Sometimes what they think they "know" is worse than knowing nothing. You will occasionally hear leading members of the bar saying things about other western countries—for example, that "in country X the defendant is assumed guilty and must prove he is innocent" or that "in country Y the defendant is not given a trial"—which are untrue for those countries. The tone of such pronouncements usually implies that our trial system is clearly superior to any other, that our lawyers and judges have it all pretty much figured out, and that we have little to learn from other legal systems. (As someone who lectures to various groups of judges and lawyers, I have to say that this attitude is beginning to change and I find many lawyers and judges much more interested in what other countries do than they were previously.)

The narrow focus of the education provided at American law schools has some unfortunate consequences when it comes to reform. It means that most students will graduate and embark on careers within our legal system where their conception of how a trial *must* be structured is reinforced every day in practice. They end up well equipped to work within the system, but very poorly equipped to think about ways in which it could be reformed. As practitioners, they may be quite excellent at what they do but as law reformers they are timid and unimaginative. They are likely to summarily dismiss almost any change that seems to make sense, such as: Why don't judges do the initial questioning of witnesses at trial to make them feel a bit more comfortable in the courtroom? Why not have the judge talk informally with the jury at the end of the trial about the law and the evidence instead of reading a set of technical instructions? Sometimes they will even throw in some legal terminology, claiming, for example, that the proposal violates "due process," in an attempt to bluff the person who made the suggestion into thinking that he or she is completely off base. Sadly, the narrow training American lawyers receive in law school and their experience of always working *within* the system become obstacles to reform, when, as those who know our system best, they ought to be leading efforts at reform.

There is actually considerable variety among western trial systems and it often turns out that what seems unthinkable to many American lawyers and judges exists in some other system (and sometimes even seems to work pretty well). It is my hope that after we have taken a look at these four trial systems, we will better understand, in Mann's words, "who we are."

Continental Trial Systems: Adversarial or Inquisitorial?

American lawyers sometimes speak of our own trial system as an "adversarial system" and of European systems as "inquisitorial." The term "inquisitorial" has obvious pejorative connotations. One pictures a system in which there is hidden investigation, the results of which are kept secret from the suspect and are handed over to a judge for trial. But the trial is little more than a formality because the judge freely uses the secret investigative file to determine the defendant's guilt. Few or even no witnesses are called, and the defendant has no way of disputing or challenging this secret information. Perhaps the trial judge even expects the defendant to take the initiative at trial and prove his innocence.

Obviously, such a criminal trial system would be something out of the Inquisition and an affront to fairness. Among its most glaring deficiencies, the defendant has no opportunity to study the evidence assembled by the police and thus no opportunity to challenge either the thoroughness of the investigation or the quality of the evidence in the file. The police may be incompetent and might fail to pursue important evidence that would exculpate the defendant. If the defendant cannot see the contents of the investigative file in advance of trial, he or she cannot see gaps in the investigation. Even worse, the police may be dishonest and may not record the evidence from interviews and other sources accurately and completely. Certain witnesses may never have said what the police have indicated or these statements may have been far more qualified in incriminating the defendant than the written record suggests. Without some opportunity to hear from these witnesses in court and challenge what they are saying, a defendant could be readily convicted on the basis of evidence manufactured by the police.

Today a trial system along this inquisitorial model would be quickly condemned for all the obvious reasons. There are now some forty European countries that are signatories to the European Convention on Human Rights. Article 6 of the Convention guarantees each citizen the right "to a fair and public hearing within a reasonable time by an independent and impartial tribunal"; the right to be "presumed innocent until proved guilty according to law"; the right "to examine and have examined witnesses against him"; the right to compel " the attendance . . . of witnesses on his behalf"; and the right "to defend himself in person or through legal assistance," including free legal assistance, "when the interests of justice so require." Citizens who believe that the trial system in the countries in which they live do not measure up to Convention standards for fair and public trials may challenge their court convictions and seek a hearing before the European Commission on Human Rights.

This is not to say that all European trial systems work well and are equally strong (any more than the trial systems in each of our states are equally strong). The strength of a system depends on more than just its formal procedures. It also depends on the quality of the judges, police, and public officials; the adequacy of the resources appropriated to the system; the level of confidence citizens have in government generally; and many other factors. Among western countries today a consensus is emerging on the need for some adversarial safeguards to permit the evidence assembled against the defendant to be challenged, and to protect a defendant from an unjust conviction or an unfair sentence. For this reason, the labels "inquisitorial" and "adversarial" do not draw a meaningful distinction between western trial systems today because all western trial systems are adversarial to some degree. In each of the systems I will be describing in this chapter a defendant has some adversarial protections.

The Netherlands

The Netherlands has a highly respected criminal justice system, yet it is the least adversarial of the trial systems I will discuss in this chapter. The first major difference between the Netherlands and most other western systems, including the United States, is that there are no lay fact finders at trials in the Netherlands. The Netherlands uses panels of three professional judges for most criminal cases except the most minor, which are handled by a single judge. Most of the judges are full-time. But when needed some people, usually academics, attorneys, or civil servants sit as part-time judges.

A second difference between the Netherlands and the other countries to be described shortly concerns the central role played at trial by the investigative file assembled by the police and other authorities. This investigative file is studied by the judges prior to trial and is also freely available to the defendant, the defense counsel, and the prosecutor. In the Netherlands, unlike the other countries, including the United States, the requirement that each of the witnesses be called to testify at the trial and repeat the substance of the statements already given the police has been relaxed over the years. The file is assumed to be evidence in the case and, as such, can be freely discussed by the judges, the prosecutor, and the defense attorney at trial. Thus the trial often tends to be a discussion of the file and what it does or doesn't show. While the defense attorney (or the prosecutor) can insist that certain witnesses be brought before the court to testify in order to dispute their accounts of the crime or to challenge material in the file, this does not happen routinely and there are many cases where no one other than the defendant gives evidence.

As is true on the continent generally, the trial in the Netherlands begins with the charges against the defendant being read or summarized. Then the defendant is asked if he wishes to respond to these charges. Almost all defendants do choose to speak to the judges, though there is no obligation to speak and the law forbids the use of silence as evidence of guilt. In the Netherlands and other continental countries the timing of the defendant's evidence is thus quite different from the United States where the defendant typically offers evidence at the very end of the trial. In continental trial systems, the defendant speaks first. One other difference with respect to the defendant giving evidence in the Netherlands and other parts of the continent is that the defendant is never put under oath and cannot be punished for perjury for what he says in court. The defendant does not "testify" as such and he is not a "witness" but he does give evidence to the judges. The English and American trial systems do not have this feature; the defendant either gets in the witness box and gives testimony under oath like all the other witnesses or else he doesn't say anything. But giving the defendant special treatment when he speaks about the charges is not unknown in common law countries. For example, until relatively recently England used to have another alternative for defendants: he could choose to give an unsworn statement from his seat in the courtroom. But this has been abolished.

At the end of a Dutch trial, the judges deliberate. When they return to the courtroom, their decision is always explained. The presiding judge explains how any legal issues that arose in the case were decided, how conflicts in the evidence were resolved, and, if the defendant was found guilty, why the particular sentence was thought appropriate. (There is thus no separate sentencing hearing in the Netherlands which means that evidence in aggravation or mitigation is considered at the trial in addition to evidence relating to possible guilt.) As is true generally on the continent, the verdict only needs the support of a majority of the judges. The oral decision announced in court is usually followed by a more detailed written decision within a couple of weeks.

There is rather broad appellate review available for either the prosecution or the defense and any issues decided at the trial may be reconsidered by the appellate court. Because there is a written decision, it is easier to indicate exactly what part of the lower court's decision is being challenged and why. Both the state's attorney and the defense have the right to appeal, but an acquittal entered in the trial court can only be reversed on appeal if the appellate judges agree unanimously that the acquittal was wrong. The same applies to any increase in the defendant's sentence: the appellate court can only increase it if the judges are convinced unanimously that the original sentence was wrong and it should have been more severe.

There are many values in the Dutch system that are common to other western countries: (1) the defendant has counsel at all stages of the proceedings; (2) the investigative file is open to liberal inspection by the defense, which may challenge any evidence in it or ask that it be supplemented if it is not complete; (3) the police must warn suspects of their right to remain silent; (4) the defendant is presumed innocent at trial and need not say anything; and (5) proof beyond a reasonable doubt is required for conviction. Yet this is not a very adversarial system in certain respects. For one thing, the judges have their own independent duty to determine the truth at trial and, to that end, are ultimately in control of the trial and the presentation of evidence. It is the judges' job to look at all the relevant evidence, regardless of whether the prosecutor or the defense attorney ask them to look at certain pieces of evidence or not. Thus the lawyers play a subsidiary role to the judges at trial. The initial questioning of witnesses is handled by the presiding judge who tries to bring out all the relevant evidence—incriminating as well as exculpatory—from the witness, before permitting the other judges, the prosecutor, and the defense attorney to question him.

There are many things in this very summary overview of the Dutch system which might arouse suspicion and concern for Americans. One obvious concern is the complete reliance on professional judges in the Dutch system. One worries that they might become jaded, less open, and less objective over the years. It would also seem healthy to have citizens in the courtroom from different backgrounds who can provide a fresh perspective. Furthermore, the very informal trial system in the Netherlands seems to put a great deal of trust in the police and the pretrial investigation. Many Dutch judges and legal scholars would probably agree that the system could be improved by incorporating citizens into it and instituting a more formal procedure. But the Dutch have decided that it is better to have a high percentage of very simple trials and compensate for vesting so much power in the trial judge by using panels of judges, providing reasoned explanations for decisions, and giving each side broad appellate rights, even permitting issues to be reconsidered all over again. Obviously, we have made different choices, preferring a much more elaborate and formal trial procedure but only being able to use it for a very tiny percentage of criminal cases.

Germany

Unlike the Netherlands, the German system requires participation by laypersons in all but the most minor criminal cases. Germany uses what I have referred to in the opening chapter as "mixed panels" composed of both professional and "lay" judges at trials involving serious crimes. The ratio between the two kinds of judges varies, less serious cases being heard by a single professional judge and two lay judges, and more serious ones by two or three professional judges and two lay judges. Since unanimous decisions are not required, this means that in some courts the lay judges can outvote the professional ones.

Lay judges are citizens who are nominated and elected from the community and serve a term of four years, during which time they are required to be available a certain number of trial days each year. Lay judges can be reappointed. It will thus usually be the case in Germany (and in most other continental countries that use citizens as fact finders) that the citizens serving as lay judges at trial will have had previous experience in the courtroom.

As in the Netherlands, all the evidence gathered by the police prior to trial is placed in the investigative file on the case, which is available to both the state's attorney and the defense attorney. German trials tend to be more formal than those in the Netherlands because of the involvement of laypersons. The lay judges are not permitted to study the investigative file—the system doesn't want them to be acquainted with the evidence. The evidence in the file thus has to be revealed at trial through the witnesses. A German trial thus resembles an American trial in that it centers heavily on the testimony of witnesses.

Trials in Germany are the responsibility of the judges more than the lawyers. The professional judge who presides at the trial—the "presiding judge"—will have studied the investigative file carefully in advance of the trial and will have decided which witnesses are to be called at trial, with the understanding that the judges should consider all the relevant evidence. If the crime involved is a serious one, one of the other professional judges will also have read the investigative file and will assist the presiding judge. Thus, one or two members of the mixed panel will have studied the file in advance of trial, but the other panel members will know little more than the charges that have been brought.

Normally, the presiding judge handles the bulk of the questioning of witnesses at trial. Thereafter the other judges, the state's attorney, and the defense attorney can ask questions in that order. But a defense attorney is not without considerable influence on the conduct of the trial. If he asks for testimony by additional witnesses the judges must grant the request, unless it is clear that such witnesses have no relevant evidence to offer. The state's attorney and the defense attorney may also request permission to conduct the initial questioning of the witnesses at trial, and will sometimes do so.

As in the Netherlands, a German trial encompasses both guilt and sentencing and a nonunanimous verdict is sufficient on either issue. Again, as in the Netherlands, the judges will always explain their verdict, giving an oral explanation at trial and then issuing a longer written document shortly thereafter. This document summarizes the evidence that was heard, explains how legal issues or conflicts in the evidence were resolved by the judges and why, and justifies the verdict reached, including the sentence imposed.

As is generally true in continental systems, the defendant or the state's attorney has a right to appellate review. For less serious criminal cases, this review will take the form of a complete retrial of the case, while for serious ones, the review will focus on alleged errors in the written judgment of the trial court or on alleged errors in the trial process. An appeal contesting the sentence, on the grounds that it was either too lenient or too severe, is also permitted.

A defendant in Germany has many of the same procedural protections one finds throughout the West, including the assistance of counsel throughout the investigative and trial stage. A defense attorney has some adversary weapons at trial, including the power to insist on calling additional witnesses if he thinks they are required. The defendant is presumed innocent at trial, has the right to remain silent at or before trial, and may only be convicted if the court is convinced of his or her guilt beyond a reasonable doubt.

Because the ultimate responsibility for the production and development of evidence at trial lies with the judges, the sharp division of a criminal trial into a "prosecution case" to be followed by a "defense case" is absent in Germany. Instead, witnesses are typically called by the judges in the order that makes the most sense in terms of what they will be testifying about. Also, as in the Netherlands and on the continent generally, the defendant is always asked if he or she wishes to respond to the charges at the very start of the trial. While the defendants need not respond, they almost always do because the fact finders want to hear from them. Also, in contrast to the United States, the defendant offering evidence in Germany does not present the same tactical problems. In the United States, a defendant's decision to testify is greatly complicated by evidence rules that permit a defendant to be questioned about prior convictions if he or she testifies. But in the absence of such testimony, he or she will keep those convictions from the jury's knowledge. In Germany (and other continental countries), because the trial involves both guilt and possible sentencing, the judges will know about the defendant's prior convictions whether or not he speaks in court. A defendant's prior convictions are therefore not a factor in the decision to testify, as they are in the United States. Also, as in the Netherlands, a defendant who responds to the charges in court is not under oath.

German trials tend to be more informal in tone and structure than American ones. Some of this informality results from the fact that judges want to and are supposed to consider all the relevant evidence. The sort of highly technical rules to which evidence must conform to be admissible in the United States—often resulting in objections, huddled sidebar arguments, and subtle legal rulings—are rare in Germany (or the Netherlands). The judges want to hear the relevant evidence from the witness with as few interruptions as possible.

Norway

Norway has an interesting trial system which has features one would expect only in common law countries. Yet it also has characteristics that one associates with other countries on the continent.

One feature of the Norwegian system that seems to be unique is its commitment to providing a second trial if a defendant or the prosecutor does not believe the original trial was fair. Many countries, indeed even many jurisdictions in the United States as well, traditionally provide for a second trial for defendants when the offense is very minor. But Norway is willing to allow a second trial for any criminal offense, even a very serious offense, and either the defendant or the state's attorney may seek a second trial if dissatisfied with the first.

This is a relatively new feature in the Norwegian legal system—it has only been in effect a few years. The motivating force for moving to a two-trial system was Article 14 of the International Covenant on Civil and Political Rights (to which Norway as well as the United States and almost all other western countries are signatories). This article guarantees that "[e]veryone convicted of a crime shall have the right to his conviction and sentence being reviewed by a higher tribunal according to law." Norway interprets this provision broadly, as guaranteeing the right to an appeal of not just some issues from the trial, but as a right to have the actual judgments in the case—the conviction and the sentence—fully reviewed. To best achieve compliance with this provision, Norway decided that reconsideration of the issue of guilt or sentence would be hard to achieve without hearing from the witnesses a second time. Hence, either the prosecutor or the defense may ask for a second trial. Because providing a second trial is expensive, there is a strong incentive to keep trial procedures simple and, of course, to provide an initial trial that is fair and that reaches an accurate verdict and a just sentence so that a second trial will be sought in only a small percentage of cases.

As far as the trials themselves are concerned, some features seem to suggest Anglo-American trials but others seem closer to those in the Netherlands and Germany. Norwegian trials are closer to American (or English) ones with regard to the way evidence is brought out at trial. In Norway, the production of evidence at trial is generally the responsibility of the prosecutor and the defense attorney with the judges asking questions after the lawyers have finished with the witness. This represents a reversal of the usual order of questioning in continental countries. But this may not be as big a distinction as might appear because the presiding judge at a Norwegian trial (called the "president of the court") is responsible for ensuring that witnesses are questioned in such a way as to produce clear and truthful evidence. If not satisfied with the way a witness is being examined, the law provides that the president of the court may simply take over the questioning. And, just as the state's attorney or the defense attorney in Germany can ask for additional witnesses to be called at trial if either thinks they have relevant testimony to add, the judges in Norway can order additional witnesses to be heard at trial.

Norway is an interesting blend with respect to the fact finders at trial. The vast majority of trials are tried before mixed panels—a single professional judge and two lay judges for minor crimes, and two professional judges and three lay judges for more serious ones. This is similar to trials in Germany. But what makes Norway interesting is the tradition of jury trials, which are much more closely associated with common law countries and which Norway borrowed from England. But jury trials are only available for a small category of serious offenses. Now, with the change in the law to provide two trials in Norway, if a crime is eligible for a jury trial the first trial is before a mixed panel. A jury trial is available if a second trial is sought.

When a jury is used in Norway, its structure and the relationship between it and the judges are different from that in the United States. For one thing, a jury in Norway consists of ten jurors, with a vote of seven required for conviction. Second, jury trials in Norway take place before three professional judges, instead of one, and the judges have considerably more authority over the jury than does an American judge. For instance, at the end of the trial the presiding judge summarizes the evidence and then instructs the jury on the principles of law. Most American judges are forbidden to summarize the evidence for the jury and may only instruct on the law.

A third difference between jury trials in Norway and those in criminal cases in the United States is that the Norwegian jury does not just return a verdict of guilty or not guilty as in an American criminal trial. Instead the jury is given a written list of questions that it is supposed to work through in reaching its verdict. The questions track the issues as they relate to the evidence in the case, including possible defenses and mitigating factors. In the United States we call such verdicts "special verdicts" as distinguished from "general verdicts." While special verdicts are common in the United States in civil cases, they are rare in criminal cases and are discouraged.[3] The submission to the jury of questions to be answered as part of its decision-making process gives judges in Norway more control over the jury than is the case at an American criminal trial. If the judges consider the jury's answers confused, contradictory, or incomplete, they may ask the jury to retire and reconsider the relevant questions.

When there is a jury trial, the trial determines guilt but does not award a sentence. If the defendant is convicted, a mixed panel procedure is used for sentencing. Four of the members of the jury sit with the three professional judges to decide the appropriate sentence.

Although it shares some important features with our trial system, the Norwegian system also has many features in common with the continental trial tradition. For one thing, the defendant is expected to respond to the charges and offer a defense or explanation before witnesses are called. As in Germany, the defendant is given the option of responding to the charges after they have been read at the start of the trial. While the defendant may choose to say nothing, he or she is under pressure to answer questions. In Norway this is made explicit, as the presiding judge warns the defendant that the failure to respond might be viewed unfavorably by the judges. As in other continental systems, almost all defendants choose to respond to the charges. The defendant is not placed under oath, however, and faces no risk of perjury for whatever he may say in defending himself.

On balance, it is very difficult to categorize the Norwegian trial system as it has elements common to trials in the United States and England as well as others found only on the continent. Perhaps there is a lesson in this: trial systems are more flexible than we might think and the range of possibilities for a country wishing to reform its system is greater than we might imagine.

England

England and the United States are both heir to the common law tradition. First-year students at American law schools continue to study, as did prior generations of law students, famous nineteenth-century English cases, such as *Hadley v. Baxondale*[4] dealing with contract law and *Regina v. Dudley and Stephens*[5] in criminal law.

As one would expect, this common heritage has produced trial systems that are similar in some respects. If one visits a Crown Court in England—Crown Courts being the courts that hear jury trials—one sees a number of similarities: a jury of twelve, the presentation of a prosecution case followed by a defense case, and even many of the same restrictive evidence rules as are found at American trials. But beneath the surface similarities there are big differences. One of these major differences is that juries are not nearly as widely used in England as they are in the United States, and even when the option of a jury trial is available, the system is set up to encourage defendants to accept nonjury trials in Magistrates Courts where cases are tried more informally, more expeditiously, and more cheaply. It is estimated that roughly 98 percent of all criminal matters are handled in Magistrates Courts. Thus, to understand the English trial system one needs to understand the special nature of Magistrates Courts, of which there is no equivalent in the United States.

In the United States, a nonjury trial simply means a trial before a single trial judge. In England most criminal trials take place before a panel of "magistrates." Like many legal terms, the term "magistrate" has different meanings from country to country. In the United States, the term "magistrate" refers to a legally trained judge of comparatively low rank, while in England "magistrates" are citizens not formally trained in the law who are appointed to their position and receive no salary for their service. (The only exception to this is a small group of professional magistrates, called "stipendiary magistrates," who serve in urban centers and are trained in the law and receive a salary.) It is often said that the magistrates—retired persons, housewives, those with flexible employment schedules—are the backbone of the English legal system. Sitting usually in panels of two or three, they handle the great bulk of English criminal matters. There are some thirty thousand of them in England. They are appointed for a fixed number of years, during which time they must be available to sit in their local community a certain number of days each year, usually about two weeks. They receive training prior to going on the bench and the less experienced magistrates usually first hear criminal matters on a panel with experienced magistrates.

Magistrates are in many respects rather like the lay judges in continental countries, such as Germany and Norway. They grow to have some familiarity with the system as they continue to serve, but at the same time they have other jobs and other careers so they bring the perspective of outsiders to the system. While they do not serve on a mixed panel with professional judges, lay magistrates do have a law clerk available, usually an experienced attorney who can advise them on the law and procedure should they need such advice.

For fiscal reasons the English criminal justice system wants as many cases tried before magistrates as possible and encourages it in a number of ways. First, even though magistrates cannot impose prison sentences exceeding six months, they may hear a trial and then send the case to a Crown Court for sentencing if they decide that a sentence in excess of their authority is appropriate. Second, although in a number of cases the defendant has the option of being tried in either Crown Court or Magistrates Court, Crown Court judges tend to sentence more severely, making the jury trial option risky for many defendants. Obviously, trials before a panel of citizens tend to be informal and mistakes can be made. To offer protection against those mistakes, a defendant convicted in Magistrates Court has the right to obtain a complete retrial before a mixed panel of a Crown Court judge and two to four magistrates. But at that trial the sentence imposed by the magistrates is also reconsidered.

Crown Court trials, which are always jury trials, are similar to American jury trials but with important differences. Some of these differences are evident immediately upon entering a Crown Court: the defendant is required to sit alone in the "dock," a small box at the back or side of the courtroom, often a considerable distance away from his lawyer. The latter sits at a bench in the well of the courtroom with the opposing lawyer. If there are multiple defendants, they are all seated in the dock in alphabetical order, usually with a guard or guards next to them. While American defense lawyers often want to try to "humanize" defendants before the jury, perhaps by talking to them during the trial or by putting an arm around them at some point in the trial, neither tactic would be physically possible in an English courtroom. When one enters an English courtroom it is easy to tell who is on trial (and that is true on more than one level). I mentioned the Colin Ferguson case in the previous chapter—Ferguson being the deranged gunman who killed and wounded commuters on a railroad train in New York—and suggested that someone coming into that New York courtroom might have been confused as to who was on trial and who was conducting the defense. In England, that confusion would not arise: if a defendant wishes to conduct his own defense, he must do so from the dock. The well of the courtroom is reserved for members of the bar.

Another striking difference is the highly theatrical way that lawyers and judges in England are dressed. While it is not unusual to see lawyers as well as judges wearing black robes in other trial systems, the full outfit—black robe, starched dickey collar, and a gray powdered wig with tightly wound ringlets of curls around the sides and back of the wig—is English to the core. This highly stylized costume marks out English lawyers in Crown Court as members of the bar. The way the courtroom is structured, with a large physical separation between the defense lawyer and the defendant, is also indicative of a bar that views the role of a trial lawyer quite differently than we do in the United States. To understand that difference, a few words about the special character of the English bar are required.

As initially explained in chapter 3,[6] the English bar is a "divided bar" consisting of two types of lawyers: solicitors and barristers. Solicitors handle the traditional legal work done by lawyers in most countries around the world: they draw up contracts and corporate documents, draft wills, handle the transfers of title in real estate matters, represent defendants in civil and criminal matters, and the like. However, when a case comes to trial in Crown Court, whether civil or criminal, it has to be turned over to a barrister hired by the solicitor. This is true not only for the defense but for the prosecution as well. The case is investigated by the police, then turned over to the Crown Prosecution Service (CPS), a government agency, to decide whether it should be prosecuted. If it is to be prosecuted, the CPS must employ a barrister to present the prosecution side.

American prosecutors and defense lawyers are involved in a case usually from shortly after the arrest up through trial and any sentencing. By contrast, a barrister comes into the case very late by American standards, often a day or two before trial. The barrister will be given a "brief" from the hiring solicitor, basically a set of instructions that (1) explains the nature of the case and its strengths and weaknesses; (2) provides the barrister with copies of the important documents, witness statements, etc.; and (3) indicates the nature of the defense, the witnesses who have been subpoenaed to testify at the upcoming trial, and what they are expected to say. The defense barrister often only meets the defendant on the morning of trial.

Again, barristers are different from defense lawyers in another respect: they are hired by solicitors to handle the trial. It is thus sometimes said that barristers have no clients. This is true in the sense that solicitors hire them and also in the sense that barristers cannot be hired directly by clients. Barristers are not permitted to form partnerships but usually work out of a set of chambers with several other barristers. They are "professional advocates" who make their living going to trial and it is in their economic interest to go to trial often. Barristers who specialize in criminal trials are often scheduled to begin a new trial only a day or two after concluding an earlier one.

Another remarkable feature of the English system that sharply distinguishes it from other trial systems is the practice of switching sides, with a barrister appearing for the prosecution in one case and defending someone charged with a crime in the next. While not all

English barristers who practice in the criminal area switch sides—some get associated with one side rather than the other—the tradition of switching sides is very much alive in England. This tradition seems to fit well with the professional expectation that the barrister is an advocate who ought to be able to present competently and efficiently either side of any matter within his area of legal expertise. It also fits with the principle known as the "cab-rank rule." This analogizes the barrister to a cab driver who must take the next person willing to pay the fare, and cannot decline a client in order to wait for another more to his or her personal liking.

With respect to the function of judges at jury trials, English judges seem closer to Norwegian judges than they are to American ones. Like Norwegian judges, English judges will always summarize the evidence at the end of the trial for the jury, even if the trial lasted only a day or two, and they sometimes add to their summaries their own comments and opinions about the evidence. While commenting on the evidence is more controversial, the judge's summary of the evidence is considered an important part of the trial. English judges usually take careful notes so as to be well prepared for the summation. Because of this responsibility, they seem more willing than American judges to intervene during the trial to see that the examination of witnesses remains focused and to ask clarifying questions. While judges vary in each system, of course, Americans who have studied both the English and American trial systems conclude that English judges are much more in control of the trial and more willing to intervene than are American judges. The latter tend to be more passive and to intervene only when asked to make a ruling by one of the parties.[7]

With respect to jury verdicts, England represents a sort of middle ground between the United States, where unanimous verdicts remain the overwhelming preference, and the continent, where less than unanimous verdicts are the rule. In England, a judge may accept a verdict of 10–2 after at least two hours of deliberation. In other words, the system would prefer a unanimous verdict, but if at some point that appears impossible, the judge may accept a nonunanimous verdict. This represents a sort of fiscal pragmatism that would like to avoid a second trial if possible. It may also constitute recognition of the fact that jurors can be unreasonable. Perhaps this is more likely in England since there are no peremptory challenges and no opportunity for barristers to question jurors.

Obviously, trials in the Crown Court are very expensive—many times more so than trials in Magistrates Court. While appellate review from the Magistrates Court is broad and a new trial can easily be obtained at which both guilt and sentence will be reconsidered, appellate review from a conviction in Crown Court is very limited. It is hard to get a case heard by the Court of Appeal in England; a defendant usually has to make a preliminary showing of merit in order even to get permission to file an appeal. This is not lightly granted. It is even harder to get a case reversed on appeal. Unless the Court of Appeal believes that there was a serious injustice involved in the conviction, even clear trial errors will not result in a new trial. This contrasts sharply with the approach taken by appellate courts in the United States where appellate review after all criminal trials is encouraged and reversals of conviction are far more frequently granted.

Which of the Four Systems Is a "Real" Adversarial System?

In the days of black-and-white television, *To Tell the Truth* was a popular game show. Four people would come on stage and introduce themselves to the three panelists as people with the same name. The moderator would give the panelists a hint by explaining what the real person of that name had done, for example, he or she may have been the first to have climbed X mountain, invented Y gadget, or written Z book, and so on. Then the panelists would ask each of the four guests a limited number of questions aimed at determining which of the four was the real person and which three were impostors. After this, they would announce their vote. After each panelist had explained who he or she had voted for and why, the game show moderator would ask the guests, "You have heard the votes of our panelists and now: would the real X please stand up!" There would be a pause, perhaps some murmurs in the audience as one or another of the four persons pretended to rise, and then finally the true "mountain climber," "inventor," or whatever, would dramatically rise to applause—loud applause if all three panelists had been fooled.

Having described four different trial systems, I am tempted to ask the obvious question, "Which of the four is the real adversarial system?" The problem is that I don't know the answer. If we mean by the term adversarial that at trial there is a lawyer for the defendant prepared to challenge the evidence and, when appropriate, ask hard questions of witnesses, then each of the trial systems would seem to qualify as an adversarial system. If adversarial means that the judges must be impartial and neutral, then too each of these systems would seem to qualify, as they expect the professional judges to go about their task in a neutral and impartial way. If by adversarial we mean a system in which the lawyer for the state and the lawyer for the defense call witnesses and ask questions, with the judges playing a secondary role in the development of evidence, then maybe only the Norwegian and the English system qualify. If we mean that the trial is divided more formally into a prosecution case followed by a defense case, then only England would seem to qualify.

Certainly, the traditional way of thinking about trial systems among American academics is to see a bright line between "adversarial" systems and "inquisitorial" systems. I think this line is a lot less clear today and that many countries see their systems as a combination of the two traditions. But there is one important difference between the English system and the other three described in this chapter that I have not drawn attention to up to this point. It has to do with the role of the police. Historically, in England the police have been the prosecuting authority. That is, the police either directly handled the prosecution on their own if the crime was minor or else they hired a barrister to handle it for them if the case was more serious. This was changed a decade or so ago with the establishment of the Crown Prosecution Service. Now the prosecution of serious cases is not handled directly by the police. But the police are still viewed as part of the prosecution effort, despite the additional screening now done by the Crown Prosecution Service.

This is somewhat different from the way the police are viewed in the other three systems. In those systems the police are investigators and are expected to conduct a thorough and professional investigation. But the decision whether to prosecute is usually handled by the state's attorney or a judge or someone more clearly independent of the police. It is not seen as the job of the police to "get convictions." This may seem like a rather technical difference. Certainly the police on the continent want to see serious offenders convicted at trial; but the conceptual differences in their role in England as compared to their role on the continent lead to differences in the way evidence for trial is shared.

In England, because the police are viewed as being on the side of the prosecution, the issue arises as to how much information the police and prosecution should be required to share with the defense prior to trial and, conversely, how much information the defense should be required to share with the prosecution. Instead of a single investigative file, the prosecution has one file and the defense may have another with evidence it intends to use at trial.

This is not the way evidence tends to be assembled in continental countries like the Netherlands, Germany, and Norway. The latter have a single investigative file for the case, which is expected to contain everything connected with the investigation. It should normally contain all the police reports, all statements obtained from witnesses, all reports of scientific examinations of evidence, and so on. This file does not "belong" to one side or the other, but is supposed to be the result of a full investigation. Thus it makes sense that it ought to be available to the state's attorney, the defense attorney, and the presiding judge who want to prepare for the trial. The idea that the state's attorney should be able to use the file freely to prepare for trial but then parcels out pieces of information to the defense is considered offensive in the Netherlands, Germany, and Norway because just as the state's attorney wants to prepare for trial, so too does the defense attorney.

This means that the police are supposed to investigate for both the prosecution and the defense. If, in preparation for trial, the defendant should tell his lawyer that a friend was present at the time of the stabbing and that this friend will certainly confirm that the defendant stabbed the victim in self-defense, the defense lawyer will usually ask the police to interview this witness. It is not seen as the function of the defense lawyer to conduct a separate investigation of the crime from the police. Indeed, a defense lawyer will want to be careful not to interfere with the latter's investigation. If the witness supports the defendant's claim of self-defense or actually ends up undercutting a claim of self-defense, the results of any such interview will be put into the investigative file. On the continent, all the evidence in the case, except for privileged discussions between the client and the lawyer, is thus usually accessible to the state's attorney, the presiding judge, and the defense attorney when they prepare for trial.

But in England and the United States there is no common investigative file; each side has its own file which it keeps close to its chest and it only parcels out information as required by "rules of disclosure" (England) or "rules of discovery" (the United States). Obviously, the nature of the trial changes in such countries. Instead of a shared body of information that will be developed and tested at trial, each side has its own information, some of which may not be known at all by the other side.

I originally raised this question of the identity between the police and the prosecution in the United States in chapter 2 when I talked about the exclusionary rule in which the police and prosecutor are treated as a single entity, "the state." I expressed the concern that the conceptual identity of the police and the prosecutor encourages a sense of loyalty on the part of the police that can distort what gets investigated or what gets placed in prosecution files. Now, in discussing trial systems, the failure to draw a conceptual difference between the police and the prosecution in England and the United States seems to raise additional problems. First, if the police are on the side of the prosecution, then doesn't the defense need its own investigative personnel? This gets expensive, and much of it may duplicate the prosecution's staff. Second, won't there always be an enormous disparity in resources between the prosecution and the defense and won't the timing of the entry of defense counsel into the case, which will often occur days or even weeks after the crime was committed, make it impossible for the defense to undertake as thorough an investigation as the prosecution has done? Third, doesn't the existence of separate files controlled respectively by the prosecutor and the defense attorney encourage advocates to view trials not as a testing of all the evidence gathered during the investigation, but instead like a card game in which the prosecutor and the defense attorney lay individual pieces of evidence on the table but keep the rest of their hands close to their chests?

Finally, does not the conceptual identity of the police and the prosecution make it less likely that the police will conduct an independent and balanced investigation if they are directly responsible for the trial outcome? I mentioned at the start of this chapter the crisis of confidence in the English criminal justice system which resulted in large part from corrupt police work in certain terrorist cases. (One of these, the so-called Guilford Four, was made the basis of the movie *In the Name of the Father*.) In chapter 2, I mentioned the serious problems that were found to exist by the Justice Department at the FBI crime laboratory, including lab reports that were slanted or falsified to support prosecutorial objectives. Given these problems, if the "real" adversarial systems of England and the United States are premised on the police identifying with the prosecution and seeing themselves as being "on the prosecution side," I have to ask: why would such identity ever be considered a good attribute of a trial system?

Some Concluding Thoughts on the Variety of Western Trial Systems

I have offered in this chapter thumbnail sketches, admittedly hurried and incomplete, of four European trial systems. I intend to build on these sketches in the next chapter to contrast our trial system with these four. But even this limited glance at four trial systems gives us some idea of the variety that exists in western countries. If one were to go on and look at still other countries, such as Sweden, Scotland, or France, other major differences would become apparent. Some countries rely heavily on laypeople in the system; others not very much or even at all. Some prefer to keep trials informal and simple but to protect against errors by providing for broad appellate review or even a complete second trial if either side wishes. Some prefer to build more protections into the trial system and save money by allowing much more limited appellate review. In some countries the presiding judge at trial plays a central role in the production and development of evidence; other systems believe that lawyers should have that responsibility; yet others believe that responsibility ought to be shared by the lawyers and the judge.

I could go on with these comparisons and add more contrasts from system to system on such matters as the number of fact finders thought desirable in important criminal cases, the ratio of votes among fact finders thought necessary for conviction, the way judges are selected and promoted, the way victims are treated in the courtroom, and so on. We would find considerable variation from country to country. That such a wide variety of procedures exists among western countries, even though all are trying to provide a fair and public trial before impartial fact finders, suggests that the task of providing a fair and efficient trial system that can handle modern caseloads is not an easy one for any country. But at the same time the variety of specific procedures is heartening because the options for improving a weak trial system are many if a country has the courage to pursue reform.

CHAPTER SIX

Criminal Trials in the United States

Trials without Truth

In the previous chapter I presented sketches of four western trial systems, demonstrating the considerable variety among them. Indeed, even within a single country there is often more than one model for criminal trials. For example, England and Norway use juries for some serious criminal cases but most trials take place before panels that have no parallel in the United States: mixed panels of professional and lay judges in Norway and panels composed solely of lay magistrates in England.

The responsibility of the judge or judges for the development of evidence at trial also varies considerably, with the judges in some countries assigned primary responsibility while those in other countries play a secondary role to the parties. But in none is the judge viewed entirely as a passive referee who has no responsibility for what happens at trial or for the outcome of the case. In each of the systems reviewed the judges may question the witnesses. In some, the judges are themselves among the fact finders with responsibility for determining whether the evidence supports the charges or not. In other situations, such as when a jury is used in Norway or England, the judges review the evidence with the jury at the end of the trial in the hope that the jury can base its decision on a clear understanding of the evidence.

What is different about the United States from these four countries is not that the American parties have the primary responsibility for the production of evidence at trial: one sees the same thing in England and in Norway. Nor is it the fact that there are lawyers for the state and for the defense putting hard questions to certain witnesses or disputing, sometimes strenuously, the strength of the evidence or the credibility of particular witnesses. Nor is it that the judges feel that primary responsibility for the direction of the trial should be left to the advocates. What is different about criminal trials in the United States is *the degree* to which control over the direction and conduct of the trial has been ceded to the advocates and, obviously related, *the degree* to which judges see themselves as somehow removed from the contest and as thus less responsible for the conduct or outcome of the trial.

What Distinguishes Our Trial System from Other Trial Systems

The Degree to Which Trials Are Personalized

Despite the fact that lawyers play a major role in the presentation of evidence at trial in some countries around the world, I have no hesitation in saying that the American system of criminal trials is far more adversarial than any of the four trial systems I described in the previous chapter or any other with which I am familiar. For a number of reasons, our trial system encourages excesses of advocacy that do not occur as frequently in other parts of the world and we find it much harder to control these excesses than do other countries. The latter problem is especially obvious in very serious criminal cases where a great deal is at stake.

To begin with, American lawyers—be they prosecutors or defense attorneys—tend to be more closely identified with a case and its outcome than are lawyers in other systems. In other countries, the prosecutor handling the trial will often come into the case toward the end of the investigation, review the evidence, and seek a trial if there is sufficient evidence. The prosecutor is not as closely identified with the police and it is less his job to control or manage the investigation. In the United States, we tend not to draw a distinction between the investigation and the prosecution or defense of a case. In chapter 2, I argued that the highly technical system of pretrial investigation rules that the Court has erected, as well as the serious exclusionary consequences for any violation, push the police and the prosecutor close together. In any serious case the local prosecutor's office will want to be involved early in the investigation to make sure no evidence is jeopardized and to assist the police on the many legal issues that will arise.

A subtheme of that chapter was that this failure to distinguish between the role of the police and that of the prosecutor is a bad way to conceptualize the investigation of crime as it can discourage a thorough, impartial, and complete investigation on the part of the police. Evidence may be withheld from the police file or leads that could weaken the case may not be pursued so as not to jeopardize a prosecution; reports of witness interviews and even scientific tests may also be slanted consciously or unconsciously to help "the team" prevail at trial. In this chapter I want to raise another problem caused by this heavy investment in criminal cases by the advocates: they become tied to the success of a case because they are identified with it from its initial stages through trial. It is "their case" from beginning to end and they bear the major responsibility for its success, however such success is defined. When they "win," colleagues will congratulate them for a victory that depended on them. When they "lose," friends are likely to console them, but they are also susceptible to attack for having "blown it" by having adopted the wrong strategy or made some other error, such as allowing the wrong person or type of persons to serve on the jury.

This is also true of defense attorneys. In chapter 3, in discussing police interviews of criminal suspects, I explained how defense lawyers like to be involved in the investigatory stage in order to prevent the suspect from giving incriminating evidence and thereby improving his or her chances of securing an acquittal. It is an advantage to have a good defense attorney as soon after the crime as possible because he or she can prevent the prosecution from gathering any incriminating or useful statements from the client. Because indigent suspects don't get an attorney until they are arrested and brought into court, which can be rather late in the process, wealthy suspects often have a big advantage during the investigatory stage. As seen in chapter 3, a good defense lawyer can prevent the police from even interviewing the suspect between the commission of the crime and arrest. This makes it easier for defense attorneys to "win" cases.

Contrast the prosecutor and the defense attorney in our system with those in England in an important case. England, because of its history of a divided bar, uses a complicated and incredibly cumbersome trial system in which the prosecution case goes from the police to the Crown Prosecution Service and eventually to a barrister on the eve of trial. The prosecution barrister is not responsible for the investigation. Much the same is true of the defense side of the case. The barrister only gets the case from the defense solicitor just before the trial is to begin. The barrister does not supervise pretrial investigation or even go to the police station if a suspect wants an attorney—that is the job of the solicitor.

I don't want to exaggerate the differences between the two systems. What I am talking about here, as elsewhere in this chapter, are differences in degree: the advocates on either side in England are not as involved in the case as are American lawyers. They haven't made the decision whether or not to prosecute, they haven't advised the defendant all along the way, they are present simply to conduct the trial, which is distinct from what has gone before. Responsibility for the outcome of a criminal case is more diffuse in England.

The same applies to European trial systems as well. The police are expected to conduct a thorough investigation and a defense lawyer has to be careful not to interfere with their investigation. Again, this is a matter of degree, for certainly defense lawyers can advise suspects during an investigation and can undertake an independent investigation. But they tend to leave the actual investigation to the police and to ask the police to interview additional witnesses if necessary. By contrast, in the United States we are used to defense lawyers playing a more active and sometimes aggressive role during the investigation. Conceptually, the investigation and the trial are not distinguished in our system: both adversaries are often involved and both try to position the case or the evidence so that they can increase their chances of "winning."

Evidence Never Seen by the Opposing Side

As suggested in the previous chapter, evidence relating to a criminal case tends in the United States (and England) to have been assembled and segregated into two separate files by the time trial approaches. The prosecution file will have police reports, reports from experts, statements from witnesses, crime scene photos, and the like. The defense file will usually not be nearly as extensive but it may contain information obtained from witnesses interviewed by the defense lawyer or a defense investigator, reports from defense experts, information from friends of the defendant, memos of interviews with the defendant, and so on, depending on the nature of the case and the resources available to the defense.

The tendency toward separate investigations and the existence of separate files with information that may not be known by the opposing side makes the American system tremendously complicated. Obviously, the defense needs to know something about the evidence gathered by the police in order to prepare for trial. Consequently each American jurisdiction has a set of "discovery" rules that define what one side can "discover" about the other side's evidence. The rules are not symmetrical and typically the prosecution must give the defense much more information than the defense must give the prosecution. Even with rules of discovery in place, disputes arise about the application of these rules to the facts of a particular case. These arguments may carry over into the trial with one side or the other claiming that it did not receive the proper information from the advocate on the other side prior to trial and that therefore (1) the court ought not to permit certain information to be presented at trial, or (2) the jury should be told of this failing by the other side, or (3) the judge should grant a continuance to permit the "surprised" lawyer time to better prepare to examine the "surprise" witness, and so on.

Even after a trial is over, discovery problems can arise when the defendant, perhaps years later, learns of information that the prosecution or the police possessed that should have been disclosed to the defense but was not. Recently, for example, former Black Panther leader Geronimo Pratt had his murder conviction overturned after spending twenty-five years in prison, because the prosecution had failed to disclose prior to trial that the key state witness had been a police informant at the time and also that an important eyewitness—the victim's husband—had initially identified a person other than Pratt as the shooter.[1] (The prosecution is both ethically and constitutionally obliged to turn over to the defense any evidence that may negate the defendant's guilt in any degree. Thus this information should have been given to the defense prior to trial.)

Unjust convictions can result in any system, but problems such as these are less likely to occur when all the evidence in the case is available in a single file that is readily accessible to lawyers on either side. Instead, our trial system turns discovery of information "from the other side" into a game in which one wants to get as much information as possible but give as little as possible.

This sort of gamesmanship can work both ways. There will often be information in the defense file of which the prosecution may not be aware. Recognition is growing that both sides need information with which to prepare for trial. Thus many jurisdictions now require that the defendant give the prosecution advance notice of any alibi that the defense intends to raise. Thus, for example, if the defendant in a murder case tells his lawyer that he was not at the victim's apartment on the evening of the killing but was watching movies with a friend at the friend's apartment all evening, most American jurisdictions now require that the defense alert the prosecution to the nature of the alibi and give the prosecution the name of the alibi witness. But it gets more complicated: suppose the prosecution has the police check out the alibi and the police discover that it is only partially true—perhaps the friend says that they were together on the evening of the killing but that the defendant left early (in time to have committed the murder). Or perhaps the alibi turns out to be completely untrue—perhaps the friend originally said the defendant was with him on the evening of the killing, but then confesses that this was not true and he was just trying to help out his friend by giving him an alibi. The Supreme Court has said that information rebutting the alibi must be given to the defense so it can decide to withdraw the alibi defense. It gets worse: if the defendant decides to withdraw the alibi and offer a completely different defense at trial, the prosecution can't cross-examine him or point out to the jury that this is now the second of two inconsistent defenses that the defendant has put forward.

Other systems don't have much tolerance for these sorts of games with the truth. They expect a suspect to cooperate with the investigation and they expect the police to conduct a thorough and fair investigation and to make the results available to the prosecutor, the defense, or the judge for trial preparation. The trial is the testing of all the evidence gathered during the investigation, not just part of it. To allow the defense to test the waters in this way would be offensive to the serious task at hand. If a defendant has offered two different accounts of what happened on the evening of the crime, the judges will know that and will take the inconsistency into account. Trials are consequently more straightforward and place much less emphasis on the skill of the advocates.

The "Shaping" of Evidence for Adversarial Advantage Prior to Trial

There is another way in which our trial system is different from the four systems described in the previous chapter. All four want the evidence at trial to be received in as natural a state as possible. They don't want the attorneys to distort or shape it to serve their adversarial purposes. That is one of the reasons why they do not want the attorneys going out and interviewing witnesses prior to trial, preferring instead to let the police do it. England is also concerned with lawyers influencing witness testimony. Until very recently, barristers were not even permitted to have any contact with witnesses (other than with experts or the defendant) prior to trial. This led to a funny exchange in the comic film *A Fish Called Wanda* in which the seductive Wanda, played by Jamie Lee Curtis, went to visit a pompous barrister, Archie Leach, played by John Cleese. Leach was defending one of the thieves who had pulled off a major jewel robbery with Wanda but was captured by the police. Wanda intended to seduce the barrister in order to find out whether he knew where her partner-in-crime had hidden the stolen jewels. When an infatuated Leach started chatting with the alluring Wanda and suddenly realized that Wanda was his client's main alibi witness, he got up in a panic, telling her as he did, "I can't talk to you. . . . You're a defense witness. . . . I must ask you to leave immediately." When she asked, "What did I say?" he explained, "It's not ethical for me to talk to a witness." When she tried to reassure him that it must be okay because "[e]verybody does it in America," he replied, "Well not in England. It is strictly forbidden." (That didn't stop the eventual involvement of Leach with Wanda.)

The ban on any contact with witnesses has been softened in England in recent years so that a barrister in Cleese's position may talk to a witness prior to trial, but the rules of ethics state that a barrister must not "rehearse, practice or coach a witness in relation to his evidence or the way in which he should give it."[2]

The American trial system goes in the opposite direction: in any important criminal case, major witnesses will have their testimony rehearsed, often over and over, by the lawyer or lawyers "on their side." But it is more than simply rehearsing: each lawyer wants "to win" at trial and one way to help in that direction is to make sure that the testimony of each important witness has the maximum impact on the jury. The lawyers subtly, and sometimes not so subtly, shape the witness's proposed testimony for adversarial advantage at trial. One way to do this is to bring in another lawyer to do a mock cross-examination of the witness. Witnesses learn through such cross-examination how to qualify their answers and how best to explain apparent conflicts at trial. Suggestions from the lawyers may also cause a witness to remember something he or she claims on the stand to have seen. But one wonders whether the witness is really remembering something or whether the power of suggestion is taking effect. For example, the prosecutor might tell a witness during an interview, "Your statement to the police doesn't mention whether or not the robber was wearing gloves. A couple of witnesses testified that the robber was wearing brown leather gloves. If you saw those gloves you should mention them, but, if not, fine, too." The witness may recall the gloves or may remain uncertain. But the chance that he or she will insist that the robber was not wearing gloves is strongly reduced. The end result is testimony shaped by the lawyers. Witnesses are not just witnesses in our system: they are performers who need to be coached to give their best performance from the point of view of the lawyer calling the witness.[3]

We have a trial system that on the one hand emphasizes the need for live testimony so that the demeanor of witnesses can be assessed by the jury. But on the other hand the system is frightened of spontaneity and prefers witnesses who are coached and rehearsed. Instead other trial systems want evidence presented at trial in as close to its original state as possible. In our trial system physical evidence is presented in such a way, being marked and preserved in its original state. But when it comes to witnesses our practice is very different. The United States is at the extreme in openly encouraging the presentation of evidence at trial that has the palm prints and fingerprints of the lawyers all over it as the evidence is shaped, reshaped, and sometimes distorted a bit for adversarial advantage.

Strong Emphasis on the Lawyers' "Performances" at Trial

What is different about American criminal trials when compared to those in other countries is not the fact that the lawyers ask hard questions of witnesses or challenge the quality or quantity of the evidence. A trial for rape, murder, or assault can turn into a very contentious event in any system. What is different about American trials is the relative lack of internal or external restraints on the advocacy considered appropriate at trial, and the complete control over the conduct of the trial ceded to the lawyers. To some extent the lawyers' freedom from external constraints can be seen physically in the courtroom. In the United States, it is accepted in most jurisdictions that the well of the courtroom is within the lawyers' control and lawyers are permitted to walk around that area rather freely. Sometimes they may go over to the jury box to make a point to them or sometimes to a spot distant from or close to a witness for dramatic effect.

Other systems don't permit lawyers that sort of control over the courtroom. They want the emphasis on the witnesses and what they have to say, not the lawyers. Often lawyers must ask questions while seated at the periphery of the courtroom. If they are permitted to stand while asking questions, they must stand at their place or at a podium a few feet away. Recall the football versus soccer analogy from chapter 1: like coaches at an American football game, the lawyers at a criminal trial in the United States are really closer to being "players" and it is accepted that their performance can be important to the outcome.

To reflect again on the football versus soccer analogy, American lawyers are permitted to dominate and control the testimony of the witnesses to a degree that would not be tolerated in other countries. On cross-examination, lawyers are expected to control the witness through a series of questions that permit only a "yes" or "no" answer and do not allow the witness to interject an explanation. By tone of voice, the lawyer doing the cross-examination may be criticizing the witness and implying a great deal. American lawyers may also use questioning of witnesses to smuggle information into the trial and thus come even closer to being witnesses themselves. For example, in a rape case the defense lawyer may ask the victim, "Isn't it a fact, Ms. Jones, that you have gone to the University Bar and Grill on other occasions to pick up men for the purpose of sex?" This question, even if objected to and overruled immediately, effectively permits the lawyer to convey information to the jury without having to testify him- or herself. In this way, the lawyer becomes a witness.

Finally, there is another sense in which American lawyers are players at trial and that is what they convey in the courtroom through nonverbal expression. In dozens of ways—smirking at a witness whose testimony is damaging to the lawyer's side of the case, rolling one's eyes in response to answers the lawyer doesn't like, derisive laughter, turning one's back to the witness, the use of an incredulous or sarcastic tone of voice for effect—lawyers are able to convey to the jury what they personally think about the testimony they have heard or of opposing counsel's arguments. While there is an ethical rule that forbids lawyers from stating "a personal opinion as to the justness of a cause, the credibility of a witness . . . or the guilt or innocence of an accused,"[4] lawyers don't need to directly state their personal views on the credibility of a witness or the merits of the case, when they can do so just as powerfully indirectly.

Other countries see the role of lawyers differently and do not want them injecting their personal beliefs into the facts of the case. The lawyer's job is to test the evidence, not to give evidence even indirectly. Regarding the balance between lawyers and witnesses, for example, they don't want witnesses to be controlled by the lawyers in an American-style cross-examination that won't let the witness come up for air. Instead of the lawyer putting him- or herself into the battle of credibility between the victim and the defendant in a rape case by snidely implying in the cross-examination that the victim left the bar with the defendant with the full intention of having sex with the latter, the lawyer must put the question directly to the witness and allow her to explain why she left the bar with the defendant. This doesn't mean that there cannot be follow-up questions that dispute the victim's version of events or that inconsistencies between the victim's testimony and her prior statements to the police cannot be pointed out to her and be made the subject of questioning. But the sort of control over the witness that lawyers exert in the United States is not permitted. The focus remains on the witness who is permitted to provide any explanation she may have to the point raised in the question.

Even in England, a country with the same legal heritage as ours, there is a marked difference between the way barristers see their role in questioning witnesses and the way American lawyers see theirs. Barristers may ask hard questions of witnesses but are expected to do so in a detached manner. Extremes of partisanship are far less likely to occur in England for a number of reasons. First, the judges have more control over the trial than do American judges—a subject I will discuss below. Second, barristers are part of a legal culture that believes that restrained advocacy is the most effective form of advocacy and that encourages it in many ways. Peter Tague, a professor at Georgetown Law School, provides a detailed comparison of English and American criminal advocacy. Far from encouraging a bitterly partisan performance from the barristers, Tague writes: "Whether representing the Crown or the defendant, the barrister should act as if he were objective and impartial, as if he were uninterested in how the witness answers. If the witness falls short of the promise in his or her statement, the barrister accepts this disappointment with equanimity."[5] Tague suggests that almost every aspect of the English system—such as the way barristers are hired, the tradition of switching sides, and the greater authority judges have over the trial—discourages the extremes of advocacy one sees in the American trial system.

I say "extremes of advocacy" in our trial system, but perhaps it would be more accurate to say that our system encourages trial lawyers to think of themselves as actors on a stage as well as advocates. Some evidence that the line between acting and advocacy is at least blurred is evident in a small book called THEATER TIPS AND STRATEGIES FOR JURY TRIALS[6] published by the National Institute of Trial Advocacy (NITA). NITA is the premier organization for the teaching of trial advocacy in the United States. NITA runs programs for young lawyers three or four years out of law school at a number of locations around the country and occasionally abroad. Its teachers are among the finest trial lawyers and trial judges in the United States. NITA instructs in part by videotaping participants actually doing various pieces of a trial—jury selection, opening arguments, direct examination, cross-examination, and so on. The videotape is then reviewed and critiqued by an experienced instructor working one-on-one with the participant. These methods have been copied and incorporated into trial advocacy courses at virtually every law school in the United States.

THEATER TIPS is an attempt to apply lessons from the theater to trial. It instructs lawyers in the sort of pen they should use in the courtroom, the sort of wristwatch to be preferred, the clothes they should wear, and so on. It even discusses the advantages and disadvantages of putting on a regional accent to ingratiate the attorney with the jury in the region where he or she is trying a case. In short, the book stresses that trial is theater, that props and costumes are important, and that lawyers must occasionally hide who they are from the jury or pretend they are someone they are not if this would give them an advantage in the courtroom. It is a symptom of how extreme our system has become that these sorts of tips are put forward by the National Institute of Trial Advocacy with no hint that there is anything odd, let alone demeaning to a proud profession, in suggesting that advocates not only cross the line into theater but that they jump across the line. While many lawyers would recoil from the advice in this book and prefer to be themselves in the courtroom, the book is not just theory: a friend who tries cases in a number of different states tells me there are lawyers who put on Mormon undergarments (although not Mormon) before trying a case in Utah or who put a pin of the praying hands in the lapel of their jacket (although not religious) when trying a case in the bible belt. In parts of the West, of course, cowboy boots are de rigueur.[7]

This is not a criticism of trial advocacy courses. All of us who speak in public as part of our work can benefit from practicing what we do, from seeing ourselves on videotape, and from being critiqued by those who are masters of whatever form of communication we are attempting. This is true whether one is a salesperson, a teacher, a business executive, or a trial lawyer. But there is a negative side to modern trial advocacy courses because they tend to foster a win-at-all-costs mentality in which one reaches for every advantage in order to win.

"Just Win, Baby"

In hundreds of criminal trials each week around the country the adversaries know each other well and have a certain mutual respect for each other. Perhaps they are a local deputy district attorney and a deputy public defender who have tried quite a few cases against each other over the years. The two lawyers know the applicable law well, they understand the issues involved in the case, and they are able to try the case in a relatively straightforward way. Advocacy remains within bounds and the case is put to the jury on the merits. If the evidence is close—as it often will be given the high standard of proof—the prosecutor can take satisfaction in having put the case clearly to the jury, even if the defendant is acquitted. The same is true of the defense attorney if the defendant is convicted.

Although many cases fit this mold, others do not: cases where advocacy seems to have no bounds and where the working principle of the defense lawyer is, borrowing from Al Davis of the Oakland Raiders, "Just win, baby." These tend to be cases of a more serious nature—murders, rapes, serious assaults, and the like—where there is more at stake for the defendant. Sometimes they are defended by private defense attorneys who are not a part of the local trial culture and have personally more at stake than a local public defender. In such cases the goal of the defense attorney is not to obtain a fair trial for the defendant; a fair trial might spell disaster for the client because it would likely result in a conviction, given the evidence. Instead the goal is to win above all and that means doing almost everything to win. It may require what lawyers refer to as a "scorched earth" defense in which anyone and everyone is likely to come under attack—including not just prosecution witnesses, but the prosecutor personally as well as the judge. Sometimes the case will not reach trial. If the pretrial hearings are made painful enough, and if it is clear that the trial will be a bitter angry battle it may lead to defense victory even before trial in the form of an advantageous plea bargain, offered to avoid the battle on the horizon.

Winning may also mean trying to obtain a mistrial so that the trial has to be aborted, giving rise to the prospect of having to start all over again. As a practical matter, mistrials are defense victories. It is much harder emotionally and practically to put on a trial a second time when one has the burden of proving a case beyond a reasonable doubt. To obtain a mistrial a defense attorney might try to bait the prosecutor or the trial judge into an outburst of anger and then insist that a mistrial is necessary because "the [prosecutor or judge] has so prejudiced the courtroom atmosphere against my client that a fair trial is no longer possible." If the judge refuses to grant a mistrial, perhaps the lawyer will insist on being allowed to withdraw in the middle of trial because the judge's outburst "has rendered any defense a nullity" and because the judge "is clearly biased" against the lawyer. Perhaps the lawyer will insist that a "neutral" judge be brought into the courtroom to decide on the withdrawal motion because the present judge is being so unreasonable. Perhaps the lawyer will begin asking for sidebars every few minutes to delay the trial or announce to the jury his or her anger at the judge's "obvious unfairness." In short, a defense lawyer can turn a trial into a bitter stressful event that takes its toll on everyone. The jury may become frustrated, and the constant interruptions might make it difficult for the jury to recall the evidence presented or to put the pieces of the evidence together so as to render an accurate verdict. While the jurors may hold the defense responsible for this, they may become so angry at the whole system that they simply want to go home.

Another tactic aimed at winning rather than ensuring a fair trial is for the defense lawyer to inject errors into the trial or to allow errors to go by without drawing attention to them so as to require reversal of any conviction. This can be done simply by failing to correct what defense counsel realizes is a potential reversible error or by objecting to the error in a way that hides its significance from the judge. (One way to lead a judge into error is to sandwich a legitimate objection in the middle of a series of rather frivolous and weak ones so that the judge will grow frustrated and fail to appreciate the error. Victory on appeal will then be assured.)

One hopes that most lawyers see their duties to their clients as stopping short of intentionally injecting error into trials or baiting judges, but we know it goes on. Many trial judges have talked about what they see happening in courts and how often they are put in an adversarial position with defense lawyers. In his book, GUILTY: THE COLLAPSE OF CRIMINAL JUSTICE, Judge Harold Rothwax, an experienced New York trial judge who was himself a defense attorney prior to taking the bench, describes a trial system in which defense lawyers often want neither an error-free trial for their clients nor a trial that allows for an accurate reconstruction of the events in question. Instead, they try to "seed the record" with errors and bait the judge into displays of anger. Judge Rothwax is severely critical of a trial ethic in which it seems to be assumed that "[a] victory gained by provoking judicial blunders is a victory all the same."[8]

Trials occasionally degenerate in this way in other countries, but it is much more likely to happen in the United States for a number of reasons. First, it is easier for judges in other countries to intervene at trial or even take over the examination of a witness if necessary. Second, because their systems are much less complicated there are fewer opportunities for evidentiary battles and exclusionary-rule battles than in the United States. Third, defense lawyers in other systems tend to view their purpose not as winning but as trying to see that the defendant gets a fair trial. That certainly would include making sure that all the evidence favorable to the defendant was considered and that incriminating evidence was tested and its weaknesses exposed to the court. But winning is de-emphasized in other trial systems.

Another factor that pushes American defense lawyers to the extremes of advocacy is the "public defender mentality" that encourages them to see themselves as standing outside the system and therefore not obligated to conform to its rules. Charles Ogletree of the Harvard Law School, himself a former public defender, claims that public defenders see themselves as "Robin Hood" figures "who do not always have to conform to the moral rules society reserves for others" and who take pride in "stealing" cases from the prosecution.[9] In a world where all the lawyers in the office view themselves as somehow "outside the system" with no responsibility to the legal establishment and the accuracy of its determinations (although, oddly enough, receiving paychecks from "inside the system"), adversarial extremes come to be seen as normal and acceptable.

Harsh punishments, such as habitual defender statutes, crimes that threaten tough mandatory minimum sentence upon conviction, and, of course, the death penalty, none of which exist in other western countries, also encourage extremes of advocacy. Many defense lawyers candidly admit that they will go to almost any lengths to help their clients avoid the death penalty. One way to do that is to make the trial so protracted and stressful that the state agrees to a plea bargain that avoids the death penalty. If that can't be achieved, lawyers hope that enough errors are seeded throughout the pretrial and trial proceedings to ensure that if the death penalty is imposed it will be overturned in time.

Lawyers who litigate death penalty cases have told me that you can pretty much forget the rules of ethics when it comes to such a case. Talking about a case in which the death penalty had been imposed, a friend who has litigated a number of such cases, said, "Bill, you know that when I was litigating that case I really drank way too much." What this sober and intelligent individual was telling me with a wink was that he was ready and willing to perjure himself and to declare his own trial incompetence due to his drinking, and would do so if necessary to void the defendant's death sentence. Obviously, this is an extreme example and it says nothing about nondeath penalty cases. But to the extent that extremes of advocacy are considered necessary and permissible in some classes of cases, it becomes hard to confine those extremes to such cases alone.

Regardless of whether there are many defense lawyers who engage in such tactics or only a few, the problem Judge Rothwax raises has its origins in a legal system in which the ethical balance between a lawyer's duty to the court and his duty to the client is much less clear than it is in other countries. There are many lawyers, judges, and law professors who would argue that the actions being condemned by Judge Rothwax represent nothing more than zealous advocacy by a lawyer on behalf of a client. If a judge can't control the lawyers in the courtroom or doesn't know the law well enough to give a defendant an error-free trial, that is the fault of the judge, not the lawyers.

In other trial systems a defense lawyer can cause problems at trial and turn a trial into a miniwar but it is harder to do so. On the continent the production and development of evidence at trial is a shared endeavor between the judges and the lawyers. Control over the conduct of the trial doesn't have to be wrested back from an obstreperous lawyer because it is never given to the lawyers in the first place.

Another moderating influence on defense lawyers in other trial systems is the fact that the relationship between lawyer and client is much less close. In the United States, defense lawyers stress over and over the "loyalty" a defense lawyer owes the client. The implication seems to be that a lawyer not performing or behaving the way an American defense lawyer does is being disloyal to the client. But what American defense lawyers really mean is *identity* with the client. In the ideal world of the American defense lawyer, the client would have all the lawyer's training and ability. But lacking that, the closest thing he can do is to identify with the client almost completely. This means that the lawyer does everything he can for the client short of violating the rules of ethics. But since very little is forbidden by the rules of ethics, or, as lawyers like to put it, there are "lots of gray areas," defense lawyers in our system face few limits. Certainly, aiding the client to commit perjury is forbidden, but even that turns out not to be a problem for a defense lawyer pushing for an acquittal. A common way to avoid being in that position is to be careful never to ask the client directly if he or she committed the crime. Rather, the defense lawyer waits until he knows the main prosecution evidence and can present it to the defendant, before asking the latter for "his or her story."

Naturally, lots of American lawyers don't want to handle criminal cases because they don't want to play the sorts of sordid games that the system not only permits but encourages. Other trial systems make it easier to be a defense lawyer because one is an advocate for the client—not the client's alter ego. This is evident in subtle ways, such as the physical separation of the defendant from his or her barrister in an English courtroom. It can be seen on the continent when the presiding judge asks the defendant if he or she wishes to question a witness after the defense lawyer has finished asking questions. It is not assumed that the defense lawyer and the defendant are one and the same person. They are two different people, and the defendant may have his own questions to ask. Contrast this with many American trials where the defendant might not utter a single word in the presence of the jury in a trial that could last weeks or months. The jury at the trial of Timothy McVeigh, one of the defendants in the Oklahoma City bombing trial, never heard McVeigh utter a single word at either the guilt phase or the penalty phase.

Prosecutors in the System

The criticism of defense lawyers in the previous sections may seem one-sided. After all, prosecutors are not shrinking violets and they often don't hesitate to use inflammatory language in the courtroom. But these criticisms were not about particular defense lawyers versus particular prosecutors, but about our trial system and the control over evidence ceded to the lawyers and the pressures put on them to win. Certainly, many of the problems identified above apply equally to prosecutors. For example, many prosecutors, like many defense lawyers, plainly "vouch" for their side of the case at trial and communicate their personal opinions about the merits of the case and the guilt of the defendant to the jury. Like all lawyers in a courtroom, they are theoretically forbidden to express personal opinions on the merits of the case being tried. Excesses of advocacy exist on both sides and deserve to be condemned when they occur. But I have chosen to give separate treatment to defense lawyers and prosecutors because there are different ethical restraints on prosecutors and there are also structural reasons why prosecutors usually prefer an orderly, tightly controlled trial.

One of the main differences is the fact that prosecutors operate under ethical constraints which put their obligation to the system above simply "winning" at trial. Ethical standards for prosecutors state that the job of the prosecutor is "to seek justice, not merely to convict"[10] and that a prosecutor "has the responsibility of a minister of justice and not simply an advocate."[11] American defense lawyers have no similar overriding obligation to justice, and thus the arguments they may put forward are less restricted. Thus, to recall an issue discussed earlier, where a client has admitted to the defense lawyer that he did indeed rape the victim as charged, it would seem ethically permissible (or at least not ethically impermissible) for a lawyer to argue vociferously that the victim is not telling the truth and that she consented to sexual intercourse, if there is an opening in the evidence for such an argument. Similarly, even if the defendant has admitted killing the victim in a murder case, it is not clearly unethical for a defense lawyer to claim at trial that the police planted evidence in order to frame the defendant, if an opening in the evidence permits such an argument.[12]

There is a second reason why adversarial excess in the courtroom is not as big a problem with prosecutors as it is with defense attorneys, namely, the different burden that the system places on prosecutors. Proving someone guilty beyond a reasonable doubt in a serious criminal case is a difficult task, even if there is strong scientific or videotape evidence of the crime. To get a jury to convict often requires that jurors have the opportunity to focus on each piece of evidence so that they can add it all up at the end of the trial. Because the burden of proof on the prosecution is so high, the injection of side issues or confusion into a trial is very unlikely to help the prosecutor. Prosecutors prefer an atmosphere in which the evidence can be presented in a deliberate and controlled way. Thus weak judges do not impact both sides to the same extent and prosecutors tend to prefer judges who run a tight ship and keep tight control over both the advocates.

Much the same point can be made about delay during a trial or mistrials (where some error or other problem requires that the trial begin again). Jurors can become impatient with delays at trial and begin to think there are problems with the prosecution or the prosecutor. Starting over, which is required when a mistrial is declared, also very rarely helps the prosecution. The memories of the witnesses may not be as sharp after a delay and it is hard to keep a case together—witnesses move, leave town, or disappear. In general, delay and confusion are very unlikely to help the prosecution because of the heavy burden of proof at trial.

Finally, there is a third reason for treating prosecutors differently from defense lawyers in describing our trial system: it is easier for a judge to intervene when a prosecutor becomes too strident in his or her advocacy than when a defense lawyer does so. The judge doesn't have to worry about appellate reversal. If the prosecution obtains a conviction, the prosecutor will have "won" anyway despite the judge's intervention, and if the prosecution loses, there will be no appeal because a retrial is not permitted. A judge doesn't need to be as cautious in rebuking a prosecutor whose rhetoric becomes extreme. Thus there is often a double standard in the way advocacy is controlled in American courts. A prosecutor who dares to say some of the things we have seen defense lawyers say in recent high publicity cases—Johnny Cochran's comparison of Mark Fuhrman to Adolf Hitler comes immediately to mind—would be interrupted and severely chastised for such comments, while defense lawyers who say similar things draw no comment from the judge because they are just defense lawyers "doing their thing."

My point is not to hold prosecutors blameless in the extreme advocacy that the system tends to encourage: where it occurs it ought to be stopped. But we have almost no conceptual framework for controlling such advocacy by the defense attorney.

Conclusion

The American legal system assumes that if an adversarial system is good, the more adversarial it becomes the better it must be. This is completely fallacious. The result is a trial system that gets more and more adversarial and every stage of the proceeding and every minor detail is turned into an adversarial battle. Consultants are available to help lawyers pick juries for adversarial advantage or even to help lawyers select clothing and accessories for such advantage. We fail to see not only how truth is undermined and the profession demeaned, but how depersonalizing trials have become. The American defense lawyer not only defends the client at trial but, to a degree unimaginable in many other legal systems, becomes the client.

CHAPTER SEVEN

Trials without Truth

Weak Trial Judges

As a group, the American judiciary is the most powerful in the world. We are accustomed to seeing judges at all levels strike down local, state, or federal statutes and regulations for any number of constitutional reasons. This is a power that judges don't have in countries such as England, where Parliament is supreme. But even in countries where judges do have this power, as in many parts of the continent, it is reserved for a select body of judges at the highest judicial level, usually a constitutional court designed to handle constitutional issues alone. This power also tends to be used more sparingly. By contrast, the American judiciary has tremendous influence over political and social issues and is often ahead of public opinion on a broad range of difficult moral issues, such as same sex marriages or assisted suicide. In addition to the power to strike down legislation, there have been times when individual trial judges have taken extraordinarily bold steps to remedy difficult local problems, even to the extent of taking over and running school systems, hospitals, housing projects, and prisons.[1]

But what is odd about the American judiciary is how a body of judges who are so confident as a group when it comes to difficult political and moral issues can be so weak and uncertain when it comes to a trial in which the issue is far more limited and comparatively straightforward: does the evidence show beyond a reasonable doubt that this defendant stabbed this victim or not? This chapter will explain why trial judges in the United States play such a weak role at trial compared to the roles of trial judges in other countries, and why it is much harder for American judges to reassert control over the trial.

Weak Trial Judges

Inadequate Trial Preparation by Judges

One of the reasons why American judges have trouble controlling what happens at trial is the fact that they are poorly equipped to intervene in terms of what they know about the issues and the evidence in the case being tried. The presiding judges in continental systems have access to the entire investigative file on the case and in most countries the judge will have read it very thoroughly because he or she will play an active role in the production of evidence at trial. Thus, in the Netherlands or Germany, where the presiding judge determines what witnesses need to be called and does the bulk of the questioning, a full command of the investigative file is part of the job. Even in Norway, where the parties present the evidence, the judge has access to the investigative file. If a lawyer in Norway takes too long questioning a witness or starts to badger a witness unfairly and refuses to stop when asked to do so, the judge can simply take over the questioning. This is specifically contemplated in the law and permitted. With access to the information in the file, the presiding judge can know nearly as much about the case and the witnesses as the lawyers do. It is thus easier for the presiding judge to redirect or supplement the examination of the witness if he or she thinks the witness might be able to provide additional helpful information.

By contrast, in the United States there is a large information gap between what the parties know about the case and what the judge knows about it. This makes it very hard for the judge to intervene. If the questioning of a witness seems to be slow or exceedingly cautious, a judge will usually be reluctant to intervene for fear that there is some good reason for the slow pace. Similarly, when a lawyer asks questions of a witness that seem unfair because they assume certain facts, without knowing what information the lawyer possesses about the witness, it is not easy for a judge to step in and put a stop to such questioning. In short, American judges are simply not well equipped to play an active role at trial. When combined with a system that places few restraints on advocacy and, in fact, pushes lawyers to go to the extremes of advocacy, this is a bad combination.

*Uncertainty over the Role We Expect of
Judges at Trial*

Another reason judges prefer to play a passive role at trial is the fact that our trial system equates impartiality with passivity. Other countries do not see preparation for trial or an active role at trial as inconsistent with neutrality and impartiality, but we seem to do so. This is odd because justices in our appellate courts, such as the United States Supreme Court, read briefs and cases to prepare for oral argument and often ask many questions of the litigators. But when it comes to trial before a jury, the system seems to see only dangerous risks in participation by the judge. The result is a trial culture that sees the judge having no responsibility for the outcome of the trial. Franklin Strier, in his book RECONSTRUCTING JUSTICE,[2] points out that the American Bar Association's Code of Judicial Conduct fails to assign to judges any affirmative duty to see that justice is done in their courtrooms. Instead the main adjudicative restraint on judges in the Code is that they perform their duties "impartially." When judges come to view impartiality as synonymous with passivity, Strier warns that this "can make a judge an unwilling abettor of intolerable injustice."[3]

Other trial systems that use juries believe that juries need more help from trial judges than they receive in the United States. They permit and expect judges to play an active role at trial in order to help see that justice is done. They also insist that judges try to help juries at the end of the trial by going over the evidence with them. In both England and Norway, for example, judges review and summarize the evidence with the jury at the end of trial. This is true whether the trial lasted three weeks or three days. The judges point out to the jury the main issues in the case and review conflicts in the testimony.

While there are risks to permitting judges to summarize the evidence for the jury, there are risks in not permitting juries to have this help as well. In balancing the two sets of risks other common law countries reach a different outcome from the American view which discourages judges from summarizing the evidence for the jury. This restriction on more active participation by the judge at trial is a rather late development in our legal history. In fact, the power of a trial judge not only to summarize the evidence but even to go further and comment on it by offering his or her own opinion to the jury was so well established in the United States that in 1930 the Supreme Court declared, "A jury trial in which the judge is deprived of the right to comment on the evidence and express his opinion on the facts . . . is not the jury trial which we inherited."[4] But gradually the law has changed so that in the majority of states today trial judges are prohibited from either summarizing or commenting on the evidence.

Part of the preference for judicial passivity at trial is cultural in the United States. While in some jurisdictions judges are still permitted to summarize the evidence for the jury, judges rarely choose to do so in those jurisdictions. In 1996, I spoke at a conference of federal judges from the Ninth Circuit which includes the states along the west coast from Arizona up to Washington, and Hawaii. In my talk I had emphasized the importance that other common law countries place on the judge summarizing the evidence for the jury. During the discussion that followed, the judges confessed that they never exercised their power to summarize the evidence at trial. The event sticks in my mind because it captured for me all the conflicts in the American concept of judicial power. Here was a room full of extremely smart and talented people. These were judges who had risen to the pinnacle of the legal profession, had lifetime appointments and regularly wrote opinions on important and difficult legal issues such as voting rights, affirmative action, privacy, and free speech. Yet they were reluctant to attempt a neutral and balanced summary of the evidence at the trials over which they presided. Many conceded that juries need this help. Yet, although our trial system permits and encourages more extreme behaviors on the part of trial lawyers in an effort to "win," it has evolved so that trial judges have less authority in the courtroom than ever before. This is a troubling combination.

Uncertainty over the Priorities of Our Trial System

A major reason why judges are reluctant to intervene at trial is our trial system has no clear priorities. Intervention is consequently hazardous. In most other trial systems, it is clear that the defendant is on trial and that the system wants to know whether there is sufficient evidence to support the charges against him or her. These systems place their emphasis on truth at trial and, for that reason, want all the evidence to be presented and thoroughly examined by the fact finders so they can determine whether or not the defendant committed the crime in question. The judges are permitted and expected to ask questions because they can help the system reach its goal. They will often have considerable experience and can sometimes see questions that need to be asked which might have been missed by the lawyers.

In the United States, it is much more difficult to say what the priorities of our trial system are. If it is simply winning or losing between the advocates, then judges would be well advised to play a neutral and passive role. The problem is that we don't know what we want. On the one hand, we claim to believe fervently in an adversarial system and to that end stress the importance of leaving the trial up to the lawyers. Yet often we are not willing to visit the failures of the defense lawyer—even intentional errors—on the defendant in our theoretically tough adversarial system.

It is also harder for American trial judges to play a very active role at trial when they work under an appellate system that focuses heavily on perceived trial errors and that asks whether each such error might, just might, have made a difference at trial. Because our system is so complicated and heavily proceduralized, a trial is a minefield of reversible errors. In such a system, helping the jury find the truth would raise a whole new set of possible appellate issues. (Indeed, this is what federal judges tell me: they are reluctant to summarize the evidence at the end of trial because it will certainly raise other appellate issues. Better to read a sterile set of jury instructions and be done with it.) It is safer for trial judges to remain above the fray—to rule on the many technical issues that come up in any major trial—and hope that error can be avoided, which is not at all the same as trying to see that justice is done.

To provide an illustration of the sorts of issues that can arise for a trial judge in our system—often with a new trial hanging in the balance if the judge does not anticipate how an appellate court would rule—consider a situation in which a defendant wishes to represent himself at trial. As mentioned in chapter 4, a defendant in the United States has the right to represent himself at trial if he wishes to do so.[5] Most countries permit some form of self-representation, though a few do not. In many countries self-representation is not the problem that it is in the United States because the rules at trial are relatively simple and the judges are in a position to ask questions and help elicit the evidence.

But in the United States, self-representation can be a serious problem. Is the defendant supposed to catch evidentiary errors committed by the prosecution? Is the defendant supposed to approve jury instructions? To what extent should the judge intervene on behalf of the defendant? Is it more important that a defendant get a fair trial or that the defendant do everything on his own at trial even if he does so incompetently? What if the defendant refuses to obey the court's rulings and becomes obstreperous in the courtroom, or decides midtrial that he is tired of representing himself and will no longer participate in the trial? Should the trial judge appoint the local public defender and make the lawyer take over the case with no preparation, or should he continue to allow the trial to proceed with the defense not asking a single question? What if the newly appointed lawyer insists that he or she cannot adequately undertake the defense and asks for a mistrial so the case can begin again? Must the trial judge grant a mistrial? What about a one-week continuance?

Some appellate courts suggest that trial judges split the baby on self-representation by appointing "standby counsel" to assist the defendant who is representing himself. But this adds a whole new set of trial and appellate issues. Is it a denial of self-representation if standby counsel speaks in the courtroom or if the judge requires the lawyer to handle all legal issues outside the hearing of the jury? Would it violate a defendant's right of self-representation for the judge to ask standby counsel to make all the legal objections at the trial because a lawyer is better equipped to anticipate problems with proposed testimony and make objections quickly? What if the defendant says he doesn't want standby counsel and refuses to talk to him or her? What if it becomes apparent to the judge and the jury that standby counsel is frustrated with the way the defendant is mishandling the defense? Should the judge intervene between the two and perhaps dismiss standby counsel or would that cause more problems with the jury?

What if the defendant has chosen to represent himself in a serious sexual abuse case and the victims are children, perhaps his own? Does the defendant have the right to confront and cross-examine these young victims personally, even if there is psychiatric evidence suggesting this could add to the trauma they have already suffered? Could a trial judge make the defendant ask questions from further back than normal in the courtroom or from a seated position to make it easier on the children? Would placing a screen between the defendant and the victims be unconstitutional? What about having the children sit in a chair facing the jury when testifying so that they do not have to look at their father when he cross-examines them? What about permitting the children to answer questions over a television connection from a room adjoining the courtroom so that they can hear the questions but don't have to face the defendant?

Every one of these issues is complicated and the wrong answer to most of them would automatically lead to reversal of any ensuing conviction. Notice also that all the above issues are completely unrelated to the actual evidence and have almost nothing to do with what should be the main issue in the case: does the evidence show beyond a reasonable doubt that the defendant committed the crime or not? Add self-representation to jury selection issues, constitutional suppression issues, evidence issues, jury instruction issues, and the like, and one can better understand why trials in the United States are fragile and uncertain events and why trial judges are reluctant to do more than they already have to do. The message to trial judges is very clear: they are better off remaining removed and detached from the contest as much as possible. This detachment is sometimes communicated clearly in the courtroom: I have seen American trial judges on the bench going over legal papers from other cases, reading and signing letters, and even quietly discussing other matters with the court clerk in the middle of trial when a witness is testifying. If there is an objection, they will sometimes have to have the question read back by the court reporter so they can rule on it. For judges in most other systems, this evidence is their responsibility too. They listen. They ask questions. They take careful notes.

The "Adversarial System" Excuse for Judicial Passivity and Detachment

American lawyers and judges often defend judicial passivity as necessary because "we have an adversarial system." I want to discuss the adversarial system excuse directly because it is important to see that, adversarial though our system can be at times, it is not a pure adversarial system. No one would want that.

One way in which our adversarial model is tempered in the interests of justice is by placing on prosecutors both an ethical[6] and a constitutional[7] obligation to turn over to the defense attorney any information in their possession that may, in any degree, tend to negate the defendant's guilt.[8] This obligation applies even if the prosecutor is firmly convinced of the defendant's guilt and has plenty of other incriminating evidence with which to establish such guilt, and even if the defense has never requested the information.

By contrast, defense attorneys operate under no similar obligation: if a defense attorney in the United States interviews a witness who is not known to the prosecution and that witness gives the attorney incriminating, even powerfully incriminating information, the defense is under no obligation to make the prosecutor aware of such information. If neither the police nor the prosecutor have discovered this material themselves and the defendant is acquitted at trial, we simply say that this is the result of the adversarial system. The higher obligation placed on the prosecutor to turn over evidence helpful to the defense is just one way our system tempers what a pure adversarial model would dictate. The obvious goal of such a requirement is to try to prevent an erroneous conviction. The obligation to fairness transcends what a strictly adversarial emphasis on winning or losing would dictate.

We often talk about trials as "fights" or "contests," and envisage evenly matched combatants operating under the same rules enforced by a neutral referee. But closer examination reveals the inaccuracies of this analogy. The combatants are not equal and do not play by the same rules. Prosecutors are supposed to care not just about convicting, but about justice, and so they have different responsibilities from defense attorneys. By the same token, a judge cannot simply be a neutral referee indifferent to the outcome. He or she should also be responsible for seeing that justice is done.

An Example of Our Weak/Strong Judges: The Louise Woodward Case

In the previous sections I have talked somewhat abstractly about our judges, who are very weak when they aren't very powerful. A case that puts some reality on my criticisms and that showed the system's conflicts and insecurities to an international audience is *Commonwealth of Massachusetts v. Woodward*, Louise Woodward being the English au pair charged with murdering Matthew Eappen, a nine-month-old infant in her care.

Our uncertainty over the purpose of trial was dramatically revealed at the close of the evidentiary phase of this trial, just before the case was given to the jury. Woodward stood charged with second-degree murder, which in Massachusetts carries with it a mandatory sentence of life imprisonment. If Woodward was convicted she would not be eligible for parole for fifteen years. While the evidence in the case might have supported a verdict of second-degree murder, which is interpreted very broadly in Massachusetts, a more appropriate charge for such a crime would seem to have been involuntary manslaughter, which means that the defendant committed a reckless act that caused the infant's death. Involuntary manslaughter carried no mandatory minimum sentence and would have left the trial judge free to impose a sentence ranging from no time in prison to a period up to twenty years.

But at the end of the case, the defense indicated that it wanted to gamble and only give the jury the choice of a second-degree murder charge or an acquittal. One might well ask: why would any trial system permit a defendant to do this? What is the purpose of a trial? Is it fair to the jury to be given such a choice? What about the victim and the victim's family?

In other countries around the world, this would be a nonissue. The judge would simply have no choice: if the evidence supported giving an instruction on the lesser-included offense, the judge would do so no matter what the defense wanted. Trials are not games. But Judge Hiller Zobel ruled that under Massachusetts law it was the option of the defense to gamble in this way. Clearly nervous about the gamble that was about to take place in his courtroom, he tried to wash his hands of the problem and brought in an additional attorney to warn Woodward about the risks of what she was doing and to make sure this was what she wanted to do. In open court, she affirmed that she wanted the jury to be instructed only on second-degree murder, not manslaughter. The prosecution tried to appeal the decision not to instruct the jury on manslaughter, but review of the decision was denied. Here was the quintessentially weak American trial judge: because he was uncertain what the purpose of the trial was, he was uncertain about what to do and, in the end, he deferred to the defense and allowed them to turn the trial into a high-stakes gamble.

The decision of Judge Zobel not to give the jury the option of a manslaughter verdict is controversial. On appeal, the Massachusetts Supreme Court said that Judge Zobel should have given such an instruction. But in fairness to Judge Zobel, it needs to be emphasized that there is a split in American jurisdictions on the issue. Many states would require the judge to give a lesser included offense instruction where warranted by the evidence. But some important jurisdictions, including our federal courts and the courts in New York and Illinois, see the issue as a tactical one for the defense and would leave the decision to the defense, just as Judge Zobel did. Of course, we know the result: the jury, put into a tough spot by the defense with the passive complicity of the trial judge, found the defendant guilty and Zobel duly sentenced Woodward to life in prison, as he was required to do by statute.

But shortly after Woodward had been sentenced, the defense filed a motion asking the judge to throw out the verdict entirely, or reconsider and lower it. But in our theoretically tough adversarial system, how could a judge possibly do that? The jury was entitled to find the defendant guilty of second-degree murder, as there was enough evidence to go to the jury. A team of the finest defense lawyers had insisted on this gambling strategy which foreclosed consideration of manslaughter. Woodward had herself been fully informed of the risks and had stated in open court that she agreed with the defense strategy. How could the "neutral referee" change the outcome of the game that had been played?

But like Phoenix emerging from the ashes, once the jury left the courtroom in Massachusetts, Judge Zobel revealed a different facet: a powerful judge, confident in his own judgment and prepared to strike out boldly to achieve a just decision. Using a court rule that allows a judge to enter a finding of guilty of any offense included in the offense charged, Judge Zobel did a complete about-face. Having previously approved the defense gamble, he piously announced that "a court . . . is not a casino" and imposed a verdict of involuntary manslaughter.

Later the same day, the judge sentenced Woodward on his involuntary manslaughter verdict. I say "his" because the jury never had the option of involuntary manslaughter. Again, the judge suddenly became incredibly powerful: he could have given Louise Woodward zero time, two years, ten years, or even twenty years. Of course, he sentenced Woodward to time served based on his own view of what her criminal liability was and what punishment he therefore believed she deserved.

My purpose is not to criticize the result in the *Woodward* case, but to use the case to show how the role of the judge swings from such neutrality as to be detached to such domination that the judge can, in effect, even reverse what the jury did. The case is symptomatic of the system's confusion over what is supposed to happen at trial and what role judges are supposed to perform there. Notice, for example, that if the defense gamble had resulted in an acquittal, neither Judge Zobel nor any other judge would have reviewed the decision. It would have been upheld as a brilliant piece of defense lawyering and the prosecution would have simply "lost" or "blown it."

Conclusion

This chapter has focused on the role of trial judges who are weak and passive in the presence of the jury, and yet display tremendous assurance and power at most other times, including sentencing, when they are truly inquisitorial in the role they perform. I used the performance of Judge Hiller Zobel to make this point because it is a dramatic illustration of a trial system that has lost its focus. The *Woodward* case exposes the rhetoric that surrounds our trial system as being just that. We believe in the adversarial system, except when we don't believe in it; we prefer a jury of common citizens to the arbitrary power of a single professional judge, except when we prefer a single professional judge to a jury; we prefer to let lawyers "try their cases," except when we don't like the result; we believe trial judges should be neutral referees, except when we don't like the outcome of the contest and want them to change it. We would be far better off with judges who acted consistently throughout the criminal process. The starting point has to be a trial system that puts far more emphasis on truth, and far less on gambling and winning and losing.

CHAPTER EIGHT

The Supreme Court
An Institutional Failure

The Difficulties of Criticizing the Supreme Court

One of the difficulties with the American criminal justice system is that it is heavily constitutionalized. Any reform proposal, even a rather minor one, runs up against the argument that it would violate the Constitution as interpreted by the Supreme Court. Immediately, the would-be reformer is put on the defensive—he or she is arguing against the Bill of Rights, motherhood, justice, freedom from government repression—and is assumed to be urging a return to the southern justice of the 1940s and 1950s, and to a period when few legislatures around the country seemed to care about the treatment suspects received at the hands of the police. He is also assumed to be attacking the Court—the institution that courageously rebuilt and reformed our criminal justice system to make it the best in the world. (One doesn't hear the latter part of this claim nearly as often today as one did five or six years ago.)

One way to finesse the problem posed by the Supreme Court when speaking to a legal audience is to be very careful not to attack the Court, but to limit one's criticisms to one or two major decisions and to suggest tactfully that if these decisions were modified a bit or overruled, then all would be well. Many major constitutional decisions have been decided by a close vote on the Court with strong dissenting opinions. So it seems more respectful to argue that the dissenters have been proven right in that case and that the Court could overrule this or that decision and put the system back on track. Arguments for change along these lines fit more comfortably within our legal tradition as they concede the centrality of the Supreme Court but contend that the Court got it wrong once or twice.

I wish the problems stemming from the Court's role in our criminal justice system could be solved by altering one or two major decisions. But that is simply not the case. The problem is not just this system of warnings versus that system of warnings, or this type of exclusionary rule versus a less severe exclusionary rule. It is an institutional failure that needs to be understood and acknowledged if we are to rebuild the system. Put bluntly, the Court has arrogated to itself an institutional role for which it was not designed and for which it is poorly equipped. As long as the Court insists that it is the central and dominant player in announcing rules on every aspect of the criminal justice system from search and seizure, to confessions, to jury selection, to the questioning of witnesses, to appellate review, the system will never be as strong as those in many other western countries. It will always be extreme and lacking in balance and proportion. Before explaining why that is so, I need to discuss the Court's authority over criminal matters and what the Court has been doing over the last thirty years.

The Court and the Bill of Rights

The first ten amendments of the Constitution, the Bill of Rights, contain a series of protections for citizens against the federal government. The fourth amendment states that the right of the people to be secure in their persons, papers, and effects against unreasonable searches and seizures shall not be violated. The fifth amendment provides that no person shall be compelled in a criminal case to be a witness against himself, that no one shall be deprived of life or liberty without due process of law, and that no person shall be twice put in jeopardy of life or limb. The sixth amendment guarantees those accused of a crime the right to a speedy and public trial, the right to an impartial jury from the state or district where the crime occurred, the right to be informed of the nature and cause of the accusation, the right to confront witnesses and to compel their attendance, and the right to have the assistance of counsel. The eighth amendment provides that excessive bail shall not be imposed and that cruel and unusual punishment shall not be inflicted.

These are protections against the federal government. As far as protection against state governments is concerned, the Constitution guarantees in the fourteenth amendment that a state shall not deprive a citizen of life, liberty, or property without due process of law. The term "due process of law" is somewhat vague. It implies a certain level of basic fairness in a state's procedures prior to depriving the citizen of life or liberty.

Over the last three decades the Court has begun to apply certain protections from the Bill of Rights directly to the states. We say in "lawyer talk" that the Court has begun to incorporate some of these protections into its concept of due process and to apply them to the states the same way as to the federal government. Today every right in the Bill of Rights (with the exception of indictment by grand jury) has been made applicable by the Court against the states just as it is in the federal area.

In the fourth amendment area, there are cases telling police when they can and cannot conduct various searches and seizures. To that end, the Court has established categories of cases dealing with subjects such as auto searches, searches incident to arrest, forcible stops and frisks, customs searches, drunk driving roadblocks, drug testing, and protective sweeps. There are also cases telling police under what circumstances they may make an arrest on the street, in the suspect's home, or even in the home of a third party.

In the fifth amendment area, again there are lots of cases deciding what is and is not permissible under the right not to be compelled to be a witness against oneself at trial. The leading case in this area is *Miranda v. Arizona* which requires *Miranda* warnings. But there are many other cases dealing with subjects such as whether the police may dispense with *Miranda* warnings in certain emergency situations, how specific a suspect's request for counsel must be to require the police to stop questioning the suspect, whether a suspect who has indicated he wishes to remain silent can be approached in jail and asked about a different crime, whether a suspect who has indicated he wishes to remain silent can be asked background booking questions at the police station, whether a suspect's silence at the police station can be brought out at trial, whether a prosecutor in summation can comment on the fact that the defendant chose not to testify at trial, and so on.

There are important advantages to building a strong criminal justice system in this way. Without the Court's intervention we would probably have a system balkanized to some extent by significant variations in trial and pretrial procedures. Some states might choose to rely heavily on juries, while others might not use juries extensively. Some states might use one set of warnings prior to custodial interrogation, while others might give a different set of warnings and some might prefer not to give any warnings at all in such circumstances. What the Court has been able to achieve, then, is a certain uniformity in procedures throughout the country. The Court's prestige, as well as our respect for the Constitution, make important reforms not only possible but palatable as well. Major reforms that would be difficult to achieve politically state by state can be accomplished by the Court and made instantly applicable at every trial in every courthouse throughout the country.

To be even more blunt about these political problems, there are states which have always been at the forefront in efforts to keep their criminal justice systems functioning at a high level and others, especially in the south, where criminal justice matters receive much less attention and much less financial support. This was true in the Warren Court years and remains true of some states today. However imperfect those state systems may be, without the efforts of the Court over the last few decades, they might be far worse today.

Other countries don't have the same problem we have in the United States because they don't have a federal system, or because, if they do have one, it still remains the responsibility of the national legislature to establish the procedures that govern criminal investigations and criminal trials. In England, for example, Parliament has the final word on most issues of criminal procedure and thus most of what has been done by our Supreme Court has been done by statutes in England. In continental Europe, a code of criminal procedure covers every step of the procedure from the moment a crime is committed up through trial, appeal, and the completion of any sentence. By contrast, our system of pretrial and trial procedure is based heavily on individual judicial decisions.

The Problem: Judicial Hubris

Unfortunately, the power of the Court and the impact that its decisions have on the efficiency and reliability of the system should have made the Court cautious about its actions. Instead the opposite has occurred. Today there is hardly any aspect of our criminal process that is not heavily impacted, if not directly controlled, by Supreme Court decisions. In fact, most coursebooks for law students in the area of criminal procedure are little more than collections of Supreme Court cases. Law reviews are full of articles arguing that this or that constitutional right should be expanded to solve whatever problem the author happens to be discussing. Rarely does one see articles proposing passage of a statute to solve a particular problem in the criminal justice area. Why fool around with the legislative process when the Court can get to the same result quickly, without the political battles a bill might raise, and can make it applicable in every courthouse in every state to boot?

The Court is honestly convinced that it has the kind of expertise required to make all these important decisions and that it is its function to do so. Unfortunately, the Court is trying to do what it was never designed to do and what it will never be able to do well. As a protection against clear abuses of state power, the Bill of Rights has no equal and it is rightly respected throughout the world for what it represents. When it comes to the criminal process, the Bill of Rights is an important assurance that a suspect will be treated fairly and that certain minimum procedural protections will be guaranteed. But the Bill of Rights is not a detailed code of trial and pretrial procedure. It doesn't tell us anything specific about the police questioning of suspects, or about what warnings, if any, should be given, and at what point, to a suspect. It doesn't tell us how a jury should be selected, what sorts of questions must be asked of potential jurors, how lawyers should be permitted to use challenges to prospective jurors, or how judges should best explain the law to juries.

In short, the Bill of Rights tells us nothing about lots of issues of major importance to a modern trial system, such as how to protect jurors from pretrial or posttrial publicity, how young crime victims should be treated in the courtroom, and whether juries should be encouraged to ask questions of witnesses. These are not "flaws" in the Bill of Rights but reflect the nature of the document. It is concerned with providing citizens important basic and minimal protections designed to assure fair treatment and a fair trial. As a code of criminal procedure it is incomplete and inadequate. If you insist on using it to build a strong criminal justice system, the system will lack balance and will never be as strong overall as it should be.

Consider this analogy. Imagine a young man who wanted to build himself up through weight lifting with the goal of becoming the next Arnold Schwarzenegger. Assume that this man has the initial physique that such a goal requires and he works diligently and conscientiously at his goal every day. But he works only on the muscle groups on his right arm. After a few years of such effort, it is easy to imagine what the result would be. His right arm would be incredibly powerful with each muscle clearly defined but his body as a whole would lack symmetry and balance, and his overall strength would not be nearly as great as it would have been if he had spread out his efforts so as to develop all the muscle groups in his body.

This illustrates what the Court is trying to do. How a suspect is treated is important to the strength of a strong criminal justice system. A system that tolerates the abuse of suspects or that does not permit defendants to contest the evidence against them or uses biased fact finders will always be weak and will deserve criticism, if not condemnation. But a system that treats defendants well is not necessarily a strong trial system. Treating defendants with dignity and respect is only one aspect of a healthy system. The public must be assured that the determinations of guilt or innocence can be relied upon with a high degree of accuracy. In short, it has to be reliable.

A strong trial system also has to be relatively efficient. Only a country with an extremely low crime rate can be satisfied with lengthy and costly trials so that only a few trials can be heard each year. But the crime rates of most countries these days require a trial procedure that makes wise use of scarce judicial resources.

A trial system also has to be concerned with how nondefendants are treated in the courtroom—victims, for instance. While there is a strong victims' rights movement in the United States, this is by no means an American problem. Lots of countries are struggling to improve the treatment of victims in the courtroom, especially when they are young and vulnerable. A system that is indifferent to the plight of victims caught up in the criminal justice process and that permits them to be humiliated in the courtroom could end up discouraging victims from reporting crimes and, in some cases, even inflicting additional harm on them.

It is not the fault of the Court that it is not addressing issues such as these. It is simply not the function of the Court to concern itself directly with such issues. There is no way to ask the Court the questions that need to be asked and answered: is it necessary to have a system this complicated? Is there not some wiser way to use the system's trial resources? The Court's only function is to make sure that the defendant's rights are not violated.

Similarly, it is not the function of the Court to ask whether there is a better way to treat child abuse victims in the courtroom. The Court can only tell us whether a particular procedure—for example, putting a screen between the defendant and the victim at trial—violated the defendant's right to confront his accusers. The same point can be made about the overall reliability of our trial system. The Court can tell us whether or not this particular rule or the admission of this or that specific piece of evidence violated the defendant's right to due process. But it cannot tell us whether the system as a whole is reliable and, if not, how we can make it more reliable.

Because cases come raining down from the Court and from intermediate appellate courts announcing whether some constitutional right of the defendant has been violated, the public gets the impression that all the system cares about are defendants and their rights. Like the bodybuilder's right arm, there are areas of the law such as search and seizure that are so overdeveloped as to be muscle-bound with each category and subcategory drawing very fine legal distinctions. Because the carrot of exclusion is so tempting, defendants have a strong incentive to ask whether a piece of luggage should have been lifted by a police officer, or whether an officer should have patted a suspect's coat pocket, or whether a police officer should have opened the cigarette package of an arrestee. Questions like these get raised and answered all the time. More important questions addressing the overall efficiency or reliability of the system or the treatment of victims are never directly raised by courts.

Perhaps the analogy of the bodybuilder breaks down in one respect. It is hard to imagine the bodybuilder not being aware that he needs to develop other parts of his body to have a body with overall symmetry and strength. But this imbalance is not so obvious to those who work in our criminal justice system. They tend to ignore or fail to appreciate issues that do not come up in the course of litigation. This may explain at least some of the tremendous anger that victims feel toward the system. They see judges writing countless opinions on exactly how a defendant should or should not be treated in the police station and how he may or may not be questioned in the courtroom. On the other hand, among the thousands of decisions pouring down from our Supreme Court or other appellate courts each year there are almost none asking similar questions about how victims ought to be treated. This is not to argue that victims deserve equal treatment from the courts, but some attention to their treatment is certainly appropriate. But there is no mention of victims in the Bill of Rights. This is not a glitch or an omission as long as it is understood that the Bill of Rights is intended to provide suspects with a certain basic foundation of fairness. But when viewed as a detailed blueprint that determines exactly how the criminal justice system should be erected, the document is woefully incomplete.

There are major issues that cry out to be addressed in our system, such as the amount of control over evidence that has been ceded to the lawyers or the tremendous expense of trials. But questions like these are not addressed in Supreme Court opinions. What is not included in the Bill of Rights gets ignored. No trial system can be strong if it fails to tackle issues such as these head on. As long as we rely on the Court for reform, our system will end up like our bodybuilder: a set of incredibly overdeveloped defendants' rights but a body that as a whole is not as strong as it ought to be considering the amount of time and effort that has been devoted to improving it.

The Court's Institutional Limitations: The Information Gap

The Supreme Court over the last three decades has never understood its limitations. This has led to some unwise decisions that have weakened the system. One of the problems with relying on the Court for all manner of decisions is that in the world of Supreme Court litigation there is a serious danger that complicated issues will be oversimplified. When making a decision the Court has before it a specific set of facts posing a particular constitutional problem. It has a set of highly argumentative briefs on either side, and it has heard an hour's worth of argument. The briefs and the arguments vary tremendously in quality. The Court is not without some support staff. Each of the justices has a few law clerks, usually a year or two out of law school. They are in a heady environment and are very smart, but usually know very little about the criminal justice system. Against this background, the Court, whose members are usually not experts in the criminal justice area and who have to be prepared to rule in many other important areas of the law, is being asked to make a ruling that could have important consequences for the criminal justice system in every jurisdiction in the United States.

Consider some of the things the Court may not know. First of all, how often does the problem posed by this case occur? Is this a recurring problem or not? Is it likely to come up in all sorts of settings and jurisdictions or is it limited to perhaps an urban setting or a particular part of the country? When it occurs, is the case before the Court typical of the severity of the problem, or is this an exceptionally bad example of what can happen?

Unlike a regulatory body or a legislature, the Court cannot conduct hearings and ask those who might be affected about their view of the problem or of any proposed solutions. The Court also can't commission empirical studies to evaluate the seriousness of the problem nationwide or ask one or two jurisdictions to try a particular procedure as a controlled experiment to see how effective the proposed remedy turns out to be in practice. Nor can it hire consultants to provide an accurate estimate of the costs of the proposed remedy and explain what the implications of those costs might be for various jurisdictions around the country.

When the Court is deciding whether a citizen has been the victim of a shocking abuse of state power or has been clearly deprived of fair procedures, these empirical questions are not important and the Court ought to condemn what occurred and impose a meaningful remedy no matter what the cost. But at other times the lack of an empirical framework becomes a liability and poses risks. Thus, the Court needs a framework to work out questions such as: under what circumstances can police officers make a protective sweep of a house? Should the police be able to ask someone stopped for a traffic offense (or the passengers in the car) to exit the car? Can the police bring witnesses or suspects to the police station to ask them questions? How long should the police be permitted to detain a suspect on the scene after a crime has occurred? Should lawyers be able to strike jurors based on religious affiliation? Should the prosecution be able to reveal at trial that the defendant was silent and uncooperative at the police station? And so on.

One might think the fact that the Court is writing its decisions in constitutional stone would make it nervous about what it is trying to do. But in fact it emboldens not just the Supreme Court but lots of other appellate courts around the country because, to be honest, constitutional decision making is liberating. If the Court extends a right it is doing simply "what the Constitution mandates," and this gives it considerable freedom. You can see the same attitude in the writings of law professors who love to suggest all manner of constitutional expansions to handle this or that perceived problem. Whether the proposal is to entirely bar station-house questioning of suspects by police, or to guarantee minority defendants a certain number of minority jurors, or to abolish peremptory challenges by constitutional fiat, you rarely see any serious attempt to demonstrate the extent of the problem or to estimate what the impact of the proposal might be on the efficiency or reliability of the system as a whole. Declaring rights without having to worry about costs or reliability is easy. Balancing rights for the defendant against the resources of the system and its need to determine guilt efficiently and with a high degree of accuracy is much harder. No country thinks these issues are as easy as do American judges and academics.

In the next sections I want to discuss three Supreme Court cases to demonstrate the above points about the Court and its institutional limitations. I have deliberately chosen to discuss less well-known opinions of the Court rather than its more controversial opinions to try to give readers an idea of how extensive the problems with what the Court has been doing over the last three decades are.

Institutional Arrogance: Brooks v. Tennessee

Brooks v. Tennessee is a relatively unknown case in which the Court jumped in to decide an issue that is in fact far more complicated than it appears.[1] *Brooks* involved a provision of the Tennessee constitution that required defendants who wanted to testify at trial to do so as the first witness on the defense case. The rule seems to make some sense. After all, witnesses at trial are usually sequestered, meaning that they must remain outside the courtroom when prior witnesses testify so that they are not influenced by what the other witnesses say and do not shade their testimony to more closely match the testimony of those who have testified first. Since this cannot be done with the defendant, Tennessee decided that at least when it comes to the defense case the defendant ought not to have such an advantage and ought to testify first so that he cannot shape his testimony to that of other defense witnesses.

Now this constitutional requirement might seem to place a restriction on the defendant giving testimony at trial, but in fact it was actually passed in the late nineteenth century as a liberalizing amendment, permitting defendants in Tennessee to testify at their trials for the first time. While this seems strange to us, when the Constitution was drafted and up until the 1860s defendants were not permitted to testify at trial. While today the fifth amendment is interpreted to give defendants a constitutional right to testify, the defendant's right to testify as a statutory matter was slow to come in our nation's history. Maine was the first state to give defendants this right in 1864. Thus the Tennessee provision was a liberalizing one that followed the lead of other states in deciding to permit defendants to testify at trial, albeit as the first witness on the defense case.

Although this was a state constitutional provision and therefore would seem to be a matter for the state to decide, the Supreme Court had an easy time striking it down as unconstitutional. In 1972, Justice Brennan concluded that the statute violated the privilege against compelled self-incrimination. He pointed out that a defendant "cannot be absolutely certain that his witnesses will testify as expected or that they will be effective on the stand" and "thus may not know at the close of the state's case whether his testimony will be necessary or even helpful to his cause."

I suppose the easiest answers to this are the most straightforward. First, since the defendant doesn't have to testify at all, this statute hardly compels him to testify. So how can this violate the privilege? Second, it does regulate the timing of his testimony and there are some important reasons for doing so—defendants facing prison time are under considerable pressure to lie on the stand and often do so. Third, Justice Brennan seems to want to keep defendants off the stand if possible or at least to make it easy for them to decide whether to testify or not. But even if the defendant is permitted to testify last, what has this achieved for defendants in that regard? He or she will still face a tough decision as to whether or not to testify and in many cases will still not know whether his testimony is "necessary or helpful."

Finally, what about the interest in truth at trial and the state's concern that the defendant will not testify honestly, and that his deception can be better detected if he has to testify prior to the other witnesses? Justice Brennan doesn't answer that question. He simply announces, "Pressuring a defendant to take the stand, by foreclosing later testimony if he refuses, is not a constitutionally permissible means of ensuring his honesty. It fails to take into account the very real and legitimate concerns that might motivate a defendant to exercise his right to silence."[2] Notice that nothing is said about the state's interest in the accuracy of the trial. If this is the wrong way to ensure the defendant's honesty, what then is a constitutionally permissible way of ensuring it? Justice Brennan is completely silent on that point. Rights always trump reliability.[3]

But the Court is obviously nervous with its reading of the fifth amendment, so it backs up its creative reading of the privilege against compelled self-incrimination with the claim that this state constitutional provision also violates due process. Why does this provision violate due process? Admittedly, some on the Court may think that this is an unwise provision or one that is unlikely to achieve the goal of encouraging more honest testimony from defendants. But even if it is unwise, is this provision so fundamentally unfair that the Court and indeed all right-thinking jurisdictions should condemn it? The Court tells us that the provision infringes due process because it requires "the accused and his lawyer to make [the choice of whether to testify] without an opportunity to evaluate the actual worth of their evidence," and "the accused is therefore deprived of the 'guiding hand of counsel' in the timing of this critical element of his defense."[4]

This is a rather weak objection in the American trial system where lawyers are permitted not only to interview their witnesses prior to trial but may rehearse them as much as they want. Why are the lawyer and the accused not able "to evaluate the worth of their evidence" perfectly well even with this restriction in place? But more importantly, why is this provision so fundamentally unfair? Why isn't it a sensible tradeoff to require the defendant to testify first on the defense, given the defendant's advantage from having heard what all the state's witnesses have said at trial?

There is, of course, no such thing as a knock down, drag-out argument in constitutional law, so I can't refute the Court's contention that this state provision is so basically unfair that it violates due process. But while the Court may be very confident in its abilities, I suggest the members of the Court know a lot less than they think they know. To speak specifically to the Tennessee provision, this is basically the law that exists at criminal trials in England. The English statute is phrased a bit differently, but basically it requires the defendant to testify as the first "fact witness" at trial unless excused by the Court.[5] (In other words, if there is an expert with time constraints, he or she could be called first. But otherwise the defendant is supposed to testify first.) This rule requiring the defendant to testify first is not limited to England. The same holds true in Scotland, which has its own criminal justice system with separate procedures, as well as in Ireland, Australia, and New Zealand. In short, if one looked at countries that trace their legal heritage back to England as we do, we would have to conclude that the Tennessee provision is viewed by many countries as a sensible restriction and one that contributes to a fair trial, not one that undermines it.

While not sharing the same legal heritage, the three continental countries mentioned in chapter 5—the Netherlands, Germany, and

Norway—always ask the defendant to respond to the charges at the very start of the trial. They don't, however, put the defendant under oath as is done in England or the United States. They want to hear his testimony and for that reason don't want to threaten him with perjury if he does not tell the truth or shades it in important respects. (Perhaps they don't want to cheapen the oath either, a lesson we might learn.) But in each of those countries, the defendant is asked to speak first. In some ways the timing of the defendant's testimony at trial fits along a spectrum, like so many issues—exclusionary rules, the right to remain silent, the role of counsel, and the like—with continental countries toward one end, a number of countries in the middle, and at the other end of the spectrum, the United States.

Brooks v. Tennessee is symptomatic of the Court's amazing self-confidence, bordering at times on arrogance, on criminal procedure issues. Here is a Court that condemns a Tennessee constitutional provision in a conclusory and one-sided opinion that is blissfully unaware of the strong contemporary support for it among other English-speaking countries. I suggest the Court, even aided by its raft of bright young law graduates, knows a lot less than it thinks it does about this and many other issues. Looking at the way the state's interest in truthful testimony was cavalierly dismissed and even depreciated by the Court, it should not surprise us late in the 1990s to find a system that badly undervalues truth.

The Differences between Courts and Legislatures: Batson v. Kentucky

The Court's efforts to build a strong criminal justice system by interpreting the Bill of Rights will never succeed for many reasons. As suggested above, the issues that the Court can address are limited because of the Bill of Rights, and because the empirical data the Court has before it are almost nonexistent. Moreover, the nature of constitutional adjudication makes it impossible for the Court to make the sorts of compromises one sees frequently in legislation. The Court cannot say, for example, that "the remedy that we are putting forward is tentative and for that reason it has a sunset provision such that it will go out of effect three years from now unless renewed." Legislators sometimes also confess that the bill that was passed was not a great bill but that it was the best compromise that could be worked out. The Supreme Court can't do that. Constitutional adjudication encourages rhetorical extremes. In order to justify the burdens and costs imposed on the system throughout the country, the Supreme Court will often exaggerate the seriousness of the problem as well as the likely effectiveness of the remedy being put forward. Some of this bold language can lead to further expansive readings of the decision by lower courts that are trying to interpret and apply the Supreme Court decision to new situations. The result is a system in which doubts and uncertainties get buried by rhetoric that is overconfident and too strong.

Another difference between what legislatures do and what the Court is doing concerns the level of institutional discipline in the two branches. In these days of tight budgets, when legislators propose increases in spending for a particularly meritorious new program, the legislator is often expected to show a source of funding for the new program or, alternatively, to propose budget cuts elsewhere so that the cost of the new program does not cause an overall increase in expenditures. Even the very brief comparison with four other countries in chapter 5 shows that there are many ways to simplify our trial system. Our rules of evidence and our rules on search and seizure could be simplified, certain pretrial hearings could be eliminated, and the number of frivolous appeals could be reduced, for a start. The Court has no way to make these tradeoffs in its opinions because the focus of each case is so narrow. In addition, some of these suggested cutbacks in procedure (such as simplifying evidence rules) are not matters for the Court at all. As a result, the

Court can always add procedure, usually in the form of expensive after-the-fact hearings, but it is extremely difficult for it to take procedure out of the system or to offer remedies that might help keep the problem at hand from arising or at least make it less serious when it does occur.

A case that nicely illustrates the Court's limitations as an institution for reform compared to legislatures and other rule-making bodies is *Batson v. Kentucky*,[6] decided by the Court in 1986. *Batson* dealt with a serious problem that plagues our trial system (and continues to do so despite *Batson*[7]), namely, the use by prosecutors (and sometimes by defense attorneys) of peremptory challenges, meaning challenges that don't have to be explained, to remove jurors on the basis of race. In *Batson*, the prosecutor had used four peremptory challenges to remove all blacks from the jury, resulting in a trial in which a black defendant was convicted by an all-white jury.

The use of peremptory challenges to remove all members of a certain race directly affects public confidence in our trial system and aggravates racial tensions in this country. We have had riots and civil disturbances in urban areas following acquittals in which the defendants (police officers) used peremptory challenges to remove all or almost all prospective black jurors. Understanding that this is a serious problem, how might our legal system attack it? One obvious way of at least reducing the problem, and perhaps speeding up jury selection a bit, would be to cut way down on the number of peremptory challenges permitted each side at trial so that it becomes more difficult to "stack the deck" as in *Batson*. The number of peremptory challenges varies from jurisdiction to jurisdiction but many give each side eight or even ten. Why not reduce that number to two or three so that lawyers have to be more careful in using them and cannot do what was done in *Batson*? But while legislators or other rule makers in a given jurisdiction could pass a comprehensive statute or rule that cuts down drastically on the number of peremptory challenges, perhaps providing for only two but giving the judge discretion to add one or two more in certain specified situations, this sort of a solution is not an option for the Court because it is not a legislative body.

Another option would be to declare all peremptory challenges unconstitutional. But making that change in isolation could be a dangerous experiment that could result in many other problems, such as an enormous increase in hung juries or perverse verdicts. England has abolished peremptory challenges, but it did so statutorily, going from seven to three and finally to zero. But England also permits a judge to accept a nonunanimous criminal verdict after two hours of deliberation so that the problem of a hung jury as the result of an irrational holdout on the jury is less likely to arise. Also, while the Court has tremendous freedom in interpreting the Constitution, as we know from everything it has done in the last few decades, it does seem a bit much to declare all peremptory challenges in all sorts of cases unconstitutional by judicial fiat.

Unable to come up with a procedure that might have prevented what occurred in *Batson* from happening so frequently, the Court's only alternative was the most expensive and possibly the least effective. The Court imposed on the trial judge the burden of determining whether the jurors who had been struck were struck for the wrong reason. But how well does this solve the problem? Sure, it stops attorneys from quickly and automatically removing jurors on the basis of race, but if the attorneys are more subtle can't they achieve much the same result by looking for other reasons to strike jurors that mask what is basically a racial motive? Because peremptory challenges can be made for any reason—other than race or gender—how effective will this after-the-fact hearing be when a lawyer can insist that he or she struck the juror because "I was concerned that she didn't look at me directly when I was talking to her," "She is approximately the same age as the defendant and I was worried that she would be overly sympathetic on that account," "I noticed that her brother lived in the same general area as the defendant and for that reason I was worried that she might have some knowledge of this case already," and so on.

My objection to this line of cases—and *Batson* was only the starting point—is not that there isn't a problem with jury selection and racial discrimination. Rather I want to show why the Court cannot solve every problem on its own as it is strongly inclined to do. In *Batson*, the Court had little choice but to opt for an expensive and time-consuming solution. The time spent on jury selection in the United States was already a scandal, often nearly doubling the trial time required in minor criminal cases. *Batson* aggravated that problem. And how well does it solve the problem of racially based peremptory challenges? Certainly, if the *Simpson* case is any indication, race continues to play a big role in jury selection despite *Batson*. (Jeffrey Toobin, a former prosecutor-turned-writer, claims that the prosecution in the *Simpson* case made a big mistake by not striking jurors on the basis of race during jury selection as the defense was clearly doing.[8])

Unintended Consequences of a Decision: *Anders v. California*

One of the problems with any major change in the law is that it is likely to have unanticipated consequences or consequences that were anticipated but turned out to be far more serious than expected. This may happen even with legislation or administrative regulations that seemed sensible in theory and that were prompted by excellent reasons. The legislation may not work out the way it was intended. With legislation it is always possible to go back and amend the original bill or even repeal it if it turns out to have terrible side effects. (Who remembers the problems generated by the seat belt warning system that would keep a car from being started unless seat belts were fastened? It was quickly jettisoned when it became impossible to start one's car if even a small package was placed on the passenger seat.)

When it comes to Supreme Court decisions it is not always easy to reverse a decision that has serious unintended side effects. The Court cannot go back and say a year or two down the road, "You know, now that we look at the fifth amendment privilege against compulsory self-incrimination again, we were mistaken to have required a set of four warnings. Now that we look more closely, we think that only two warnings should be required." Laws passed by legislatures or rules put out by administrative agencies are constantly being modified and changed, but it is hard to change Supreme Court pronouncements without damaging the integrity of the institution. The Court does cut back on earlier opinions. But these revised opinions are not very elegant and not very honest—they claim fidelity to the earlier opinion but then go on to limit it in such a way that the impact of the earlier opinion is almost completely undercut. The result is often additional confusion about what the law really is.

The Supreme Court has never appreciated the sort of unintended and indirect consequences that its opinions can produce. I have argued throughout this book that the Court has tended to the extreme in right after right and the consequences have been far more serious than the Court realizes. For example, in chapter 2 I argued that the problem with our extreme exclusionary rule is less the amount of evidence suppressed by trial judges than the indirect effects on the system. A harsh rule that fails to understand the difficulties police face in applying vague fourth amendment pronouncements encourages dishonesty on the part of police and tolerance of that dishonesty on the part of judges who don't want to suppress evidence in important cases. The system becomes more cynical about what the oath means. Add that to the host of other decisions—including *Brooks v. Tennessee* above—in which the Court always seems to put truth low on the scale of values it wants our trial system to serve, and it is not surprising that the system has serious problems.

One area that the Court has influenced indirectly and for the worse is our system of criminal appeals. Basically, among western countries, there seem to be two main approaches to appellate review. In the liberal approach both the defendant and the prosecuting authority are given considerable opportunity to challenge the results at trial or the sentence. Sometimes, especially if the crime is minor, the appellate review may even consist of a whole new trial. Norway is the most extreme example of a liberal appellate system because it provides that either side can seek a completely new trial if dissatisfied with the original result.

Most continental countries tend toward the liberal approach to appellate review, generally permitting the defendant or the prosecuting authority to appeal the trial result or the sentence. Appellate review on the merits is made easier in such countries because the verdict of the trial is explained and justified, so that the evidence that led to the result and the reasons for the result are before the appellate court. If the trial judges misapplied the law to the facts or if there was no factual support for some aspect of the trial judges' decision, it is easier for an appellate court to order reconsideration of that issue. The same is true of the sentence imposed. If the trial judges decided not to impose a custodial sentence and the reasons for that sentence do not support their decision, it is easier for an appellate court to review the decision and determine the appropriate sentence.

In contrast, some countries go in the opposite direction and are very conservative about allowing appeals. This tends to be true where the trial procedures are complicated and expensive and where the particular form of trial does not lend itself well to appellate review. The classic example of a conservative approach to appellate review is that taken in England when appeal is sought from a conviction at a jury trial in Crown Court. Because jury trials are expensive and complicated, and a jury verdict, being unexplained, is not easy to review, England takes a very conservative approach to appeals from jury verdicts. Unless it is purely a point of law, a defendant (there is no appeal from an acquittal) needs to obtain permission to appeal, which is not readily given. To further discourage appeals, even if it is determined that there was a mistake at trial, reversals are given only if the Court of Appeal believes a miscarriage of justice has occurred. This means that even a rather serious error in the jury instruction, for example, will not result in a reversal of the conviction where the evidence at trial was strong.

Before turning to Supreme Court opinions that have had a tremendous effect on our appellate system and on the relationship of appellate and trial courts in this country, I want to emphasize that even in countries with liberal appellate review it is not thought desirable for all defendants (or, where available, all prosecutors) to routinely seek appellate review. It is always hoped that the defendant will conclude that the trial was fair, that the judges worked hard to reach the verdict, and that the sentence imposed was justified. Amazingly the United States uses the worst form of trial for appellate review—jury trials for every criminal case except extremely minor offenses—and yet it *insists* that all criminal trials be appealed. The Court has encouraged this dreadful combination.

The starting point is *Anders v. California*,[9] an early Warren Court case, in which the defendant's lawyer, a public defender, had written to the state appellate court that he did not file a brief because he did not think there was any merit to the appeal. The Supreme Court held that this letter was insufficient to protect the defendant's right to counsel under the sixth amendment. The Court ruled that in such a situation, after "a conscientious examination" of the case convinces the lawyer that an appeal would be "wholly frivolous," the lawyer must write a brief to the appellate court that goes through any possible appellate issues and shows why each issue has no merit. A copy of this brief, said the Court, must also be furnished to the defendant so that the defendant has a chance to raise any points he chooses. The appellate court is then supposed to go through the trial record on the matter and the lawyer's brief to decide whether any appellate issues are frivolous. If so, it may dismiss the appeal. If, however, the court finds appellate merit, the court must appoint new counsel to brief the issues and argue the matter on appeal.

This is a full employment bill for appellate courts. In effect, it requires an attorney to file a brief in every case because to avoid doing so the lawyer still has to file a brief going over any possible error and explaining why the apparent error was not an error at all. This is an awkward position in which to put a public defender because the Court is asking the attorney, who probably represented the defendant at trial, to write a brief that helps the prosecution by essentially refuting any of his client's possible appellate issues. Notice another aspect of *Anders*—only if an issue is "wholly frivolous" is it appropriate for a lawyer not to raise it on appeal. What the Court seems to be saying is that a defense attorney should raise any possible appellate issue even if he believes that overall the trial the defendant received was fair and the result just. When someone looks at our trial system and wonders why defense attorneys are constantly objecting and refusing to stipulate even the most obvious facts, this is in part the influence of cases like *Anders*. One must raise every possible issue to fit the Court's image of a defense attorney, except for issues that are "wholly frivolous" and even then the Court wants appellate courts to scrutinize the trial record for errors lurking unseen.

As a practical matter, it is easier to write the brief no matter how frivolous the point raised. And though ethics rules condemn attorneys who raise frivolous issues at trial or on appeal, in response to *Anders* many states have changed their ethics rules to allow defense attorneys to raise and argue frivolous issues without fear of any disciplinary sanction rather than put lawyers in the odd position of having to write an "*Anders* brief" that asserts and then refutes any arguable issues.

When appellate courts complain about their caseload, the public should not be overly sympathetic. The Supreme Court wants every criminal case to be appealed, with the result that lots of time is spent on frivolous appeals. Of course, to review a trial and seek out errors requires that a transcript of the entire trial be produced, which is both expensive and time-consuming. Court reporters are busy and this alone can take months. If the defendant is out on bail, *Anders* ensures that it will be a long time before the case finishes the direct appeal and the defendant begins to serve his sentence.

But more important for the purposes of this book than the expense is the attitude *Anders* expresses toward trials and what this opinion means for lawyers and trial judges. This is a Supreme Court opinion telling us that trials are fragile and uncertain events and that errors are so common that lawyers must scour the transcript of every trial to search them out. The clear assumption in *Anders* is that there are nonfrivolous errors in a high percentage of trials that could have affected the verdict, especially if counsel is forced to look closely at the trial transcript, and the system wants them raised. Unless the only errors are, in the Court's wonderful words, "wholly frivolous"—which seems to suggest that alleged errors that are "partly frivolous" should be raised on appeal—the defense attorney has no choice but to file an appeal under *Anders*.

For a lawyer to turn to his client and say, "You know, there were some things at trial that maybe didn't go our way, but overall the trial was fair and the verdict was just. I think you should accept the result and that we should not appeal" is something every other criminal justice system encourages and sees as the proper role of counsel. But the Court doesn't want lawyers to play that role. Trials are about winning and losing and even on appeal the Constitution demands that the lawyer raise every technicality and try to win even if the chances are slim and even if the lawyer believes the verdict at trial was correct and the trial was fair. A lawyer who sees his or her role differently is to be second-guessed by the appellate court.

In the previous chapter I spoke about the relatively weak role that trial judges are supposed to play in the United States and their reluctance to intervene. *Anders* is a nice example of the pressures on trial judges. If they do anything unusual—ask too many questions, cut off a line of defense questions, or lose their temper when baited by the defense lawyer—they will be the subject of the appeal. When you look at the difference in the appellate structure between the United States and England, the reason why English judges are better able to control their courtrooms is obvious. The appellate structure encourages them to exercise control and they are much less likely to be reversed than an American trial judge.

Further distinguishing the United States, even from countries with very liberal appellate review such as Norway, is the way the Court has used the Constitution to take any risk out of appellate review for the defendant. In Norway, if a defendant wants a second trial, there will be a complete rehearing of the case, which carries with it a number of risks. Since it is a complete retrial, the defendant might be convicted of a more serious offense, or if convicted of the same one, the court may decide that the sentence the defendant received was too lenient and add more time to it. The same is true in England if the defendant wishes to appeal from the Magistrates Court and obtain a new trial in the Crown Court. The trial will be heard by a Crown Court judge and two or four magistrates and, if the defendant is convicted a second time, the judges will look at the sentence and may increase or lower the sentence.

The United States would not permit a defendant to receive an increased sentence in such a situation. In *North Carolina v. Pearce*,[10] the Court dealt with a defendant who appealed his first conviction, handed down after a fair trial. He was retried, convicted, and received a longer sentence. Worried that a trial judge might vindictively increase the defendant's punishment because he had successfully appealed, the Court ruled that due process barred any increase in punishment unless additional objective information had surfaced since the first trial that justified the increase in sentence. *Pearce* helps encourage appeals by making them completely risk-free for the defendant. Even if the defendant received a very lenient sentence, he or she has nothing to lose in filing an appeal as the sentence can't be increased. Notice that what these two opinions, *Anders* and *Pearce*, say about defense lawyers and trial judges is not very flattering. Defense lawyers cannot be trusted to evaluate the merits of an appeal and sentencing judges can't be trusted to sentence defendants fairly and for the right reasons.

When you combine *Anders v. California* and *North Carolina v. Pearce* with a trial system that is uncertain about its priorities and with our American obsession with procedure, you end up with an expensive disaster. As I showed in chapter 4, appellate courts in the United States view trials as crapshoots in which any error—constitutional errors, nonconstitutional errors, errors at pretrial, or errors in jury selection—could have changed the outcome. The result is a very unstable system. While England won't reverse unless the appellate court concludes that there was a serious injustice, appellate courts in the United States must decide whether any trial or pretrial error was harmless beyond a reasonable doubt. But when the jury functions as a black box with no way of inquiring into the reasons for the verdict and what moved the jurors to convict the first time round, how can an appellate court ever be sure that the particular error—an outburst of anger by the judge, an improper question from the prosecutor, a piece of evidence admitted that should have been excluded—did not affect the verdict? Obviously, it can't. In a highly complicated trial system with elaborate rules of evidence and with skilled defense attorneys some error could always qualify as reversible error if an appellate court wants to reverse a case. Obviously, appellate courts don't reverse every case or even a high percentage of cases. But the indirect consequences on trial judges is powerful. Trial judges like to be considered fair and don't like appellate courts telling them that they deprived the defendant of a fair trial. The safe route is to remain passive and comfortably seated above the fray, resolving close questions in favor of the defense and letting the adversaries go at one another with a passion if they choose to do so.

One of the ironies of our appellate system is that while it is certainly not a conservative approach to appeals, it isn't a liberal approach either. Although the trial transcript must be scoured for all errors, the most important issue at trial doesn't get reviewed, namely, did the jury get it right and is the defendant really guilty— or not guilty—of the offense with which he was charged? *Anders* helps us understand why some cases in the American criminal justice system have been under constant appellate review for years as they go up through state systems and then over to the federal system, then back to the state systems. And yet, colorable claims are still made that the defendant is innocent of the crime and the jury was wrong to convict. Our appellate system—unlike other western appellate systems—is set up to spend countless hours on every issue but the most important ones. Is the verdict that the jury reached correct and do we have confidence in it? The result is an appellate system that loves to micromanage trial judges and often finds fault with what they did. It encourages judicial passivity. Yet when it comes to the jury, it is assumed that its verdict is always correct. Judges make mistakes, but so do juries.

Conclusion

It is plain from the earlier chapters of this book that I disagree with many Supreme Court decisions and think that the balance the Court has drawn between defendants' rights and the truth is much too heavily weighted on the defendants' side and that truth is badly undervalued in the system. In this chapter I have continued to make this argument by singling out some less well-known decisions for criticism. But my main point in this chapter has not been to attack individual decisions by the Court but rather to show why our trial system will never be strong if we continue to rely on the Court to build it. The Court as an institution is simply not designed for that task. It is not surprising, given the limited issues the Court can consider, the unbalanced nature of appellate review, and the limited options for change the Court has at its disposal, that we would end up with an extremely complicated and expensive trial system that is not all that reliable.

CHAPTER NINE

A Weak Trial System

Who Benefits?

A Macro Effect of a Weak Trial System: A System That Avoids Trials

A weak trial system can have serious consequences for any country. While it is naïve to think that the problems of race, drug abuse, the breakdown of the family, and the like can be solved by a criminal justice system, the latter can certainly exacerbate such problems. No one should expect a perfect trial system—it is run by humans—but citizens have the right to expect a system that works very hard to find the truth at trial and that tries to treat all who come in contact with it, whether as police officers, victims, witnesses, or defendants, with dignity and respect. I think our criminal trial system fails on both scores. In this chapter I want to explain why very few benefit from an unreliable trial system. Even the vast majority of defendants end up being hurt by it.

This last remark—that our weak trial system hurts defendants—may seem to run counter to the logic of the earlier chapters. One might think, for example, that an unreliable trial system would benefit defendants because, even if the evidence against them is overwhelming, the roll of the dice could go against the odds, making them big winners and allowing them to walk out of the courtroom. Shocking acquittals do happen. But a criminal justice system that has a weak trial system compensates for it by avoiding trials if possible. That is what has happened in the United States. While those in the criminal justice system insist that increased plea bargaining is caused by the sheer volume of cases and limited fiscal resources, that explanation is not entirely accurate. Our criminal justice system, if pressed to the task, could put on many more trials than it does, especially in serious cases, but those in the system don't want trials and go to great lengths to avoid them. And who could blame them? From the prosecution's point of view, one puts in a lot of work preparing the case and then goes into a courtroom where the roll of the dice can do funny things. Who wants to take chances with something that important? No one likes to lose. In our system if you don't win, you lose.

Trials are also very stressful. Major trials today are often potential "wars" in which everyone is liable to attack, including the prosecutor and judge. Just as countries try very hard to avoid war if they can, so lawyers will go very far to avoid trial. America is full of "trial lawyers" who rarely go to trial, unlike trial lawyers in other countries. Sure, they go to court for hearings on this motion or that, or to handle drunk driving and other minor criminal matters. But if you were to examine how many days they have actually spent in court before a jury in felony cases, you would find many prosecutors and defense attorneys who are lucky to do one or two trials a year. If American prosecutors and defense lawyers were barristers who made their living in court trying the more serious criminal cases and were paid, as are barristers, for the days actually spent in the courtroom at trial, they would starve.

This is not a criticism of American prosecutors and defense lawyers but rather a criticism of the trial system in which they are forced to operate. The trial system is incredibly expensive, complicated, unreliable, and, if that wasn't enough, it also takes a toll on those who go to trial. As noted previously, the result is a criminal justice system completely given over to plea bargaining. When there is the occasional trial now and again, it serves to remind people why the system wants to avoid trial if it can.

This is not to suggest that all important cases should go to trial or that all plea bargaining is wrong. Given the crime rates as well as the fiscal realities of all western countries, there is always some "incentive mechanism" for resolving a significant percentage of criminal cases short of a full-blown trial. I use the term "incentive mechanism" because in most European trial systems there is often no exact parallel to plea bargaining on the American model whereby a defendant goes to court and enters a guilty plea in exchange for a specified bargain. On the continent the defendant will sometimes win some assurances with respect to his sentence in exchange for a greatly simplified trial in which the evidence is not contested.[1]

But there are good and bad incentive mechanisms for avoiding trial. When a country has a strong trial system, a defendant who has committed a serious crime knows that if the evidence against him is strong, he is likely to be convicted. The chances of distracting the fact finders from the task at hand or of obtaining a mistrial by baiting a judge into error are very slim. In this situation, if a defendant wishes to enter into an agreement that will assure him a somewhat lighter sentence in return for avoiding a full trial this makes sense, given the limited judicial resources in most countries. While the defendant does receive a break in terms of the sentence, he admits to what he did and hopefully the sentence imposed is roughly appropriate to the crime.

But when a country has a weak and expensive trial system, it is forced to accept any kind of plea bargain to avoid trial. A distinction between good plea bargaining and bad plea bargaining cannot be maintained. This is what has happened in the United States. One finds rape cases in which, as police reports make clear, the defendant sexually penetrated the victim, being pled down to "unconsented touching," as if the defendant simply brushed the victim's breast with his hand. One finds a string of robberies "rolled up" into a plea to only one robbery or an armed robbery pled down to a charge of robbery with the gun simply swallowed up in the plea. As to the sentence, it too may have to be deeply discounted to reflect the weaknesses of the case. A defendant with strong reason to suppress crucial physical evidence may be offered probation or a short prison sentence even though everyone in the courtroom concedes that he or she deserves several years of prison time, given the offense. In short, the American criminal justice system has no choice but to "split the baby" and will do so regularly to avoid trial, even if the final conviction has only a remote relationship to the crime or crimes committed and the sentence is inadequate for what the defendant actually did. To the public it seems that offenders are getting terrific "bargains" because the crime to which the defendant pleads guilty often does not reflect what he or she did and the punishment appears to be heavily discounted.

The system's complete preference for bargaining over truth is nicely captured in a type of guilty plea I have never encountered in any other country. It is called an *Alford* plea, after the United States Supreme Court case, *United States v. Alford*,[2] that upheld it. A defendant wishing to make an *Alford* plea indicates that he or she wants to plead guilty, but at the same time maintains that he or she is actually innocent of the crime. Other western criminal justice systems would not touch plea arrangements of this sort because they want to make sure, first and foremost, that the defendant committed the crime in question. The defendant's strong denial would raise serious questions about his guilt, which would necessitate a trial.

But in the United States, the guilty plea, not the evidence, is emphasized above all. You can see this very graphically when judges accept pleas in American courtrooms. The judge spends almost the entire time taking the plea going over with the defendant the various trial rights he or she is waiving as part of the guilty plea. To lock the defendant into the plea bargain, the judge will ask a long list of ritualized questions designed to make sure the defendant is aware of each right he is waiving by pleading guilty, such as the right to a jury, the right to counsel at trial, the right to confront witnesses, the right to proof beyond a reasonable doubt, and so on. To each of these questions the defendant must answer"yes" to show that he understands what he is waiving.

But when it comes to discussing the crime in question, the judge is unlikely to ask more than a perfunctory question or two. ("Are you pleading guilty because you committed the crime?" "Yes, your honor." "And what did you do?" "I went into the liquor store and robbed it.") He is unlikely to make any attempt to discuss with the defendant, in a spontaneous way, specific facts of the crime, such as the planning that went into it, the details of the crime, the reasons for it, what the defendant feels about it, and so on. Is it any wonder that many years after a crime, even in high profile criminal cases where there is strong public interest in seeing that justice is done, such as the assassination of Martin Luther King, genuine issues about the guilt of a defendant can still arise? Judges don't want to ask too many questions about the substance of the offense, and prosecutors and defense lawyers don't want them to either, because this might raise questions about the wisdom of the plea bargain in the minds of those involved—the defendant, the judge, and members of the public.

A criminal justice system that continually plea bargains is bound to lose public respect. The public sees a system less concerned about what the defendant actually did or what punishment is appropriate for the crime than about getting "bargains." I am reminded of a small cartoon in the *Wall Street Journal* a couple of years ago in which two people are looking up a long flight of stone steps to a giant courthouse complete with towering Greek columns across the front, not unlike the Supreme Court building in Washington. Above the columns proudly etched in stone are the words,

"Liberty, Justice, and Plea Bargaining." I am afraid the cartoon captures what our system has become.

From a defendant's perspective, plea bargaining breeds cynicism, too. Defendants see a system in which they are supposed to have all these rights—the most powerful set of defendants' rights in any western country—and yet their own lawyers put tremendous pressure on them to waive those rights and accept a bargain which everyone assures them is "a good deal." In a system of plea bargaining where there seem to be no limits to what can be bargained, how does the defendant know whether the bargain is a good one or not? A certain ambivalence is normal and, like anyone who has to be convinced to accept a bargain, inevitably he or she will wonder whether a "better deal" might have been struck if the defense lawyer had been more aggressive or if he or she had had the funds to hire a private attorney rather than a public defender. Defendants understand that the system is not about truth.

A Warning about the Synergy between Procedure and Punishment

I said at the start of this chapter that our weak trial system actually hurts the vast majority of defendants. But I have not justified that claim other than to explain that our criminal justice system today is really a plea bargaining system, not a trial system. The way to understand how this impacts defendants is to ask a very important question: what happens when citizens grow frustrated or become angry with the system? What happens when they see a system in which truth is not emphasized and defendants seem to get deals that discount their sentences?

I think citizens will try to change the system by pushing for harsher punishments for those defendants who don't "get off on a technicality." Indeed, this is what we have seen over the last ten or fifteen years—a steady increase in the punishments authorized for particular crimes. Lawyers and judges like to blame this on the "politicians" who they claim are just pandering to the public. What those in the system don't appreciate is *why* the public gets angry and *why* there is constant pressure on politicians to be ever tougher on criminals.

Certainly, a weak trial system and our complete reliance on plea bargaining are not the only reasons for increasingly harsh criminal sentences, but a system evolves to meet its needs. In a country in which plea bargaining determines the sentence, it is not surprising that there would be constant pressure to pass statutes so the defendant receives "what he really deserves" or that statutes would evolve to give prosecutors more leverage in plea bargaining so that they can get good bargains.

To accommodate our plea bargaining system, we have seen a big increase in the number of statutes with mandatory punishments or very high minimum punishments. These statutes coerce defendants to enter into plea bargains by making the risk of conviction at trial unacceptably high because, should the defendant be convicted, there will be nothing a judge can later do to ameliorate the harshness of the punishment. The statutes effectively transfer sentencing power from the judge to the prosecutor. Another device for coercing plea bargains that has become more common is habitual offender statutes which mandate a certain fixed sentence for an offender convicted of a second or third felony. Many states now have two or three different habitual offender statutes and the punishment mandated may even be life without parole.

The prosecutor can also frequently add other charges to the charging document to "up the ante" and increase the risk of trial for defendants who might otherwise choose to go to trial. For example, sometimes prosecutors can raise the defendant's sentencing range dramatically by adding an additional count of having "committed a crime of violence." Or they can add additional counts for having committed a crime "against an elderly person," against a "vulnerable person," a "handicapped person," and so on. These will usually dramatically increase the sentence the defendant faces if convicted and put pressure on a defendant to enter into a plea bargain that will avoid the sentence such aggravating counts would require.

Mandatory minimums, the possibility of extra aggravating charges, high sentencing ranges, and the like, reflect the importance of plea bargaining in our system and show that we put a lot of pressure on defendants to get them to waive their trial rights and enter into plea bargains. As a result, we are fundamentally inconsistent in the way we treat defendants. If a police officer offers lenient treatment toward a suspect in an effort to get him to admit his involvement in the crime in question, judges immediately condemn such tactics and bar the use of his statement on the grounds that it was unfairly "coerced" from him. Yet defendants are routinely put under much more severe pressure to get them to waive their right to trial and courts not only find such guilty pleas to be voluntary and constitutional, but the judges themselves accept guilty pleas where the defendant's choices are, to put it euphemistically, rather unpleasant.

The leading Supreme Court case on plea bargaining, *Bordenkircher v. Hayes*,[3] shows how the system works and the pressures it puts on defendants. In *Hayes*, the prosecutor offered a defendant charged with burglary a five-year maximum sentence if he pled guilty to the charge, but warned the defendant that he would charge him as a habitual offender if he insisted on going to trial. If convicted, the defendant would then receive a mandatory life sentence. When the defendant insisted on trial, the prosecutor followed through on the threat and charged him as a habitual offender. The defendant was convicted of the burglary and of being a habitual offender, with the result that he received a life sentence. Notice that the prosecutor would have been quite willing to limit the defendant's sentence to five years in prison if he had pled guilty to the burglary. But by exercising his constitutional right to have the case proven at trial, the defendant got a life sentence and there was nothing the judge could do.

The Supreme Court upheld the life sentence in an opinion that basically said, "Hey, it's plea bargaining." Indeed the Court was being honest: this is American-style plea bargaining. If you dare to exercise your right to trial, you will pay if you "lose." Today prosecutors have powerful clubs with which to coerce defendants to accept plea bargains so that even when they have strong defenses, they often have no choice but to plead guilty. If the prosecutor has at his disposal counts that would require a minimum sentence of ten years in prison, but offers to dismiss some of the counts and recommend a two-year sentence, it is hard to take the risk of going to trial even if one has a strong defense.

I am not arguing that people who commit a crime and do it again and again don't deserve substantial sentences and, in some cases, life imprisonment. But mandatory sentences that treat all offenders as if they were the most serious offender capable of committing the particular crime can be the source of terrible injustices. People commit crimes, even very serious crimes, for all sorts of reasons. People kill others out of anger, out of stupidity, out of mercy and love, out of revenge, out of greed, out of jealousy, and so on. To fail to consider the offender's individual culpability for what he or she has done is a serious mistake. But in a world where trials are viewed as "rolls of the dice" and punishments determined largely by barter and bargain, it is not surprising that individual culpability will often take a back seat to expediency.

Obviously, I am oversimplifying the relationship between punishment and procedure in suggesting that procedure influences punishment. Certainly there are other pressures that influence punishment such as a high crime rate and a general fear of crime on the part of citizens. Harsh punishments also put pressure on the system for ever more procedure, because the system worries about mistakes.

There is no better example of that than the death penalty. Many special procedures in matters such as jury selection must be followed to the letter if a death penalty sentence is to be upheld.

Some years ago I read that there is a synergy between asbestos and smoking, such that the fatality rates of those who had breathed in asbestos fibers and also smoked was many times greater than those who had done only one or the other. The asbestos fibers increased the harmful effects of smoking and smoking increased the harmful effects of asbestos. I think much the same point can be made about punishment and procedure—they feed off one another and tend to extremes together.

I admire the Netherlands for its courage in attempting to find alternatives to incarceration for drug addicts, and even for those accused of relatively serious crimes. It is sad that an American politician who advocated trying a similar approach in the United States would likely die a quick death at the polls. But if you looked at the trial procedures of the Netherlands as I described them in chapter 5, you would not use "rolling the dice" as a metaphor for its trial system. When a country has an efficient trial system that puts a high priority on truth and expects defendants to own up to what they have done and accept responsibility, it is easier to maintain a high level of public respect and confidence. That, in turn, permits the system to try alternatives to incarceration that would not be politically possible in the United States. If some of these alternatives turn out to be ineffective, the system has a sufficient reservoir of trust and goodwill to right those mistakes and move on. It can also fend off calls for harsh mandatory minimums or other statutory changes that can cause more problems than they will ever solve. Meanwhile our system of criminal law grows harsher every year and the number of our citizens in prison continues to grow.

Just as surely as our trial system discourages honesty and remorse from suspects, it discourages forgiveness and rehabilitation. Unfortunately, harshness breeds harshness until two years in prison is considered "a slap on the wrist." Having spent most of its political capital defending the Court's extreme expansion of right after right, the criminal justice system doesn't have much credibility left when it tries to head off tough sentencing laws that even many prosecutors in the system would concede to be draconian.

An Additional Warning: More Procedure May Mean Less Accuracy

For too long, the American legal system has deluded itself into thinking that more procedure will lead to more fairness and more accuracy at trial. But it doesn't work that way: excessive procedure, especially procedure not directed to the factual accuracy of the charges against the defendant, can lead to injustice. A heavily proceduralized system forces defense lawyers to make some hard decisions regarding the issues on which they will concentrate their efforts. A defense lawyer who chooses to spend a substantial amount of time on an important suppression motion may not be able to spend as much time going over the evidence or seeking out additional evidence which may help the defense. William Stuntz warns that more procedure may lead to less reliable verdicts even in death penalty cases:

> Not only does more procedures not mean more accuracy, more process may actually mean less accuracy, because it encourages defense lawyers and courts to shift energy and attention away from the merits and towards procedure. In their desire to construct the best possible process for determining who must die, appellate courts may make the determinations worse.[4]

It is not that the procedural issues totally supplant concern for the defendant's guilt, but they take time away from such concern. Only the very wealthy can afford to hire an attorney, or more commonly these days a team of attorneys, so that every possible issue can be anticipated, studied, and litigated. This leads to the public perception that the system favors the wealthy. This is accurate: a complicated and highly proceduralized trial system will greatly favor sophisticated and wealthy defendants.

Procedure has to be proportional to the system's resources for other reasons. Public defender agencies don't get automatic boosts in support every time a court adopts a new set of procedures that will increase the time and cost of representing indigent defendants in criminal cases. Caseloads remain high and, in fact, funding for public defenders has remained flat. So there is actually less money available for the defense of criminal cases today than there was five or ten years ago. Forced to ration their time over a large number of clients, public defenders have to choose how best to spend their time. If upon quick examination of a case a public defender thinks the case is weak he may press the defendant to plead guilty, thereby freeing up time to work on other cases. Or the public defender may invest the limited amount of time he or she has preparing a suppression motion. If unsuccessful, this may mean the lawyer has devoted less time to evaluating the facts of the case than he or she should have. The same is true of appointed lawyers, especially in states which place caps—often very low caps—on the amount of money that appointed lawyers can receive for handling a case. This forces lawyers to make some hard choices about the issues that will be raised and pushed hard and those that will be ignored.

Admittedly, some of these pressures on public defenders and appointed lawyers could be alleviated by additional appropriations. But it is difficult to convince legislators of the need for greater appropriations when the system presently spends vast amounts of resources on issues unrelated to the guilt or innocence of the defendant. If there is no limit to the amount of procedure in the system, the system is capable of eating up enormous quantities of resources on a very few cases. The five-week trial of Timothy McVeigh is reported to have cost $14 million in attorneys' fees.

The Micro Effects of a Weak Trial System: A System That Doesn't Listen Well to Citizens

In the opening chapter, I compared our trial system to professional football and continental trial systems to professional soccer. I suggested that American football coaches who prowl the sidelines are closer to being the players of the game because they call every play and every defensive alignment. I compared their influence over the players on the field to the influence of American trial lawyers over the testimony of the witnesses at trial.

I want to return to this point and discuss briefly the problem that nonlawyers face in our trial system. We badly overemphasize the role of lawyers and end up demeaning nonlawyers in the courtroom. I mentioned in the previous section the way the system speaks to the defendant when he or she enters a guilty plea—there is no real attempt to communicate with the defendant, to find out who he or she is, what exactly happened, and why. In our system, if such questions do get asked they are asked by a probation office outside the courtroom. The judge concentrates on ritualized questions that could just as easily be asked by a law clerk.

I would make the same point about defendants who don't plead guilty and who go to trial. Perhaps the best result for such a defendant will be obtained by a lawyer who makes sure that the defendant volunteers no statement to the police prior to trial, thereby permitting the defense lawyer to develop a strategy to prevent the defendant's conviction. But ultimately the system demeans and depersonalizes the defendant. At the end of trial we usually know very little about the person on trial. His or her lawyer may have put on a terrific defense but who is this defendant? By contrast, in continental trial systems after the defense lawyer has questioned a witness, the judges will often ask the defendant whether he or she wishes to ask any questions. They will also often ask the defendant during the trial if he wishes to respond to something a witness has just said. This seems strange and unthinkable to an American defense lawyer, but the lawyer is not the defendant and continental trial systems are respectful of the defendant.

Consider the problem for crime victims in the American system. In chapter 2, when I discussed the exclusionary rule I mentioned "the adversary mentality" that grips many lawyers and judges, convincing them that a criminal case has two and only two sides. On one side is the impersonal state with its awesome power. On the other is the defendant. The reality is that criminal cases, especially serious ones, may have more than two sides, and if trials are wars between the prosecution and the defense, victims are often caught in the cross fire. They didn't hire the police officer who conducted the investigation or get to select the prosecutor trying the case. The prosecutor is not their lawyer and doesn't represent them, yet their credibility and reputation may come under bitter attack at a trial at which they are not represented. To the extent that our trial system is more about winning and losing than it is about truth, victims often pay the price. Yet because the chances of a civil recovery are usually zero, the criminal trial is often the only forum in which the victim can ensure that the defendant's conduct will be recognized as wrong and condemned.

I want to discuss just one aspect of the problems that victims face in our trial system, namely, the way they are treated in the courtroom. I begin with a remarkable statement from the victim of a horrific crime, Betty Jane Spencer, whose four sons were murdered in an Indiana farmhouse and who was herself injured by the attacker. In an article she wrote about her experience, Ms. Spencer said the following:

> I spent long hours discussing the murder with the Parke County Prosecutor. . . . I was treated with kindness and respect, but I soon began to feel like another piece of evidence. I felt no different than

the shotguns or the many other pieces of evidence that has been collected."[5]

I think this statement is very revealing. Although she described her treatment by the prosecutors as kind and respectful, there was something wrong with it. She began to feel "like another piece of evidence," not unlike the shotgun that had killed her sons.

To understand the problem from the point of view of a victim (or any other witness at trial), imagine how confusing trials must seem. The victim is put under oath "to tell the truth, the whole truth, and nothing but the truth." Yet the system doesn't want the victim to tell what she believes is the whole truth about the crime. If the victim's testimony is not carefully confined to the mechanics of the crime and if she dares to explain what was running through her head at the time—what she thought, feared, and dreaded—there will be immediate objection ("Your honor, please ask the witness to confine her testimony to what happened at the time"). Perhaps there will be a huddled sidebar with the lawyers and judges talking in loud whispers to each other while the victim sits on the stand, knowing that they are talking about her or at least about her testimony and about the rules of evidence and whether or not her anticipated answer might or might not fit within the rules. Polite and well-meaning though the prosecutor and judge might be, something tells the victim that this is not right: "What am I that the system will not let me tell them what happened in my own way and in my own words? I am trying to tell the whole truth."

To an extent that is almost unimaginable and would even be unethical and wrong in other trial systems, our adversary system turns witnesses into weapons to be used against the other side. They need to have their testimony shaped to bring out its maximum adversarial potential and they need to be coached about what they should or should not say in court. For example, it is standard practice to tell witnesses not to volunteer any information on cross-examination.

(A victim might well wonder: how is this consistent with telling the "whole truth" on the stand?) They also need to be prepared to fend off the standard cross-examination tricks of defense attorneys. In short, their testimony must be made to fit what the system wants to hear and it must be honed by the lawyers for maximum adversarial advantage.

Contrast this with the way victims are treated at a continental trial. Countries such as the Netherlands, Germany, and Norway want witnesses to testify in their own words—not those shaped or even supplied by the lawyer—and in their own way. They will always ask a witness—whether police officer, victim, defendant, or expert—to tell the whole truth about the incident and not to hold any information back. They want the witness to tell everything she remembers, including what she thought at the time, what she felt, what she may have said or may have been said to her, and what she may have feared. Only when she has finished will questions be asked of her.

Studies suggest that witnesses who are permitted to give evidence in an uninterrupted narrative are able to remember more about events and to remember things more accurately than are witnesses who have to break up their recollection to fit a tight question-and-answer format. But whether this is true or not, in our trial system the heavy imprint of the lawyers on the testimony of witnesses overemphasizes the role of the former and demeans the latter. Our trial system doesn't do a very good job of *listening* to people other than the lawyers.

Conclusion

For too long, the legal establishment has deluded itself into thinking that more procedure and more powerful rights for defendants would lead to a system that was just and respected. Instead, respect for our trial system has never been lower. What has gone wrong?

This chapter has explained what happens when a trial system is too expensive and too unreliable to be used with regularity: in the United States the criminal justice system works to avoid its trial procedure by passing statutes that shift sentencing authority to prosecutors. These then use their power to pressure defendants to waive their trial rights. In the end, a trial system that placed a higher priority on truth and that was simpler and less expensive to use would better serve almost everyone in the system, including the vast majority of defendants.

CHAPTER TEN

Juries

The Loss of Public Confidence

The Need to Rethink Juries

A criminal justice system is an organic whole that is only as strong as its weakest part. A system may have the greatest trial procedures in the world, but if the rules governing the investigation do not allow the police to gather a sufficient amount of reliable evidence or to conduct a complete and thorough investigation, the system will always be weak. Similarly, even if the procedures governing criminal investigations are sensible and fair and the police carrying out the investigation are highly competent and professional, the system will be weak if its trial procedures do not allow important pieces of reliable evidence to be admitted at trial or if the trial procedures do not permit the evidence that has been admitted to be sufficiently examined and tested. In short, a good trial system is just as important as sound investigative practices for a strong criminal justice system.

In this chapter I want to talk about another crucial link in the system: the fact finders who ultimately determine the defendant's guilt or innocence. No matter how strong a system's investigative and trial procedures may be, if the fact finders are not up to the task of evaluating the evidence fairly and competently, or cannot be trusted to understand and apply the law to the facts, that trial system will never be strong. Right now we are suffering through a crisis of confidence in our jury system. Probably everyone is familiar with some juries' stunning acquittals or failures to convict in important cases in recent years. In 1991, a jury in Manhattan acquitted El-Sayyid Nosair of murdering Meir Kahane, the founder of the Jewish Defense League. The judge who had presided over the trial declared the jury's verdict "against the overwhelming weight of the evidence and devoid of common sense and logic."[1] Jews in both New York and Israel took to the streets in protest.

In 1992, a Brooklyn jury acquitted Lemrick Nelson, Jr., of stabbing Yankel Rosenbaum to death during a violent encounter between blacks and orthodox Jews. Before his death, Rosenbaum had identified Nelson as his attacker and the murder weapon was found in Nelson's possession.[2] Thousands of orthodox Jews marched to protest the acquittal. The evening after the verdict was returned jurors and their spouses attended a celebration hosted by the defendant's attorney.[3]

The worst race riots in American history began on April 29, 1992, the day that a California jury failed to convict any of the four Los Angeles police officers videotaped beating Rodney King with batons as he lay on the ground. The jury's action precipitated two days of violence that resulted in fifty-eight deaths and almost one billion dollars in property damage.[4] The Los Angeles riots were strikingly similar in their origin to the Miami riots twelve years earlier, when four white police officers were acquitted of any criminal liability by an all-white jury for the beating death of a black motorist stopped for a traffic violation.

The trial of the Menendez brothers and the O. J. Simpson trial are so well known that little need be said. The Menendez brothers drove to San Diego in an Alfa Romeo given them by their father in order to buy a shotgun which they then used to kill their parents as they watched television. The gun was fired sixteen times. Although these handsome young men claimed they had been victims of their father's abuse, why their mother should also have been gunned down was never very clear. Neither of the original juries—there was a joint trial but separate juries for each of the brothers—was able to agree on whether the brothers had murdered either of their parents.[5] After eight months of trial, the jury in the O. J. Simpson case deliberated for just three hours before reaching its not guilty verdict. (The *Simpson* jury, like all criminal juries, had been instructed numerous times by the trial judge not to discuss the case among themselves until the end of the trial.)

This handful of cases is but one of many other signs of a jury system in trouble. There is the growing phenomenon of jurors who stubbornly insist on hanging the jury in the face of overwhelming evidence of guilt. In March 1997, the *New Yorker* magazine published an article about this phenomenon entitled, "One Angry Woman."[6] The article discussed the growing percentage of criminal cases that result in hung juries in general, as well as the particular phenomenon of lone black female jurors hanging juries in the District of Columbia. Eric Holder, the then-U.S. Attorney for the District of Columbia, told Jeffrey Rosen, the author of the article, that these days the preeminent challenge for prosecutors during jury selection is to identify what he described as the "unreachable juror," in order to strike that person from the jury. But, Holder stated, such jurors are hard to find because persons with such a motive will often lie to get onto a jury.

While the *New Yorker* article focuses on urban jurisdictions such as the District of Columbia, Los Angeles, and New York City, where race is often a factor in the decision to hang the jury, the phenomenon exists in other jurisdictions and for reasons that may have nothing to do with race. Recently, a white female juror hung a jury in Colorado and refused to even discuss the evidence with the other jurors because of her personal view that criminalization of drug use was the wrong way to solve our nation's drug problem. (The case eventually received national attention when the trial judge decided to punish the juror with contempt after the trial for failing to disclose during jury selection her strong views on drug laws.[7])

Another sign of a jury system in trouble is the tremendous emphasis lawyers place on jury selection. This reflects the common belief among trial lawyers that the composition of the jury can be just as important to the outcome of the trial as the evidence. To help "pick the winners" for the jury, there are jury consultants available for the wealthy who do such things as background checks on potential jurors, or telephone surveys of the trial venue, aimed at helping the lawyer in the case form a statistical picture by gender, race, age, religion, and the like, of persons likely to be favorable or unfavorable at the trial. Sometimes a jury consultant with a background in psychology may sit in the courtroom in order to study the body language and manner of speech of a potential juror and thereby help the trial lawyer determine which jurors should be struck from the panel. This focus on who gets on the jury is demeaning to the entire system. It reinforces the view, described in detail in chapter 4, that trials are just a "crapshoot" or "a roll of the dice" and that the right or wrong juror can determine the outcome despite the evidence.

A rethinking of our jury system is long overdue.

The Supreme Court and Jury Trials

Among western countries, the United States is far more committed to trial by jury than any other country. Norway and Denmark use juries on occasion, but only for a handful of serious cases each year. Although England uses juries more frequently, moderately serious crimes, such as the sale of drugs, burglary, possession of stolen goods, theft, forgery, or even a simple assault—cases for which the defendant may even spend a short amount of time in prison if convicted—are tried by a panel of magistrates without the use of a jury. (If the magistrates decide after trial that the offender deserves a longer sentence than they can impose they will transfer the case to Crown Court for sentencing.) These criminal justice systems are cautious about using juries because jury trials are expensive.

We are at the other end of the spectrum when it comes to jury trials. The Supreme Court in two important Warren Court era decisions tied our criminal justice system heavily to trial by jury. Its attitude in those decisions was "hang the expense." Today every criminal case, except the most minor ones involving "petty offenses," must be tried by a jury. The leading Supreme Court case on jury trials is *Duncan v. Louisiana*[8] decided in 1968. In *Duncan*, the Court held that the sixth amendment right to a jury trial, which applied to the federal government, should also be applied to the states as part of the state obligation to provide due process of law to citizens. In other words, to be fundamentally fair a trial must have a jury.

Duncan was a controversial decision because it guaranteed defendants a jury trial in any criminal prosecution in which they faced a possible sentence of more than a year in prison. But two years later the Court expanded a defendant's right to a jury trial even further. In *Baldwin v. New York*,[9] the Court held that it was unconstitutional for the City of New York to fail to provide a jury trial to defendants in any case where there was even the possibility of a sentence of more than six months in jail. (These minor crimes are what the system calls misdemeanors.) Notice that we are talking in both cases about possible sentences, not actual ones. Even if it is clear that the defendant will not spend any time in prison for his offense, perhaps because it is a first offense and he has no previous convictions, the Supreme Court requires that states provide the same trial procedures that would be used for serious crimes for which the defendant may spend five, ten, or twenty years in prison. Obviously, given the staggering number of minor criminal cases filed daily in low-level criminal courts in our urban jurisdictions, a jury trial cannot possibly be provided for a significant percentage of these cases. The result is courtrooms so given over to plea bargaining that they more closely resemble third-world bazaars than courts of justice.

In chapter 8, I argued that the institution of the Supreme Court is poorly designed for building a strong criminal justice system. I pointed out that one of the main limitations of the Court is the limited number of options it has available to address problems before it. The question of how to provide fair trials in minor criminal cases is a nice example. Some countries provide a level of lay participation in minor criminal cases. Norway and Germany use mixed panels in which citizens serve along with a professional judge as "lay judges," while England uses lay magistrates—part-time "judges" who belong to the community, are not trained in the law, and volunteer their time to sit on panels to handle minor criminal cases. But the Supreme Court didn't have the option of imposing on the states some middle position between trial before a single professional judge and a full-blown jury. So it chose the latter. Today, the United States has only one trial model—the Indy 500 car that is expensive to run and requires constant tuning and a crew of specialists to keep it running well—for all felony and misdemeanor cases. We need to consider whether it is better to have such a vehicle available in *theory* for a great number of cases but in *reality* only to a minuscule percentage of them, or whether it would be better to offer a much higher percentage of citizens a simpler type of trial, perhaps using citizen judges or a mixed panel that would be considerably less expensive—more like the slightly battered ten-year-old Chevy that still runs well. The nature of Supreme Court adjudication never permitted discussion of other options. The Court was presented with a stark choice: to impose a jury trial requirement or to permit trial before a single professional judge acting alone.

The Changing Composition of Juries

We tend to view juries, somewhat romantically, as a cross section of the community that goes into the jury box and applies the law to the facts as they find them. But jurors have never been much of a cross section of the community. I have read trial transcripts of old criminal cases from the early 1800s and been struck by how different juries must have been then from what they are today. Summations by the lawyers at the end of trials were full of classical and literary illusions that would be lost on the vast majority of jurors today. Clearly, juries were not drawn from a random mix of all citizens.

This is not a plea for a return to those early days when juries were handpicked by the court clerk or the local judge and were clearly "blue ribbon" groups of wealthy citizens from which minorities and women were excluded. But it is important to see that although in theory our present system is open to all citizens, it is probably closer to the other end of the spectrum in terms of who gets to sit on the jury in important criminal cases. Many citizens with responsible positions—physicians, small shopkeepers, college students, business executives, teachers, and the like—cannot afford to serve on a jury if the trial is likely to last a week or two, let alone a few months. The trial judge therefore permits them to opt out of jury service. (Today many citizens called for jury service are opting out in another way—by just not showing up.) Also, in many two-income families it is hard for one spouse to take over child-care and other family responsibilities from the other if one of them is called for jury duty. This means that juries tend to be disproportionately weighted in favor of individuals without daily responsibilities or low-level government employees or low-level employees of large companies. This is not to say that such citizens should not be jurors, but rather that many others are forced to opt out because they cannot serve and still take care of their other responsibilities. Complicating this issue is the uncertain duration of American criminal trials. A scheduled one-week trial may end up taking two or three weeks, which discourages citizens who could serve on a one-week trial jury from attempting to serve.

Another important factor discouraging citizens from doing so is the jury selection hurdle. There is an excellent chance that an educated person, or one with experience making difficult decisions based on the evidence, or with some knowledge of statistics, and the like, will not be considered desirable by one of the lawyers and will end up being removed from the jury anyway. Trial lawyers often joke that if a citizen wants to get out of jury service, he should show up in a suit and tie.

For these reasons, juries in the United States are often very ordinary in terms of their background and education, at a time when the evidence at criminal trials has grown increasingly sophisticated. It is hard to understand DNA evidence, for example, without some background in statistics. It is difficult to provide that background in the middle of a criminal trial. Added to these problems, the courtroom itself has become a somewhat intimidating place for nonlawyers. Even among lawyers, increasingly only the specialists who understand evidence law, the substantive issues in the case being tried, constitutional rules, local court rules, and so on, can follow the issues fully. Yet into this intimidating world our system marches a group of twelve very ordinary citizens, who don't know one another, who may never have been in a courtroom before, and who may never have done anything remotely like what they are being asked to do, with very serious consequences hanging in the balance. Nonetheless, the system expects them to adjust to this strange environment and reach the correct verdict—unanimously— based on the law and the evidence. I think this is asking a lot of a jury in a serious and hotly contested criminal case.

What Are Juries Supposed to Do at Trial?

The confusion in the United States over what a trial is supposed to accomplish causes other problems for juries. In western countries with strong trial systems, trials are designed basically to do one thing above all else—to decide whether or not the evidence shows that the defendant committed the crime in question. An American trial seems by contrast to be intended to accomplish many things, including punishing the police in order to deter violations of constitutional rules, giving defendants the right to self-representation at trial, assuring defendants a fair trial, and assuring the public and victims that criminals will be made to answer for crimes they have committed. Obviously, these many goals conflict and no trial system can expect to do all these things at the same time and to do them all equally well. Without a strong priority on determining the truth, trials become difficult to manage. It is hard for a judge to control a trial without a clear understanding of where it should be going.

This uncertainty impacts juries as well. They are likely to be exposed to a range of arguments and attempts to sway them that they would not have to deal with in other countries. To make this point, let me focus on one particular issue that continues to be much debated in our trial system: jury nullification and delivery of a verdict inconsistent with what the law would demand. In a passage in *Duncan v. Louisiana*, Justice White responded to the claim that juries are "unpredictable, quixotic, and little better than a roll of the dice" as follows:

> [T]he most recent and exhaustive study of the jury in criminal cases concluded that juries do understand the evidence and come to sound conclusions in most of the cases presented to them and that when juries differ with the result at which the judge would have arrived, it is

usually because they are serving some of the very purposes for which they were created and for which they are now employed.[10]

The reference is to a study by Harry Kalven and Hans Zeisel published in 1966[11] that found a substantial difference in the conviction rates of judges and juries. Judges were asked at the end of the trial to state whether they agreed with the jury's verdict and would have reached the same result. Judges disagreed with the jury's decision to acquit in 19 percent of the cases and with its decision to convict in 3 percent of them. (One suspects that this discrepancy would be much greater today.)

What I want to concentrate on is Justice White's assurance that this discrepancy of roughly 20 percent between the amateur fact finders and the professional fact finder should not be viewed with alarm because juries in these cases "are serving some of the very purposes for which they were created and for which they are now employed." What Justice White is telling us in this obscure passage is that juries do not always apply the law to the facts before them, but instead come to verdicts, despite the law or despite the evidence, for reasons of their own. Justice White seems to be approving this practice. He tells us it is one of the reasons for which juries "were created" and "are now employed."

This passage beautifully captures just how ambivalent our criminal justice system is about jury nullification. Notice how indirectly Justice White deals with the topic. On the one hand, he seems proud of jury nullification and tells us it is one of the reasons why our system uses juries, but, on the other hand, he seems timid about even using the words "jury nullification" and instead speaks in a veiled way about this function of the jury.

Considering the rather reverential way Justice White alludes to the jury's power to nullify, one might think that our system encourages jury nullification. But, in fact, jurors are not supposed to nullify the law. During jury selection they are asked whether they will follow the law as given them by the judge. Anyone who says that he or she will not do so is removed from the jury. To reinforce the duty to apply the law to the case, when jury selection is concluded the jury is put under oath to follow the law.

Yet our system is proud of jury nullification. Lawyers and judges justify the importance of juries by recalling the jury's refusal to convict Peter Zenger in 1735 for libeling the governor of New York, an English appointee, in his newspaper. At Zenger's trial, despite intense pressure from the trial judge, the jury refused to convict Zenger for seditious libel. (At that time it was not a defense for seditious libel that what had been published was in fact true.)

Obviously, if we accept jury nullification, any of the verdicts described at the start of this chapter can be justified as simply situations in which the jury put aside the law or the evidence for what they considered more important reasons. I mentioned a Colorado case in which a juror refused to convict and hung the jury because she believed that the criminalization of drugs was a mistaken way of solving our drug crisis.[12] In a representative democracy, one might think this a matter for the legislature, not an individual jury or a single juror. But one could argue just as well that this was a juror "serving one of the purposes" for which we have juries.

But jury nullification makes a mockery of our whole intricate trial system. Once the oath is stripped away and jurors are free to "do their own thing" the system heads quickly for terrible problems. Jury nullification—whether it is blacks acquitting blacks in urban jurisdictions today or whether it was whites acquitting whites of the murders of civil rights workers in Mississippi in the 1960s—is a dangerous concept and we are, as a general matter, scared to death of it. But despite the rules, lawyers often argue for jury nullification in this country—"Hey, it's a way to win and trials are about winning." And there is evidence that jury nullification is going on more and more today.

Some people even applaud it. In an article in the prestigious *Yale Law Journal* in 1995, Paul Butler called for more instances of jury nullification in cases involving black defendants because of the racism he sees built into the system.[13] (But what about the oath, Professor Butler?) Meanwhile, the Fully Informed Jury Association, a group based in Montana that includes among its members tax protesters, gun-control opponents, and citizens who are worried about what they perceive to be the tyranny of the legal system, has been trying to get state constitutional initiatives passed that would require trial judges to instruct juries in their power to determine the law for themselves.[14] Unsuccessful so far in their legislative efforts, some members of the group have taken matters into their own hands and have been arrested trying to intercept jurors at courthouses in order to give them leaflets that would instruct them on jury nullification.[15]

When we see outcomes like those described at the start of this chapter as well as reports of very high acquittal rates in urban jurisdictions, I wonder whether Justice White would be quite as eager to embrace juries as he was in *Duncan*. But part of the problem with building a system through Supreme Court decisions is that one is sometimes tempted to believe the rhetoric of the Court, which is designed to convince us of the merits of its decision. I think the Court in *Duncan* glossed over the problems with juries that existed in 1966 and that are even more serious today.

How Well Does the System Treat Jurors?

It has frequently been observed that our legal system is deeply ambivalent when it comes to juries. On the one hand, we profess a deep respect for juries and trust them to do everything—to sift through complicated evidence, to understand expert testimony on scientific topics, to have the wisdom to decide whether the law being enforced is "Just" with a capital J (though on the basis of no evidence at trial directed to this question), to have the intelligence to grasp sophisticated legal instructions on a single reading at the end of the trial, and so on. But at the same time, we give every indication that we don't trust juries at all, think they are stupid, and are frightened of them. Evidence has to be carefully screened for them because they cannot be trusted to make the sorts of judgments that are made routinely by judges. Thus, to give but a couple of examples, in the trial of the Menendez brothers, the fact that Erik Menendez had written a play several months before the trial in which a young man kills his parents with a shotgun for their money had to be kept out of the trial.[16] In the trial of Alex Kelly in Darien, Connecticut, the jury was not informed that he was charged with raping two teenage women in a four-day span. The women did not know each other and each claimed she was forced into the back seat of a sport utility vehicle and raped. The two charges were separated and the second rape was not mentioned at Kelly's first trial, which resulted in a hung jury.[17] (After the trial, some of the jurors expressed shock when informed of the second rape charge and frustration that they had not gotten more information.[18])

Other systems seem more confident about the abilities of lay fact finders. Some of that confidence may stem from the fact that they usually sit with professional judges who are in a position to help the laypersons better assess the evidence, and that lay judges on the continent and lay magistrates in England are usually appointed for a term of three or four years so that they can gain experience as time goes on. Whatever the exact reasons for the treatment of American jurors, I think the description put forward by Albert Alschuler of the University of Chicago Law School is accurate. Alschuler notes that the system treats jurors like children: "Like good children, good jurors are to be seen and not heard."[19] He goes on to say that they are treated like children until the end of the trial. Then the system suddenly treats them as if they were law professors as the judge reads them a complicated set of instructions in legalese which they are supposed to grasp on the basis of a single reading.

Part of the reason we are afraid of spontaneity is that we do not want jurors playing an active role at trial. A few jurisdictions are beginning to move beyond this prejudice and allow occasional questions, but even there the juror wishing to ask a question must write it down and have it approved by the judge and the lawyers before it can be asked. The result is an odd system in which the judge and the lawyers may interrupt a witness to ask a clarifying question or to repeat something more loudly, but a juror is not allowed to make such a request. I have spent many hours in American courtrooms, but cannot recall ever hearing a juror ask spontaneously, "I'm sorry. Could you repeat that?" or "I'm sorry. You said he was wearing gloves. Could you describe what kind of gloves they were?" To return to a theme from the opening chapter, spontaneity, even of this mild sort, is something the system has grown to fear.

How many times must jurors sit there and puzzle over the terminology that occasionally slips into trials whereby cars become "motor vehicles," robbers and rapists become "perpetrators," a brief exterior pat down of a suspect's clothing for a weapon becomes a "frisk," and normal words like "discovery" or "brief" mean something quite different to lawyers and judges than they do to laypersons? Yet we don't want puzzled jurors to ask questions that might easily clarify their confusion: they are to remain silent. It would be as inappropriate for them to ask questions as it would be for an audience to interfere with the performance of a play.

Alschuler's observation about the way jurors suddenly assume a high level of sophistication at the end of the trial when they are instructed in the law is also accurate. At that point a complicated set of instructions is read to the jury, a substantial portion of which jurors fail to understand. Like any set of rules or regulations, it is difficult to make sense of them when they are read to you in this way.

Pause on one of them in order to figure out how it might apply to the issues in the trial and you are likely to have missed the next instruction. Not surprisingly, jurors' eyes often begin to glaze over after ten minutes of listening to instructions as the judge drones on.

Some instructions are simply common sense, but many draw subtle distinctions that even law students who have studied criminal law for a semester could not easily understand. A homicide statute may draw a distinction based on whether the killing was done with premeditation and deliberation as opposed to whether it was done knowingly, recklessly, or negligently. Each of these terms will be defined by statute or court decision in a way that departs significantly from what ordinary usage would suggest to citizens. In addition, there may be complicating factors that need to be considered by the jury in a murder case in deciding the defendant's criminal liability. For example, a jury may have to decide whether the defendant was high on drugs or alcohol or whether he was suffering from a mental disease and how these conditions affected the way the murder was committed: whether knowingly, or with premeditation and deliberation, and so on. Each of these complicating factors will have its own precise legal definition that will need to be explained to the jury.

These instructions may seem to draw rather technical distinctions, but the consequences for a defendant in terms of the range of his or her sentence can be significant. Because instructions are so dry and technical, a judge might be expected to want to make them less abstract and easier to understand by offering the jury some concrete examples or analogies from ordinary experience. But this could be risky for a trial judge, as an appellate court might find the examples misleading and require a new trial. Pragmatism or "the art of not getting reversed" usually dictates that the trial judge stick to the dry wording of the model instruction. In short, the rule for American judges is: "Just read the form instruction and be done with it."

Today some states are beginning to move away from complete reliance on oral instructions and now permit jurors to take a written copy of the instructions into the jury room to consult during deliberations. It is a mark of just how conservative our system is that this is considered a rather daring reform.

Another feature of our system with respect to juries is the prohibition in many courtrooms on jurors taking notes during the trial. Like the prohibition on juror questions or the requirement that jurors aurally pick up the law, the prohibition on note-taking is a reflection of the system's insistence that everyone—witnesses, victims, jurors—adjust to it rather than the system adjusting to the needs of citizens.

Today we know that people at all levels of education learn in different ways. We probably all know people with whom we studied in high school or college who mastered the same subject in different ways. I recall friends who took very detailed notes in lectures and seemed to capture the gist of everything that was being said. I myself took decent notes, but they were rather incomplete and contained lots of phrases and half-sentences that I would often puzzle over when I reviewed them for exams. Then there were a few people who didn't take any notes at all but who just listened and yet seemed to understand and recall what was said. Much the same can be said for the way students read textbooks: some students underline, some prefer to highlight passages from the text in different colors, some limit themselves to a few notes and questions in the margin, and some just read the text and make almost no notations at all.

What is the best way to absorb new information on a new topic? I suggest there is no single way, but that we each have learned what works best for us. Instead of appreciating that people absorb new information in different ways and being tolerant of the differences among us, our trial system insists that jurors absorb the evidence at trial in a single rigid way. Our legal system is reluctant to permit jurors to take notes on the testimony they are hearing in the courtroom during the trial, although the lawyers and judges are scribbling like crazy. Of course, even in courtrooms where judges permit jurors to take notes, it is very hard to do so as there is typically no writing surface to support a pad. The lawyers have a table; the judge has a bench; jurors have nothing.

Judges have rationales for this prohibition—that the juror who can take good notes will dominate the jury deliberations or that one who is not a good note taker will miss important pieces of the testimony. But what is the empirical evidence for these worries and does it outweigh the benefit to those jurors who wish to take notes in being able to follow complex testimony the way they are most comfortable? Instead of a system that understands how hard it is for citizens to adjust to the strangeness of the courtroom, we have one that doesn't seem to care how individual jurors learn and recall best. To use Alschuler's analogy: jurors are children who cannot be trusted to make these sorts of decisions for themselves.

I have already mentioned how strongly the system prefers fact finders who are passive. While questions from jurors are technically permitted, the system does not want jurors asking questions and discourages it, often by neglecting to tell them that they can ask questions. Again, I doubt you would find any study that suggests that completely passive absorption of material works best for those who are trying to master a lot of new information.

The final example of the way the system demands that citizens adjust to it, not vice versa, is the way we expect jurors to learn the law. Legal instructions on the elements of the crime with which the defendant is charged are not explained to the jury until the very end of the trial, that is, until *after* they have heard all the evidence. It is like beginning a trip in a new place with no road map. In addition, reading the instructions to the jury puts those who have trouble absorbing things aurally at a tremendous disadvantage.

Does the Supreme Court Really Respect Juries?

Over the last thirty years our criminal trial system has been so completely tied to juries that states have had no choice in the matter and, for better or worse, have been obliged to provide jury trials for all but the most minor criminal offenses. One might think that the Court's expression of confidence in juries—whatever misgivings trial judges and trial lawyers have about them—would translate into a deep respect for jury verdicts on the part of the Court. But the deep ambivalence one sees in our trial system also manifests itself in Supreme Court opinions.

A case that nicely demonstrates the Court's lack of respect for juries is a 1997 decision by the Court in *United States v. Watts*[20] in which it upheld an increased sentence for Vernon Watts by the trial judge on the basis of conduct for which he had been acquitted by the jury. Vernon Watts was a dealer in cocaine base (more commonly referred to as "crack") whose house was lawfully searched by the police. In the course of the search the police found more than five hundred grams of crack in a kitchen cabinet and, hidden in a bedroom closet, two loaded guns and ammunition. Watts was charged in federal court with possessing cocaine base with the intent to distribute and with using a firearm in connection with a drug offense. The jury convicted Watts of the first charge but acquitted him of the second crime.

But despite the acquittal, Watts's problems with the gun charge were not over. At sentencing the trial judge concluded that Watts had possessed the guns in connection with the drug offense and decided to increase the sentencing range under which Watts was to be sentenced. Under the tight sentencing guidelines in federal courts, the judge's finding had the indirect effect of raising Watts's sentence rather substantially: his already hefty sentence of eighteen years went up an additional four years, bringing the total to twenty-two years of imprisonment.

Because jury verdicts in the United States are never accompanied by a formal explanation or justification—although some jurors have been known to grant press interviews or even to go on talk shows to discuss the trial and reasons for the verdict—we don't know as a formal matter why the jury acquitted Watts of the gun charges. The jury may have felt that the guns could have been used by persons in the house other than Watts, or that there was not a sufficient connection between the guns in the bedroom and the drugs in the kitchen. Or, in a system that is sometimes proud of jury nullification, by acquitting Watts on the gun charges the jury may have been making a statement about our very high drug penalties, especially for crack cocaine. Perhaps the jury did not want to add any more years to what it knew would be a long sentence for the cocaine alone.

Having committed our trial system to the use of juries, one would think this would be an easy question for the Court: the verdict of acquittal must be respected and no additional punishment can be meted out by a judge for conduct of which a jury of citizens have found the defendant not guilty. But the Court found it easy to decide the other way: without even hearing oral argument in the case, the Court ruled that the trial judge was free to add four years to the defendant's sentence for conduct for which the jury had acquitted the defendant.

I suspect the result in *Watts* would probably not be approved in any other western country. In fact, I received a phone call from the editor of an English law journal asking me to write a short article on the decision because it seemed so extraordinary by English standards. The editor was frankly puzzled by *Watts*: "A trial judge added years to a defendant's sentence specifically on the basis of criminal conduct for which the jury in the case had just found the defendant to be not guilty? How can this be?"

We have ended up with a trial system in which federal judges are discouraged from summarizing the evidence for the jury at the end of the trial—it might influence the jury's decision—but they can ignore a jury's acquittal and sentence a defendant specifically for a crime on which the defendant has just been acquitted. When it comes to juries, even the Court seems deeply ambivalent.

Conclusion

The goal of this chapter has been to suggest that we rethink the role of citizens in our criminal justice system. In some ways we have combined the worst elements in our jury system—inexperienced fact finders with no professional training are brought in for a single case, important categories of citizens are deselected from jury service, lawyers are permitted the most adversarial arguments and behaviors, and the judge renders the least amount of help in reaching the verdict. Is it any wonder that confidence in the jury is weak and that many verdicts seem driven by raw emotionalism and not by an attempt to apply the law to the facts?

Criticizing the jury and exposing the weakness of our jury system does not mean that we need to reduce the role of citizens in our system. In fact, we might well expand citizen participation but change the form it takes. One of the ironies of the American trial system is that while we proudly proclaim the importance of citizens in our system, that importance has been increasingly diminished except for a small percentage of cases. The average criminal case is a plea bargain worked out by the professionals: the prosecutor, the defense attorney, and the trial judge. Most of our prisoners were incarcerated without any citizen participation in the process. By contrast, if we look at other legal systems, such as those in England, Norway, or Germany, they use citizens much more extensively though not in the form of juries. Ninety-eight percent of English cases are handled by lay magistrates in England, while in Norway and Germany a high percentage of criminal cases go to trial and there is lay participation on mixed panels of professional and lay judges in all but the most minor criminal cases.

Perhaps just as important in Norway and Germany is the fact that nonprofessionals participate in the sentencing decision as well, so that citizens will help decide what sentence is appropriate for those who go to prison. By contrast, the United States talks rhapsodically about citizens as a buffer protecting the people from the power of the state, but in fact the trial judge determines whether the defendant will go to prison for two, ten, or twenty years. This places a great deal of power in the hands of a single judge, especially when his decision is unreviewable.

In the United States, we swing between two extremes: on the one hand, we place extreme emphasis on citizens at trial, allowing them to decide the issue of guilt without any accountability for their determination, and with very little help in reaching their decision. When there is a conviction, however, we swing back in the other direction and place tremendous sentencing power in the hands of a single judge who will decide how many years in prison a defendant should serve. Almost any tempering of the power at either extreme would be welcome. The goal should be a system that makes wiser use of what citizens can contribute to the fact-finding process while recognizing that fact-finding experience can also be valuable and important. We ought not to look at the issue as if it were a choice *between* juries versus judges but rather at how we can best *blend* the talents of both sorts of fact finders.

CHAPTER ELEVEN

Starting Down the Path to Reform

For the last decade the American public has been told over and over by bar leaders that our trial system is basically sound and that whatever problems have emerged in recent trials they are isolated occurrences that can be attributed largely to human error. This book has showed readers that the problems in the system are structural. They are not going to go away and, indeed, they are likely to get worse over time as citizens become more cynical about the system. In this chapter, I want to review some of the structural problems in the system and discuss the issues that must be faced if we are to reform it.

The System's Overemphasis on Winning and Its Failure to Place a Priority on Truth

A strong trial system has to place a high priority on truth and work hard to achieve that goal. Our trial system does not do this and, as a result, our trials lack focus. Without a clear goal to work toward, trial judges cling tightly to procedure almost as an end in itself because they have nothing else to guide them and are unsure in what direction the trial should go. In this situation a lawyer who sees adversarial advantage in a confusing, prolonged, and bitterly contentious trial finds it easy to create such a trial.

A trial, be it more or less adversarial, is simply a way of testing the evidence that has been gathered during the investigation in order to determine whether or not the defendant is guilty of the crime. Trial systems can vary considerably in the way they carry out this task. But the goal of the system has to be the same: an accurate and reliable evaluation of the evidence in order to determine the defendant's guilt.

The System's Preference for Weak Trial Judges

One structural element that needs to be reconsidered is the role expected of trial judges. Our system is confused about what it wants trial judges to be doing at trial, in part because it is unsure about what trials are supposed to accomplish. American judges are poorly prepared to control trials and are more passive and tentative than are judges in other systems. As I have shown, one of the reasons for this is a disastrous appellate system that insists on reviewing all possible errors that occurred at trial and that orders new trials for what would be considered minor errors in other legal systems. Yet this appellate system does not review the most important issue of all, namely, the accuracy of the jury's verdict. In the end, our trial system ends up emphasizing what our appellate system emphasizes—procedure above all else, not substantive accuracy. If we want judges to exercise more control over trials, they need to be given more authority to do so and they need to prepare for trial differently.

The System's Failure to Distinguish the Role of the Police from the Role of the Prosecutor

We need to rethink the adversary alignment that seems so natural and comfortable to American lawyers and judges, whereby the police and the prosecutor—"the state"—are conceived of as working together "against" the suspect (who later becomes the defendant) from the time the crime has been committed. A criminal justice system should not encourage the police to see themselves as being "on the same side" as the prosecutor during the investigation. Instead, the police should be encouraged to carry out thorough and complete investigations and to see their role as independent from the eventual prosecution of the case.

England and the United States differ noticeably from the other trial systems I have described in tending to see the police as being "on the same side" as the prosecutor. Both countries appear to be paying a price for blurring the roles of the police and the prosecutor into a single joint identity. Whether a system uses trial procedures that are more or less adversarial, the investigation of a crime should not be structured as an adversarial undertaking.

The System's Failure to Set Limits on Advocacy and Its Willingness to Cede Complete Control over the Evidence to Advocates

No other system permits the kind of behavior from advocates that is not only tolerated in American courtrooms, but considered completely normal and ethical. The line between advocacy and acting is nonexistent in the United States, and the limits on advocacy that do exist in ethical codes are so easily evaded as to be nearly nonexistent. When a trial system is unsure of the purpose of a trial and ends up by default heavily stressing winning and losing, it becomes hard to limit what advocates can or can't do in the courtroom.

The level of control over the evidence that has been ceded to the advocates in the United States contradicts what was traditionally thought to be one of the important reasons for having a trial in the first place. We have always stressed the importance of witnesses being brought to court to testify in person so that the fact finders can assess the credibility of the witness as he or she testifies. But we undermine this objective by permitting the advocates to shape the testimony of their witnesses and to coach them in their delivery.

The System's Complexity Has Become Part of the Problem

In chapter 1 I compared the sports of football and soccer, and I poked fun at football's devotion to a false precision in rulings that interrupts the flow of the game while referees confer or as chains are dragged across the field to make sure the ruling is exactly right. What we see in our national sport, we see in our trial system: we love procedure and have a tendency to lose ourselves in it, despite our self-image as practical individuals who prefer to do things simply and efficiently.

Throughout our system, lawyers and judges struggle to achieve the same false precision in an effort to draw precise lines, sometimes well after the fact, between reasonable and unreasonable suspicion, reasonable suspicion and probable cause, the relevant and irrelevant, the relevant and the prejudicial, and so on. The rules become ends in themselves and they end up distorting the system as lawyers spend more and more time trying to anticipate and prepare for every possible trial ruling. Our system of evidence rules particularly needs simplification. At present our rules of evidence are so technical and complicated that they actually drive spontaneity out of the system. A strong trial system should *listen* to what the witnesses have to say and give them the freedom to testify about the events in question in their own words and in their own way. We do not do this.

The System's Use of Its Resources Is Unfair and Inefficient

Like most other western countries, we have a high crime rate, yet we have only one model of trial for all felony and misdemeanor offenses and it is incredibly expensive and cumbersome to operate. How much of the expense can really be justified? Do we need juries and jury selection in every felony case? Most countries have two or three different trial models. We ought to consider mixed panels or some simpler procedure—still involving lay people—for less serious criminal cases. Perhaps it would even be better, following Norway's example, to give the defendant or the prosecutor the right to request a second trial if dissatisfied with the first, while keeping the trials very simple.

When we do use a jury, how well are we using our resources? If seating a jury in a robbery case takes ten or fifteen minutes in many other common law countries, why does it take a day in the United States?

The System Needs Rules That Encourage the Cooperation of All Citizens, Including Suspects, in Criminal Investigations

I suggested in chapter 3 that the police are often able to assemble less evidence in the United States than in other countries because sophisticated suspects will not talk with the police and there is no downside to refusing to answer questions. I contrasted our system with that in England where not only is the defendant's refusal to answer questions introduced at trial—a longstanding practice—but now the jury may be told that it may draw an adverse inference from silence in certain circumstances. If we were to compare the United States with other criminal justice systems, the United States would be at an extreme in the way it limits police access to a suspect as a source of evidence.

It is not just that the suspect may make admissions or lead the police to important physical evidence. Without some access to a suspect during the investigation, a trial becomes a game in which sophisticated defendants aided by crafty defense attorneys have the advantage when it comes to explaining, well after the fact, any incriminating evidence that the police have put together and that has been produced during the trial. Apart from the implications for truth, this lack of access infects the system in other ways. For example, it encourages the prosecution to try to keep its evidence hidden from the defense as much as possible. It would be much better to have all the evidence in the case freely available to the defense as in Europe. In those systems cooperation with the police during the investigation is more common and is expected.

Our Jury System Has Become Such a Serious Problem That the Way Citizens Participate in Criminal Trials Needs Reexamination

Our jury system seems to have the worst combination of elements. First, the system is extremely complicated and intimidating for citizens. Nevertheless we want our fact finders to be citizens who come in off the street with no prior experience in the courtroom and almost no preparation for the task, which they are expected to carry out perfectly. A prospective juror who has had prior experience on a jury is often disqualified for service by one of the lawyers. Second, it is extremely difficult for citizens with other obligations and responsibilities to serve on a jury in the United States because it is hard to estimate how long the trial may take, particularly if the case is an important one. Because the judge has imperfect knowledge of the evidence in the case he cannot easily predict its length. Also, hearings within the trial can arise unpredictably, often causing jurors to spend hours midtrial in the jury room wondering what is going on in the courtroom. Third, while preferring fact finders who have never done any fact-finding, misplaced American populism results in a trial system that gives the jurors much less advice and help from the judge than they get in other trial systems.

Our jury system needs to be reformed. An immediate reform should be to cut down or even eliminate peremptory challenges, protecting against "the unreachable juror" by permitting jury verdicts that are not unanimous. Oregon and Louisiana have permitted nonunanimous verdicts for some time and there is plenty of support for nonunanimous verdicts in other countries. I have also argued that American judges should be required to give juries much more help than they do at present by reviewing and summarizing the evidence for the jury at the end of the trial. Admittedly, this is controversial as the judge may be able to influence the jury in its decision to some extent. But this is an issue that needs to be confronted. If almost all continental countries use mixed panels of professional and lay judges to decide a defendant's fate and if most common law countries at least permit the trial judge to review the evidence for the jury, do we really have that much to fear in allowing a judge to discuss the evidence with the jury? When we have got to the point where even judges talk about jury trials as "rolling the dice," isn't it time to rethink the relationship of the judge and jury in the United States?

I would prefer to move away from juries composed solely of citizens in favor of mixed panels of judges and citizens. Perhaps skeptics will be reassured if we make sure that there are a sufficient number of citizens to outvote the professional judges. What is important is not the voting ratio but getting someone on the jury with knowledge of the law, experience in the system, and experience in fact-finding. I recognize that this proposal is controversial and runs up against American populism. But for all our rhetoric about juries, the present system shows in many, many ways that it doesn't really trust them.

Many of the problems in our criminal justice system, such as the extremes of advocacy and our incredibly complicated evidence rules, are tied to the use of juries. Juries also complicate appellate review of the decision at trial, be it an acquittal or a conviction, because there is no formal way of knowing the reasoning that went into the verdict. For all these reasons, some changes are overdue in the way citizens participate as fact finders at trial, or, at least, in the relationship between judges and juries.

Starting on the Path to Reform: The Need for a "Royal Commission" for the United States

Our system has to be reformed legislatively. This is a serious obstacle to reform because we are at a period in our history when confidence in legislatures is not high. In addition, as the courts have interpreted constitutional provisions more and more freely, they have supplanted legislatures in the area of trial and pretrial procedures. But if we are to reform our system, we have no choice. Courts are ill-suited for the sorts of structural changes the system needs because the issues they can attack are too limited and narrow. We badly need a reform in which we look at the system as a whole with a view to making it more efficient and reliable. We cannot expect that from the courts.

All other western systems have been built legislatively, not judicially. European systems have been built from the ground up in comprehensive codes that lay out the procedures to be followed from the time a crime is reported, through trial and appeal. While England has no similar code, most of the major reforms in that system, such as the restrictions on police in the gathering of evidence, are legislative.

I have made it plain that I think the Court has arrogated to itself decisions that go beyond its expertise. The result has been decisions that don't achieve the Court's goals and that occasionally even have negative consequences in terms of the system's honesty. Looking at the system as a whole, we need to recognize that criminal procedure over the last thirty years has produced at best mixed results:[1] the treatment of suspects is better in many ways, but our trial system has become weaker. It has even become a bit of an international embarrassment at this point.

If we have no institution ready to consider the sort of broad reforms our system needs, we need to create one. There are models we can adapt to our purposes. Our first goal should be to seek some consensus on reform. One way to do that is to set up an institution to examine our system with an eye to reform. England seems to do this every fifteen or twenty years by setting up a Royal Commission of highly respected individuals, charged with the task of examining a particular problem. There have been a number of Royal Commissions on Criminal Justice, some looking at the whole system, others examining important pieces of it. We need to create a similar institution in the United States to study our trial system and propose major reforms.

We have created similar commissions in the past in the United States and their work has often been highly praised and influential. One example was the so-called Kerner Commission. Chaired by former Illinois governor Otto Kerner, it issued a powerful report in 1968 on the causes of civil disorders in the United States (in the wake of the Watts riot) and warned of a country pulling apart on the issue of race.[2] Another example, closer to what I am suggesting for our criminal trial system, was the Wickersham Commission which was appointed in 1929 to study and report on the American criminal justice system.[3]

What is important is that such a commission have a broad membership, including a number of members who possess expertise in areas outside the law and who can bring fresh perspectives to a study of the system. The commission ought to have the authority to carry out their own empirical research if they feel they need it or to seek the advice of experts, maybe even to bring in experts from other countries if that might prove instructive. The goal would be a series of recommendations for change which could take many different forms.

Assuming that there were concrete recommendations that a jurisdiction thought were attractive, the next step might be to try some of the suggestions on a limited basis and see how they work. This might be done informally on a "mock" basis or by a courageous jurisdiction willing to test the recommendations in actual cases. Because we use the Constitution for so many of our reforms, we rarely engage in such experimentation in the United States. That is unfortunate because unanticipated problems can arise with respect to any change, no matter how well thought-out in theory. We ought to try some reforms with simpler cases where much less is at stake and see how they work and how people affected by them like the changes.

Reasons to Be Optimistic, Not Pessimistic about Reform

There is today no leadership from the bar for the sort of structural reforms the system needs. Part of the problem is that while many American lawyers know that something is wrong with the system, they are unaware of exactly what the problems are and thus are uncertain where to begin. This book has tried to show the structural problems in the system as well as possible avenues for reform.

But there is a second reason why no one is doing much about reform in this country despite cases that often fairly scream out for it: it is easy to get discouraged about reform when any proposed change is likely to conflict with decisions of the Supreme Court. If a detail as minor as the timing of a defendant's testimony at trial, whether he is made to testify first on the defense case or permitted to testify last, violates due process,[4] what chance is there that the Court would permit more significant changes to the system, such as assigning judges greater responsibility for the development of evidence at trial, simplifying evidence rules, or changing the nature of the fact-finding body at trial? Sadly, the legal community often has a defeatist attitude toward reform. Although many bar leaders and judges freely acknowledge the need for change, they see no way to achieve it in our system. We seem, in their eyes, to be stuck with what we have or, to put it more accurately, with what the Supreme Court says we must have.

I don't share this pessimism about reform. One reason I am optimistic is that some of the Supreme Court's decisions are not quite the barriers to reform they might initially appear to be. The Court has indicated in some of its opinions that it would reach a different decision if a legislature were to put forward an alternative scheme. To give an important example, in *Duncan v. Louisiana*, which imposed the requirement of jury trial on the states, the Court conceded in a footnote that "[a] criminal process which was fair and equitable but used no juries is easy to imagine. It would make use of alternative guarantees and protections which would serve the same purposes that the jury serves in the English and American systems."[5] The Court had no option but to take this position because to insist that the lack of a jury made a system fundamentally unfair would condemn almost every western trial system in whole or part as well as international courts of justice which have never used juries. But the Court went on to note that "no American system has undertaken to construct such a system." Here is an opening for a major reform in the states that might permit us to move away from juries in their present form. We could compensate for the move by adding other guarantees of fairness, such as mixed panels, reasoned decisions, broad appellate review, and so on.

There are other reasons to be optimistic about reform. Akhil Amar, one of our best constitutional scholars and a proponent of a reconceptualization of our system of criminal procedure, believes that the time is right for reform.[6] He sees a generational change taking place on the Court, among legal academics, and even in Congress, such that there is less attachment to the failed doctrinal structures of the past and a willingness to look for what will work. As someone who lectures frequently to lawyers and judges, I share Amar's optimism about reform. I think lawyers and judges are aware of the fact that many Supreme Court decisions would really have been more appropriate for legislatures and they realize that Supreme Court doctrine on many issues is badly flawed. For the above reasons, I think that reform legislation, perhaps in the form of a national code of procedure as some have urged,[7] that was supported by empirical research and was well-thought out, would be upheld by the Court.

But I would like to conclude with an additional reason why I am optimistic. All over the world, criminal justice systems are in the midst of reform and we will not be unaffected by it. Countries such as Poland, Hungary, and the rest of the former communist bloc, as well as the new South Africa, have had no choice but to rebuild their criminal justice systems from scratch. They operate within severe fiscal restraints as well as with the additional problem of trying to find sufficient numbers of judges and lawyers not tainted by the past. These and many other countries are looking at other criminal justice systems and borrowing and adapting features from them.

On the international level as well, new criminal trial systems are being created in which lawyers and judges from different countries are expected to work together to reach results that are fair and just. The International Criminal Tribunal for the Former Yugoslavia had to invent its own procedures as it went along, not an easy task. Hopefully, what has gone well at the Hague (and what has not gone so well) will be put to use in 1998 when the procedures for a permanent international criminal court, which would have jurisdiction over genocide and other crimes against humanity, are determined at a conference in Rome.

What is beginning to emerge is something approaching an international consensus on criminal trial systems. But even if such a consensus does not emerge, the cross-fertilization that is going on will make it harder to resist change in this country. It is obvious today and will be even more obvious tomorrow that our trial system is extreme. What I hope I have shown in this book is that when the time comes for reform, whether we are considering changes in procedures for pretrial investigations, changes in the role of lawyers at trial, changes in the way citizens participate at trial, changes in the role of the trial judge, changes in our approach to evidence rules, or changes in our appellate system, the options for building a stronger trial system that places a much higher emphasis on the truth are many if we have the courage to pursue them. I am optimistic that Americans will have that courage.

NOTES

Notes to Chapter 2

1. 367 U.S. 643 (1961).

2. People v. Quintero, 657 P.2d 948 (Colo. 1983).

3. See United States v. Sharpe, 470 U.S. 675 (1985); Terry v. Ohio, 392 U.S. 1 (1996).

4. United States v. Bayless, 913 F. Supp. 232 (S.D.N.Y. 1996).

5. Alison Mitchell, *Clinton Pressing Judge for Reversal in New York Drug Case*, NEW YORK TIMES, March 22, 1996, p. 1, col. 5; Alison Mitchell, *Clinton Defends His Criticism of Judge's Ruling*, NEW YORK TIMES, April 3, 1996, p. 12, col. 1.

6. United States v. Bayless, 921 F. Supp. 211 (S.D.N.Y. 1996).

7. Clifford Krauss, *Rights Group Finds Abuse of Suspects by City Police*, NEW YORK TIMES, June 26, 1996, p. B4, col. 6.

8. Dan Barry, *2 More Officers Held in Attack on Haitian Man*, NEW YORK TIMES, August 19, 1997, p. 1, col. 3.

9. Associated Press, *Inmate Set Free after Account of Corruption*, NEW YORK TIMES, January 1, 1997, p. 13, col. 1.

10. See Christopher Slobogin, *Testilying: Police Perjury and What to Do about It*, 67 U. COLO. L. REV. 1037 (1996).

11. David Johnston, *Report Criticizes Scientific Testing at F.B.I. Crime Lab*, NEW YORK TIMES, April 16, 1997, p. 1, col. 6.

12. People v. Temple, 42 Cal. Rptr. 888, 36 Cal. App. 4th 1219, 1995 Cal. App. LEXIS 672 (1995).

13. YALE KAMISAR, ISRAEL LAFAVE, JEROLD R. ISRAEL, MODERN CRIMINAL PROCEDURE 12 (8th ed. 1994).

14. See Stephen Kines, *Why Suppress the Truth? U.S., Canadian and*

English Approaches to the Exclusion of Illegally Obtained Real Evidence in Criminal Cases, RES PUBLICA Vol. II, no. 2, p. 147 (1996).

15. Id. at 159–61.

16. See Craig M. Bradley, *Criminal Procedure in the "Land of Oz": Lessons for America*, 81 JOURNAL OF CRIMINAL LAW & CRIMINOLOGY 99, 106–13 (1990).

Notes to Chapter 3

1. 384 U.S. 436 (1966).

2. Watts v. Indiana, 338 U.S. 49, 59 (1949).

3. ANTHONY G. AMSTERDAM, 5 TRIAL MANUAL FOR THE DEFENSE OF CRIMINAL CASES § 51, p. 61 (American Law Institute-American Bar Association, 5th ed. 1988).

4. Id.

5. Id. at §87, p. 120.

6. THE LAW SOCIETY'S GUIDELINES: ADVISING A SUSPECT IN THE POLICE STATION (3d ed. 1991).

7. Id.

8. *Code of Practice for the Detention, Treatment and Questioning of Persons by Police Officers* C:10.4 in 1997 ARCHBOLD CRIMINAL PLEADING, EVIDENCE AND PRACTICE 15–295.

9. 638 F.2d 582 (3d Cir. 1980).

10. The leading critic of the *Miranda* line of cases is Joseph Grano. See JOSEPH D. GRANO, CONFESSIONS, TRUTH AND THE LAW (U. Michigan 1993).

11. See, e.g., Charles Ogletree, *Are Confessions Really Good for the Soul? A Proposal to Mirandize Miranda*, 100 HARV. L. REV. 1826 (1987); Janet Ainsworth, *In a Different Register: The Pragmatics of Powerlessness in Police Interrogation*, 103 YALE L.J. 259 (1993).

12. JEREMY BENTHAM, 5 RATIONALE OF CRIMINAL EVIDENCE 229–40 (1827).

13. DAVID SIMON, HOMICIDE: A YEAR ON THE KILLING STREETS 193–207 (Houghton Mifflin 1991).

14. Id. at 193–207.

15. See The Criminal Procedure (Scotland) Act 1975, Section 20A.

16. Id. at 200.

Notes to Chapter 4

1. See, e.g., JOHN H. MERRYMAN, THE CIVIL LAW TRADITION 132 (Stanford Univ. Press 1985).

2. See, e.g., Kevin R. Reitz, *Sentencing Facts: Travesties of Real-Offense Sentencing*, 45 STAN. L. REV. 523 (1993); David Yellen, *Illusion, Illogic, and Injustice: Real-Offense Sentencing and the Federal Sentencing Guidelines*, 78 MINN. L. REV. 403 (1993).

3. To show just how extreme American law is: the United States Supreme Court ruled in United States v. Watts, 519 U.S. 148 (1997), that a defendant's sentence may be increased by a trial judge based on criminal conduct for which the jury concluded that the defendant was not guilty. This controversial decision is discussed at pp. 217–18 infra.

4. United States v. Ruiz, 47 F.3d 452 (1st Cir. 1995).

5. United States v. Graves, 98 F.3d 258 (7th Cir. 1996).

6. State v. Doleszny, 146 Vt. 621, 508 A.2d 693 (1986).

7. State v. Ramos, 211 Wisc.2d 12, 564 N.W.2d 328 (1997).

8. Moore v. State, 525 So.2d 870 (Fla. 1988).

9. People v. Scott, 170 A.D. 627, 566 N.Y.S.2d 399 (1991).

10. People v. Macrander, 828 P.2d 234 (Colo. 1992).

11. State v. Sexton, 163 Ariz. 301, 787 P.2d 1097 (1989).

12. 684 So.2d 1378 (Dist. Ct. App. Fla. 1996).

13. 476 U.S. 79 (1986). The case is discussed in more detail at pp. 171–73 infra.

14. 96 F.3d 1132 (9th Cir. 1996).

15. 76 F.3d 638 (5th Cir. 1996).

16. People v. Damiano, 87 N.Y.2d 477, 663 N.E.2d 607, 640 N.Y.S.2d 451 (1996).

17. United States v. Ottersburg, 76 F.3d 137 (7th Cir. 1996).

18. Robert D. McFadden, *Teen-Ager Acquitted in Slaying during '91 Crown Heights Melee*, NEW YORK TIMES, October 30, 1992, p. 1, col. 4.

19. See Alan Abrahamson, *Lyle Menendez Case Ends in a Mistrial; D.A. To Retry Brothers*, LOS ANGELES TIMES, January 29, 1994, p. 1, col. 6.

20. The leading case on a defendant's right to self-representation is Faretta v. California, 422 U.S. 806 (1975).

21. Andrew Blum, *Poll: More Lawyers See O.J. Walking*, NAT'L L.J., April 10, 1995, p. 1, col. 1.

Notes to Chapter 5

1. See JUSTICE IN ERROR (CLIVE WALKER & KEIR STARMER, EDS.) (Blackstone Press 1993).

2. THOMAS MANN, JOSEPH IN ÄGYPTEN (1933), citation and translation from DAVID P. CURRIE, THE CONSTITUTION OF THE FEDERAL REPUBLIC OF GERMANY V (1994).

3. See United States v. Spock, 416 F.2d 165 (1st Cir. 1969).

4. Ex. 341, 156 Eng. Rep. 145 (1854).

5. 14 Q.B.D. 273 (1884).

6. See p. 57 supra.

7. See PETER W. TAGUE, EFFECTIVE ADVOCACY FOR THE CRIMINAL DEFENDANT: THE BARRISTER VS. THE LAWYER 210–18 (W.S. Hein 1996); MICHAEL H. GRAHAM, TIGHTENING THE REINS OF JUSTICE IN AMERICA: A COMPARATIVE ANALYSIS OF A CRIMINAL JURY TRIAL IN ENGLAND AND THE UNITED STATES 83–84 (Greenwood 1983).

Notes to Chapter 6

1. Edward J. Boyer, *Judge Reverses Conviction of Geronimo Pratt*, LOS ANGELES TIMES, May 30, 1997, part A, p. 1, col. 1.

2. Paragraph 607(b) of the Code of Conduct for the Bar of England and Wales (5th ed. 1996).

3. Sometimes lawyers go a bit too far in coaching witnesses and actually provide them with a script to help them "remember" factual details that will be important at trial. One such law firm—which represents plaintiffs in asbestos cases with millions of dollars in damages and in attorneys' fees at stake—was based in Dallas. See Holman W. Jenkins, Jr., *How about a Tony for Best Asbestos-Related Script?* WALL ST. J., October 7, 1997, p. A23, col 3.

4. Model Rule 3.4(e), American Bar Association Rules of Professional Conduct (1991).

5. PETER W. TAGUE, EFFECTIVE ADVOCACY FOR THE CRIMINAL DEFENDANT: THE BARRISTER VS. THE LAWYER 71 (W.S. Hein 1996).

6. DAVID BALL, THEATER TIPS AND STRATEGIES FOR JURY TRIALS (NITA 1994).

7. If lawyers are worried that they might not be able to pull off their impersonations, the Wall Street Journal reports that there are consultants who will help the trial attorney learn to "walk the walk" and "talk the talk" in order to impress juries. Edward Felsenthal, *Lawyers Learn How to Walk the Walk, Talk the Talk*, WALL ST. J., January 3, 1996, p. B1, col. 4.

8. HAROLD ROTHWAX, GUILTY: THE COLLAPSE OF CRIMINAL JUSTICE 135 (Random House 1996).

9. Charles J. Ogletree, Jr., *Beyond Justification: Seeking Motivations to Sustain Public Defenders*, 106 HARV. L. REV. 1239, 1275 (1993).

10. AMERICAN BAR ASSOCIATION STANDARDS FOR CRIMINAL JUSTICE PROSECUTION FUNCTION AND DEFENSE FUNCTION, Standard 3–1.2 (3rd ed. 1993).

11. AMERICAN BAR ASSOCIATION MODEL RULES OF PROFESSIONAL CONDUCT (1997), Model Rule 3.8 Comment [1].

12. Harry I. Subin has argued that a defense lawyer should not be permitted to present a defense he knows to be false. See Harry I. Subin, *The Criminal Lawyer's "Different Mission": Reflections on the Right to Present a False Case*, 1 GEO. J. LEGAL ETHICS 125 (1987).

Notes to Chapter 7

1. So important has the judiciary become in our political system that scholars such as Mary Ann Glendon and Robert Nagel have warned that such heavy reliance on the judiciary is actually eroding democratic principles and undermining important moral values. See MARY ANN GLENDON, RIGHTS TALK (Free Press 1991), and ROBERT F. NAGEL, CONSTITUTIONAL CULTURES (U. California 1989).

2. FRANKLIN STRIER, RECONSTRUCTING JUSTICE: AN AGENDA FOR TRIAL REFORM 83 (U. Chicago 1994).

3. Id.

4. Patton v. United States, 281 U.S. 276 (1930).

5. See pp. 84–86 supra.

6. AMERICAN BAR ASSOCIATION MODEL RULES OF PROFESSIONAL CONDUCT, Model Rule 3.8 (d) (1997).

7. See Brady v. Maryland, 373 U.S. 83 (1963).

8. Because this had not been done in the case of Geronimo Pratt, a former Black Panther leader, Pratt's conviction was overturned in 1997 after he had spent twenty-five years in prison. See Edward J. Boyer, *Judge Reverses Conviction of Geronimo Pratt*, LOS ANGELES TIMES, May 30, 1997, part A, p. 1, col. 1.

Notes to Chapter 8

1. 406 U.S. 605 (1972).

2. Id. at 611–12.

3. For a powerful exegesis of the way that individual "rights" tend to overwhelm other values in our political discourse, see MARY ANN GLENDON, RIGHTS TALK (Free Press 1991).

4. Id. at 612–13.

5. The Police and Criminal Evidence Act 1984, s. 79 contained in ARCHBOLD CRIMINAL PLEADING, EVIDENCE AND PRACTICE (P.J. RICHARDSON ed.) (Sweet & Maxwell 1997) §4–311, p. 434.

6. 476 U.S. 79 (1986).

7. For two cases in which the trial judges made errors in applying *Batson*—one in wrongly upholding a *Batson* challenge and the other in wrongly denying a *Batson* challenge—resulting in new trials in both cases, see pp. 79–81 supra.

8. JEFFREY TOOBIN, THE RUN OF HIS LIFE: THE PEOPLE V. O.J. SIMPSON 191–94 (Random House 1996).

9. 386 U.S. 738 (1967).

10. 395 U.S. 711 (1969).

Notes to Chapter 9

1. See Joachim Herrmann, *Bargaining Justice—A Bargain for German Criminal Justice?* 53 U. PITT. L. REV. 755 (1992).

2. 400 U.S. 25 (1970).

3. 434 U.S. 357 (1978).

4. William J. Stuntz, *The Uneasy Relationship between Criminal Procedure and Criminal Justice*, 107 YALE L.J. 1, 44 (1997).

5. Betty Jane Spencer, *A Crime Victim's Views on a Constitutional Amendment for Victims*, 34 WAYNE L. REV. 1, 2 (1989).

Notes to Chapter 10

1. Ronald Sullivan, *Judge Gives Maximum Term in* Kahane *Case*, NEW YORK TIMES, January 30, 1992, p. A1, col. 2.

2. Robert D. McFadden, *Teen-Ager Acquitted in Slaying during '91 Crown Heights Melee*, NEW YORK TIMES, October 30, 1992, p. 1, col. 4.

3. Patricia Hurtado & Curtis Rist, *Nelson Jurors Angry at Judge and Critics*, NEWSDAY, October 31, 1992, p. 4.

4. Irene Wielawski, *Riot Aftermath*, LOS ANGELES TIMES, May 6, 1992, part A, p. 3, col. 2.

5. Christopher Reed, *Death in the Family*, GUARDIAN, October 11, 1993, p. 2; Alan Abrahamson, *Jury Told Erik Menendez Confessed*, LOS ANGELES TIMES, July 27, 1993, part B, p. 1, col. 2.

6. Jeffrey Rosen, *One Angry Woman*, NEW YORKER 54 (February 24–March 3, 1997).

7. David A. Rovella, *Judge: Juror Didn't Nullify, She Lied*, 19 NAT'L L.J. 26, February 24, 1997, p. A8, col. 1. David A. Rovella, *A Judge Mulls: Did Juror Lie, or Did She Nullify?* 19 NAT'L L.J. 7, October 14, 1996, p. A9, col 1.

8. 391 U.S. 145 (1968).

9. 399 U.S. 117 (1970).

10. Duncan v. Louisiana, 391 U.S. 145, 157 (1968).

11. HARRY KALVEN & HANS ZEISEL, THE AMERICAN JURY (Little Brown 1966).

12. See p. 205 supra.

13. Paul Butler, *Racially Based Nullification: Black Power in the Criminal Justice System*, 105 YALE L.J. 677 (1995).

14. Reynolds Holding, *Group Tries to Sway Jurors*, SAN FRANCISCO CHRON., December 11, 1995, p. B1.

15. Leslie Wolf, *Can Jury Void Law: Proponent Faces Jail*, SAN DIEGO UNION-TRIBUNE, December 6, 1993, p. B1.

16. Alan Abrahamson, *Jury Told Erik Menendez Confessed*, LOS ANGELES TIMES, July 27, 1993, p. B1, col. 2.

17. See Maureen Down, *Liberties: The Sound and The Jury*, NEW YORK TIMES, November 21, 1996, p. 29, col. 1; George Judson, *Returned Fugitive Prevails in His Bid to Have Separate Rape Trials*, NEW YORK TIMES, May 4, 1996, p. 21, col. 2.

18. See William Glaberson, *The Nation: For Juries, the Truth vs. the Whole Truth*, NEW YORK TIMES, November 17, 1996, p. 5, col. 1.

19. Albert W. Alschuler, *The Supreme Court and the Jury: Voir Dire, Peremptory Challenges, and the Review of Jury Verdicts*, 56 U. CHI. L. REV. 153, 162 (1989).

20. 117 S. Ct. 1024 (1997).

Notes to Chapter 11

1. Some would consider my assessment of what the Court has done as "mixed" to be quite charitable. Craig Bradley, though sympathetic to what the Court is trying to do, terms the Court's work a "failure." See CRAIG M. BRADLEY, THE FAILURE OF THE CRIMINAL PROCEDURE REVOLUTION (U. Pennsylvania 1993).

2. See Report of the National Advisory Commission on Civil Disorders (1968).

3. National Commission on Law Observance & Enforcement (1931).

4. See pp. 165–69 supra.

5. 391 U.S. 150 at fn. 14.

6. Akhil Reed Amar, *The Future of Constitutional Criminal Procedure*, 33 AM. CRIM. L. REV. 1123 (1996).

7. See CRAIG BRADLEY, THE FAILURE OF THE CRIMINAL PROCEDURE REVOLUTION (U. Pennsylvania 1993) urging that Supreme Court doctrine be replaced by a comprehensive national code of criminal procedure.

FURTHER READINGS

Chapter 1: Soccer, Football, and Trial Systems

PAUL CAMPOS, JURISMANIA (Oxford 1997), a witty attack on American popular culture and its addiction to law.

JANET LEVER, SOCCER MADNESS (Waveland 1983), a book with unique insights into the relationship between sport and national identity, using Brazil and the world's most popular sport as its central example.

Chapter 2: Technicalities and Truth

Dallin H. Oaks, *Studying the Exclusionary Rule in Search and Seizure*, 37 UNIVERSITY OF CHICAGO LAW REVIEW 665 (1970), a classic article pointing out some of the defects of the exclusionary rule in practice.

Myron W. Orfields, Jr., *Deterrence, Perjury, and the Heater Factor: An Exclusionary Rule in the Chicago Criminal Courts*, 63 UNIVERSITY OF COLORADO LAW REVIEW 75 (1992), an article reporting the results of a survey of prosecutors, defense attorneys, and judges showing that police perjury is a serious problem in Chicago courts.

Christopher Slobogin, *Testilying: Police Perjury and What To Do about It*, 67 UNIVERSITY OF COLORADO LAW REVIEW 1037 (1996), an article that examines the emergence of "testilying" and suggests among possible solutions replacing the exclusionary rule with other alternatives.

Chapter 3: Truth and the Amount of Evidence
Available at Trial

JEREMY BENTHAM, 5 RATIONALE OF CRIMINAL EVIDENCE 229–40 (1827), a beautifully written attack on the rationales offered in defense of the notion that someone suspected of a crime should not have to answer questions about the crime. This work is made all the more remarkable by the fact that it was written some hundred seventy years ago. Yet it remains just as powerful today as when it was written.

MARVIN E. FRANKEL, PARTISAN JUSTICE 87–101 (Hill & Wang 1980), a highly respected federal judge questions the honesty of the balance established by the Court in *Miranda* by which trial judges routinely find waivers of rights to be "knowing and intelligent," when they are often not so. Argues instead for a system that would automatically give a suspect in custody counsel but permit the refusal to answer questions to be admitted at trial and commented on by the prosecutor.

Henry J. Friendly, *The Fifth Amendment Tomorrow: The Case for Constitutional Change*, 37 U. CINCINNATI LAW REVIEW 617 (1968), a powerful attack by one of the foremost American judicial scholars of the late twentieth century on the privilege and, in particular, what the Court has done in interpreting the fifth amendment privilege against self-incrimination. The article ends with a proposed constitutional amendment.

JOSEPH D. GRANO, CONFESSIONS, TRUTH AND THE LAW (U. Michigan 1993), a powerful sustained critique of *Miranda* and other major Supreme Court decisions on interrogation.

WALTER V. SCHAEFER, THE SUSPECT AND SOCIETY (Northwestern 1967), a set of lectures at Northwestern Law School given by a justice of the Illinois Supreme Court. In one of them Schaefer argued for taking interrogation out of the back rooms of police stations and instead having questioning done before a judge with a refusal to answer admissible at trial. Justice Schaefer argued that this balance reflects the practice of many other countries and better accords with both fairness and morality.

DAVID SIMON, HOMICIDE: A YEAR ON THE KILLING STREETS (Houghton Mifflin 1991), a terrific book about the difficulties police face investigating serious crimes. Includes fairly scathing looks at what the Supreme Court has done and the position in which it has put the police.

Chapter 4: A Trial System in Trouble

Albert Alschuler, *Implementing the Criminal Defendant's Right to Trial: Alternatives to the Plea Bargaining System*, 50 UNIVERSITY OF CHICAGO LAW REVIEW 931 (1983), one of a series of articles in which Alschuler attacks the American plea bargaining system and the hypocrisy involved in offering defendants an elaborate system of trial rights but then threatening them with heavier punishments if they dare to exercise those rights.

HAROLD ROTHWAX, GUILTY: THE COLLAPSE OF CRIMINAL JUSTICE 135 (Random House 1996), an experienced New York trial judge describes the sorts of shocking courtroom behaviors that are often alleged to be "zealous advocacy" in American courtrooms. Judge Rothwax also explains how extreme the law he must apply in the courtroom has become.

Chapter 5: Discovering Who We Are

MIRJAN R. DAMASKA, THE FACES OF JUSTICE AND STATE AUTHORITY (Yale 1986), a sophisticated and rather theoretical examination of western legal systems and the views of state authority each system tends to reflect.

CRIMINAL JUSTICE IN EUROPE: A COMPARATIVE STUDY (Phil Fennell editor) (Oxford 1995), a comparison of the criminal justice systems in the Netherlands and England. Each chapter contrasts some aspect of either trial procedure or criminal justice policy in the two countries.

J. DAVID HIRSCHEL & WILLIAM WAKEFIELD, CRIMINAL JUSTICE IN ENGLAND AND THE UNITED STATES (Praeger 1995), an excellent overview of all aspects of the English criminal justice system.

JOHN LANGBEIN, COMPARATIVE CRIMINAL PROCEDURE: GERMANY (West 1977), while now dated and inaccurate in some details, this remains the best introduction to continental trial systems because its focus is an actual trial which could just as easily take place today.

PETER W. TAGUE, EFFECTIVE ADVOCACY FOR THE CRIMINAL DEFENDANT: THE BARRISTER VS. THE LAWYER (W.S. Hein 1996), a book that explores the sharply contrasting trial cultures of England and the United States.

CRIMINAL PROCEDURE SYSTEMS IN THE EUROPEAN COMMUNITY (Christine Van Den Wyngaert editor)(Butterworths 1993), each of the thirteen chapters of this valuable book provides an overview of a different European trial system.

Chapter 6: Criminal Trials in the United States

MICHAEL H. GRAHAM, TIGHTENING THE REINS OF JUSTICE IN AMERICA: A COMPARATIVE ANALYSIS OF A CRIMINAL JURY TRIAL IN ENGLAND AND THE UNITED STATES (Greenwood 1983), follows a robbery case in England from investigation through trial and urges that our American trial system be modified to more closely follow the English model.

Kenney Hegland, *Moral Dilemmas in Teaching Trial Advocacy*, 32 JOURNAL OF LEGAL EDUCATION 69 (1982), an excellent short article that questions the morality that underlies some aspects of trial advocacy courses. A nice article because the author raises issues about the ethics of advocacy that are often not even noticed in these sorts of courses.

Harry I. Subin, *The Criminal Lawyer's "Different Mission": Reflections on the Right to Present a False Case*, 1 GEORGETOWN JOURNAL OF LEGAL ETHICS 125 (1987), a provocative article questioning whether a defense lawyer should be able to raise a defense which he knows to be completely false (e.g., that the victim consented to intercourse) in an effort to gain an acquittal for his client.

Chapter 7: Trials without Truth

FRANKLIN STRIER, RECONSTRUCTING JUSTICE: AN AGENDA FOR TRIAL REFORM 83 (Chicago 1994), while directed toward civil cases, also discusses many problems that are widespread in the criminal justice system. Many of Strier's proposals, such as his suggestions that there be more judicial involvement in questioning at trial, limits on peremptory challenges, and more use of special verdicts at trial, could be applied to criminal cases as well as civil.

Chapter 8: The Supreme Court

MARY ANN GLENDON, RIGHTS TALK: THE IMPOVERISHMENT OF LEGAL DIS-
COURSE (Free Press 1991), a powerful book in which Glendon shows how
the American tendency to see every issue as a matter of individual rights
isolates us from those around us and blinds us to responsibilities owed by
the individual to others and to society as a whole.

DANIEL L. HOROWITZ, THE COURTS AND SOCIAL POLICY (Brookings 1977),
a classic study of four cases that shows some of the dangers and inherent
limitations involved in judicial policy making.

Chapter 9: A Weak Trial System

William T. Pizzi, *Punishment and Procedure: A Different View of the
American Criminal Justice System,* 13 CONSTITUTIONAL COMMENTARY 55
(1996) (reprinted in POINT-COUNTERPOINT—READINGS IN AMERICAN GOV-
ERNMENT (Martin Levine, editor 6th ed. 1997), an essay in which I argued
that procedure and punishment tend to extremes together and that it
shouldn't surprise us that defendants' rights are far more extensive in the
United States than in other western countries but that defendants pay a
price for this in terms of punishment.

William J. Stuntz, *The Uneasy Relationship between Criminal Procedure
and Criminal Justice,* 107 YALE LAW JOURNAL 1, 44 (1997), an important
article in which Stuntz shows in a number of different ways why more procedure does not mean more fairness and more accuracy in the American
criminal justice system, and why excessive procedure can actually lead defense lawyers to concentrate less on possible factual defenses.

Chapter 10: Juries

STEPHEN J. ADLER, THE JURY (Times Books 1994), a journalist who remains
a strong proponent of juries provides a close look at the way juries were
selected and their performance in a number of jury trials and offers his pre-
scription for reform.

B. Michael Dann, *"Learning Lessons" and Speaking "Rights": Creating
Educated and Democratic Juries,* 68 INDIANA LAW JOURNAL 1229 (1993),

article by an Arizona trial judge who has been a leading advocate for reforming our jury system.

Jeffrey Rosen, *Annals of Justice: One Angry Woman*, NEW YORKER, February 24 & March 3, 1997, p. 54, an article that chronicles the rise of hung juries in some American jurisdictions and focuses on the problem of the "unreachable" juror in some urban jurisdictions.

Jack B. Weinstein, *The Power and Duty of Federal Judges to Marshall and Comment on the Evidence in Jury Trials and Some Suggestions on Charging Juries*, 118 FEDERAL RULES DECISIONS 161 (1988), an article by a well-known federal judge that contrasts the English and the American approach to instructing juries and commenting on the evidence at trial. Judge Weinstein concludes that juries need more help from judges than they typically receive.

Chapter 11: Starting Down the Path to Reform

AKHIL REED AMAR, THE CONSTITUTION AND CRIMINAL PROCEDURE: FIRST PRINCIPLES (Yale 1997). Amar has written a series of essays over the last several years strongly critical of the Supreme Court's decisions on issues such as search and seizure, the right to counsel and interrogation. The book pulls together these essays to offer a program for reorienting and reforming our system of trial and pretrial procedure.

CRAIG BRADLEY, THE FAILURE OF THE CRIMINAL PROCEDURE REVOLUTION (Pennsylvania 1993), a provocative book that criticizes the piecemeal, case-by-case development of criminal procedure attempted by the Supreme Court over the last thirty years, showing how confusing the law has become. Bradley shows the strengths that statutory development would bring to the task and proposes a national code of criminal procedure that would apply in both federal and state courts.

INDEX

Index

Pratt, Geronimo, 122
Prosecutors: ethical standards compared to defense attorneys, 137–38, 148; obtaining information from the defense, 121–22; strong identification with each case, 119

Quintero, People v.: dissenting opinion, 27; facts, 26–27; majority opinion, 28

Rothwax, Judge Harold, 133
Rovira, Justice Luis, 27
Royal commissions on criminal justice, 229
Ruiz, United States v., 74–75

Scotland: the questioning of suspects, 67
Search and seizure: costs in less honest judicial opinions, 39; costs in public confidence of exclusionary rule, 34, 35; costs to victim of exclusionary rule, 35; deterrence rationale of exclusionary rule, 33–34; difficulty of determining probable cause, 28; exclusionary rule, 26; illusory rules to guide police, 39–40
Self-representation, 146–47; the Colin Ferguson trial, 84–86
Simon, David: *A Year on the Killing Streets*, 66, 67
Simpson, O. J., trial of, 2, 84, 201; claimed prosecution errors, 87–88; defense tactics, 87; difficulties for trial judge, 87; high expectations in legal community, 86; stunning result, 86
Soccer, 6; enforcement of rules, 9; length of game, 14; officials, 8; pace of the game, 9, 12; prohibition on coaching during the game, 18; rules, 8; speedy rulings, 13; the value placed on spontaneity, 20
Solicitors: divided bar in England, 57;

107; Law Society guidelines for solicitors on police questioning, 57; relationship with barristers, 108
Speedy trial reform, 1
Strier, Franklin, 142
Stuntz, William, 193–94
Supreme Court, 1, 164–65; application of Bill of Rights to states, 154–56; difficulty of changing earlier decisions, 174; disrespect for jury verdicts, 217–18; institutional limitations, 182; interrogation, 65, 152; lack of empirical data, 163–64; limited options, 170; undervaluing truth, 174; Warren Court era, 63

Tague, Peter, 129
Toobin, Jeffrey, 173
Trial judges, 140; as affected by appellate system, 179; duty to apply the law, 42; indifference to outcome, 142; lay judges in Europe, 97–98; mixed panels at European trials, 15; restrictions on summarizing evidence, 143–44; trial preparation compared to European trial judges, 141–42, weak role at trial, 141–42, 181, 222
Trials. *See* adversarial trial systems; American trials; European trials; trial systems
Trial systems, 92; adversarial versus inquisitorial systems, 94, 111–12, 115–16, 148; differences in lay participation, 219–20; differing roles for trial judges, 117; inquisitorial trial systems and fairness, 92–93

Victims, 160–61, 195; child victims at trial, 161, treatment in system, 196–97; victims' rights movement, 2, 160

Witnesses: coaching for trial by lawyers, 197–98; ethical prohibitions on prepartion by barristers, 124–25;

ABOUT THE AUTHOR

William T. Pizzi is a 1971 graduate of Harvard Law School where he was a member of the Harvard Law Review and from which he graduated with honors. Following his graduation, he was an Assistant United States Attorney for the District of New Jersey. In 1975, he joined the faculty at the University of Colorado School of Law where he has taught since that time. In 1996, he received the law school's award for teaching excellence. He has also been honored by both the Colorado Bar Association and the Colorado Supreme Court for his bar service.

His main research interest is the study of foreign trial systems and he has spent a considerable amount of time in foreign countries observing trial systems, mostly in Europe, but also in countries as varied as South Africa, India, Malaysia, and China. He has twice been a lecturer in Italy at the invitation of the United States Information Service and in November 1997 lectured in China as a guest of the Center for Criminal Justice and Criminal Law Research at China University.